Esther Jordan

THE TEACHINGS OF JESUS

THE TEACHINGS OF JESUS

A Textbook for College and Individual Use

By
HARVIE BRANSCOMB, M.A. (Oxon.), Ph.D.
PROFESSOR OF NEW TESTAMENT IN DUKE UNIVERSITY

COKESBURY PRESS
NASHVILLE, TENN.

SET UP, ELECTROTYPED, PRINTED, AND BOUND
BY THE PARTHENON CRAFTSMEN AT NASH-
VILLE, TENNESSEE, UNITED STATES OF AMERICA

THIS BOOK IS DEDICATED
To
M. McG. B.

PREFACE

THIS book is an expansion of my small volume, *The Message of Jesus*. It had its origin in a number of requests for a textbook along the lines of that book but planned for college use. Accordingly, I have not hesitated to include certain chapters from that book, though the reader will find that these have been reworked and corrected.

Considerable attention has been given to the supplementary readings at the end of each chapter. It will be noted that these deal for the most part with topics related to but not adequately discussed in the preceding chapters. By utilizing these readings the instructor can expand the course as much as may be desired. No doubt many of the most useful of these have been overlooked, but each instructor will supply the omissions.

In quoting New Testament passages I have followed, as a general rule, the American Revised Version. I am grateful to Messrs. Thomas Nelson and Sons for permission to use this translation.

HARVIE BRANSCOMB.

DUKE UNIVERSITY,
DURHAM, NORTH CAROLINA.

CONTENTS

CHAPTER I

THE JESUS OF HISTORY

JESUS was a historical person, not the personification of our highest ideals and moral judgments. He lived at a particular place and time, was in contact with movements and groups of which we have definite knowledge, and was put to death by a Roman official whose place and public career are matters of historical record. When, therefore, Christian faith declares Jesus to be its moral example and religious ideal, it is committed to the one and only method by which the Example can be followed and the Ideal known, the method of historical study. We cannot know how Jesus lived nor what he taught by consulting our own desires, hopes, or prejudices any more than in the case of Socrates or Martin Luther. One must seek knowledge of him by asking certain simple questions: What records of his life and teachings have been preserved? What dependability can be placed in these records? How should the information which they supply be correlated and understood? Any other approach to the problem is purely subjective and prejudiced. Jesus has a right to speak for himself. He will never mean anything to anyone who is not willing to take him as he actually was. Unless by patient study of the facts we will do this, we have no right to label ourselves followers of him nor to regard our religious activities and programs as obedience to his commands.

I

In beginning the study of Jesus' teaching, therefore, our first task must be to ascertain what records there are to tell us of that ministry which occurred so long ago. Merely to ask such a question, however, seems at first discouraging. One calls to mind the obscure character of Jesus' career, and the nonliterary atmosphere in which he lived. He did his work on the extreme eastern boundary of the great Roman Empire. The little Galilean towns in which he spoke were unknown in the great centers of civilization. His hearers were, for the most part, simple peasants and fisherfolk. In all his life he probably never met a person above the rank of the subordinate official who sentenced him to his death. So far as we know he never wrote a line, and no official observers nor court reporters were present to record the story of his deeds. His ministry was unbelievably brief, not exceeding three years at the most. Even during his lifetime conflicting testimony concerning him was borne not only by the multitudes, but by witnesses formally testifying at his trial. The wonder is that we can recover at all the story of his life. The fact that that story is to-day reverently read in millions of homes in Christian America and other lands is indeed, in contrast with its obscure beginnings and the centuries that have gone by, the greatest of all the miracles.

The major sources for information concerning the life of Jesus are four Greek documents dating from the second half of the first century known to us to-day as the Four Gospels. Before considering these, however, it will be well to note some other sources of knowledge about Jesus.

From what has already been said concerning the humble and obscure character of the career of Jesus, one need not expect court historians or the professional literati of his day to be concerned with his deeds or fortunes. Most of what we know about Jesus we owe naturally enough to his followers.   It would be a mistake, however, to assume that the references to Jesus in ancient literature are only in Christian writings.   The greatest historian of the last days of the Roman republic and the beginnings of the empire was Tacitus; the chief historian of the closing decades of the Jewish state was Josephus; the primary literary record of Jewish religious life in the first century is the Talmud.   In all three of these the historical character of Jesus and the nature of his work are attested.

The *Annals* of Tacitus were probably the last of his works.   Written in the years 115-117 A.D., at the close of a long and honorable career by one who had been an eyewitness of much that he describes, they constitute an invaluable source of information.   In *Annals* XV, 44, occurs a famous passage describing the persecution of the Christians in Rome by Nero at the time of the great fire which the Emperor was suspected of having started. Tacitus says: "The founder of this sect was one Christus who was put to death in the reign of Tiberius by the pro-curator Pontius Pilate"—a precise note of time of great value.   He then goes on to say that by this act the spread of this "pernicious superstition" was checked for the time, but that it broke out again "not only in Judea, the original birthplace of the pest, but also in the capitol, to which place everything that is hateful and shameful flows from every quarter and there meets with sympathy."   In this passage, written by one who probably had little definite knowledge of the contents of Christian belief, is attested the foundation of Christianity by an individual named Christ (the title is taken for a proper name as in Christian writings of the same date as the *Annals*), the location of his work in Judea, his fate at Roman hands, the date of the same, and the fact that the movement which he initiated was only temporarily checked by his death and spread rapidly from Jerusalem to Rome.

Josephus' testimony consists of two passages in his monumental work, the *Antiquities.* In XX, 9, he tells of how Ananus, the high priest, in 62 A.D., taking advantage of the fact that the procurator was dead and that the new appointee had not reached the country, summoned a judicial council. The text reads: "He called before it the brother of Jesus who was called Christ—James was his name—and some others, and on the charge of violating the law he gave them over to be stoned." Here Jesus is mentioned as a person well known to his readers, the faith of his followers in him as the Messiah is affirmed, one of his brothers is named, and the charge which Judaism brought against the early Christians listed.

The second passage (XVIII, 3) reads as follows: "Now at this time Jesus appeared—a wise man, if he can be called a man. For he accomplished marvelous things, was the Master of those who receive the truth with joy, and led away many Jews and also many Greeks. He was the Christ. Upon the denunciation of the leaders of our nation Pilate condemned him to the cross, but those who had loved him from the first ceased not to revere him, for he appeared to them on the third day, raised again from the dead, as had announced the divine prophets as well as a thousand other marvelous things concerning him. There still exists to-day the sect which, after him, receive the name of 'Christians.'" That this passage was not written by Josephus in the form in which it now stands is obvious. For if Josephus had said of Jesus, "if he can be called a man," and, "he was the Christ," if he had believed in his miracles, his resurrection, his fulfillment of prophecy, he would have been a Christian. In that case

Jesus would have been for him the most important figure of history, and his appearance and work would have been the dénouement of the long history of the Jewish people. But except for the passage concerning the death of James quoted above, no further mention of Jesus is made nor is any interest in the Christian movement displayed.[1] Nevertheless, scholars who have made careful study of the writings of Josephus recognize in the passage a number of words and expressions which are characteristic of his writings, and it seems likely that the passage as it now stands is a Christian expansion or modification of a genuine reference to Jesus by the Jewish historian. Reconstructions of what Josephus originally wrote have been attempted, such as, for example, the following one by Reinach: "At this time there appeared Jesus, called Christ, an able man (for he was a worker of miracles), who preached to those eager for novelties, and he led away many Jews and many Greeks. Although Pilate, upon the denunciation of the leaders among us, condemned him to the cross, those who had loved him from the beginning ceased not to be attached to him, and to-day there still exists the sect which from him had taken the name of Christians." Such reconstructions of course are to a large extent conjectural, but the suggestions in the passage of a genuine reference to Jesus, particularly when taken with the casual reference to Jesus in XX, 9, as to a person already mentioned, is evidence from the Jewish historian of the historicity of Jesus and his influence on his countrymen.

[1] Origen, the greatest scholar of the early Church, who lived in Alexandria (185-254 A.D.), states in two places in his works that Josephus did not admit Jesus to be the Christ: *Comm. in Matt.*, X, 17, and *Contra Celsius* I, 47.

From the Talmud comes further corroboration of these points. This enormous collection of rabbinic laws and teachings, although put in writing considerably later than the time of Jesus, contains the record of religious thought and practice of the orthodox Judaism of his day. Written in a scholastic and difficult Hebrew, in an abstruse and confusing manner, often employing technical terms and expressions meaningless to all who have not given the subject a lifetime of study, the Talmud has until recently been virtually a closed book to Christian readers. Thanks, however, to the work of a number of distinguished scholars both Jewish and Christian, it has in recent years been made accessible to a wider circle, its contents made known, and its text translated into modern languages. Within its pages, concealed often under obscure terms to escape deletion by Christian censors of the Middle Ages, are various references to Jesus. These references are mostly of a vague and general character, some of them are obviously confused and inaccurate, and all of them are written from a strongly prejudiced point of view. Among them, however, one finds attested the following facts and points of views: that he was called Jesus the Nazarene, that his mother's name was Mary, that he "scoffed at the words of the wise," that he worked miracles by means of magic brought out of Egypt, that he had devoted personal disciples, that he "led astray and deceived Israel," that he was about thirty-three years of age when he was put to death, and that he was executed on the eve of the Passover.[2]

[2] See Herford, *Christianity in Talmud and Midrash* (London, Williams and Norgate, 1903), for the best list and discussion in English of these Talmudic passages.

The Talmud thus, like Tacitus and Josephus, bears witness to the historical character of the life of Jesus. Though the information that these three give is meager, scarcely going beyond the fact of his existence and the nature of his work, these three great secular sources for our knowledge of the Palestine under the Romans, all of them non-Christians, are three solid mountain peaks of facts which assure us that the story of Jesus is not a beautiful mirage created by pious imagination.

II

For the details of that story we must turn to the extant writings of early Christian teachers and leaders. These writings are of various types. There are letters to individuals like Paul's letter to Philemon, letters to particular churches like 1 and 2 Corinthians, messages of an encyclic character such as the Epistle of James, Christian apocalypses such as that of St. John, manuals of Church discipline and organization like the second century "Teachings of the Twelve Apostles," apologetic works like those of Justin Martyr, an account of certain important events in the early history such as "The Acts of the Apostles," brief lists of sayings of Jesus like those found at Oxyrhynchus in Egypt, and longer collections of teaching and narrative called Gospels. In this varied literature we will find the historical record of what may be known about the earthly life of Jesus.

The men who wrote these letters and tracts, however, had in each case certain specific purposes in mind. Philippians, for example, is a letter of thanks to friends in Philippi who had sent a gift to the imprisoned apostle. First Corinthians was written to answer a list of questions which his converts in that city had sent to Paul as well as to rebuke the division of the Church into a number of definite factions. Except in those works dealing specifically with the life of Jesus, references to his deeds or his sayings would be only occasional and incidental to the main theme of the work. The further fact that each Christian community no doubt possessed in some form or other a gospel tradition made largely unnecessary repetition of incidents or teachings. Thus while early Christian literature repeatedly testifies to the character of Jesus and certain of the chief incidents of his life, its contribution of material not recorded in the gospels is slight.

The earliest Christian writings which have been preserved are the letters of the Apostle Paul. Confining ourselves now to the teachings of Jesus, we find in Paul's letters four passages where he quotes by name sayings of the Lord. These are 1 Thessalonians 4: 15; 1 Corinthians 7: 10 f.; 1 Corinthians 9: 14 (cp. also 1 Tim. 5: 18); and 1 Corinthians 11: 23 ff. Three of these sayings are to be found in the gospels. In addition to these in which the authority of Jesus is expressly cited, there are numerous passages in which Paul virtually repeats sayings of Jesus without so designating them. Thus he writes that his readers are aware that the day of the Lord comes as a thief in the night (1 Thess. 5: 2; cp. Matt. 24: 43 or Luke 12: 39); he speaks of love as the fulfillment of the law (Gal. 5: 14 and Rom. 13: 10; cp. Mark 12: 29), and he speaks of a faith that can remove mountains (1 Cor. 13: 2; cp. Mark 11: 23). In these cases we can check the parallel passages in our gospels and see that in all probability Paul is quoting from the stream of tradition familiar to his readers.[3] No doubt there are other cases where he

[3] The student should note the echoes of Jesus' teachings in the passage Romans 12: 6–13: 10.

is also quoting which we cannot identify because the saying has not been preserved. Beyond question Paul's ethical teaching taken in the large is at one with that of his Lord, but his writings supply little definite data which would enable us to recover the teachings of Jesus.

The same is true of the other writings of the New Testament. The Epistle to the Hebrews alludes in general terms to a number of aspects of Jesus' character—his faithfulness (3: 6), his obedience (5: 8), his courage under pain (12: 2), etc. But no specific sayings of his are quoted. First Peter similarly speaks of the example which he gave in suffering unjustly without retaliation (2: 21 f.). The First Epistle of John makes it clear that the essence of Jesus' teaching was love: "This is his commandment, that we believe in the name of his Son Jesus Christ, and love each other, as he commanded us to do" (3: 23; cp. also 3: 11). The same thought is to be found in verses 6 and 9 of the Second Epistle of John. But none of these passages go beyond general statements. They give us no word of Jesus. But there is one saying preserved only incidentally in one of the speeches in Acts, without which the Christian tradition would be immeasurably poorer. We read that Paul, leaving the territory around the Ægean Sea in which he had labored so long, summoned the elders of the Church at Ephesus to meet him at Miletus, and there he bade them farewell. Among other final exhortations, he urged them to "remember the words of the Lord Jesus, how he said, It is more blessed to give than to receive." [4]

From Christian writings of the sub-apostolic period a few more sayings of Jesus which are not found in our

[4] Acts 20: 35.

gospels can be collected. "In what state I find you, therein shall I judge you," is quoted by two writers.[5] Origen, the great scholar of Alexandria, in his treatise on prayer, quotes as a saying of Jesus the following: "Ask for greater things, and the small shall be added unto you: ask for the heavenly, and the earthly shall be added to you."[6] From a number of writers comes, "Be ye wise money changers" (or bankers).[7] It has been suggested that the words of Paul, "Prove all things, holding fast to that which is good" (1 Thess. 5:21), are a comment on and explanation of this saying. In the *Apostolic Church Order* is attributed to Jesus the striking saying, "The weak shall be saved by the strong."[8] Sometimes one finds additions made by scribes to gospel accounts which they were copying. Thus in Codex Bezæ one finds introduced at Luke 4:4 the statement, "And on the same day, seeing one working on the Sabbath, Jesus said to him, Man, if thou knowest what thou doest, blessed art thou; but if thou knowest not, cursed art thou and a breaker of the law." Such sayings seem to echo the spirit of the gospels, and some or all of them may be genuine recollections of words of Jesus. Others, however, are attributed to him which sound a different note. "The Lord said in a mystery, If ye make not the left hand as the right and the right as the left and the things that are above as those that are below and the things that are before as those that are behind, ye shall not know the kingdom of God."[9] Papias, an elder of the early second century, attributed

---

[5] Justin Martyr, *Dialogue with Tryho*, 47, and Clement of Alexandria.

[6] *On Prayer*, 2.

[7] Clement of Alex., *Strom.*, I, 28, 177, and others.

[8] Page 26.

[9] *Martyrdom of Peter*, 17.

to Jesus the following: "The days shall come when vines shall grow, each having ten thousand branches, and on one branch ten thousand shoots, and on every shoot ten thousand clusters, and in every cluster ten thousand grapes, and every grape when it is pressed shall yield five and twenty measures of wine." And when any of the saints take hold of one of the clusters another will cry out, "I am a better cluster; take me, through me bless thou the Lord." [10]   It is evident that these sayings must be considered with caution. One cannot accept as genuine every saying attributed to Jesus one to three centuries after his death. In attempting to distinguish between those which may be genuine and those which are not, about the only test which can be applied is whether or not the saying in question conforms to the content and character of Jesus' teaching as we have it in the canonical gospels. These clearly are the standard authority. Isolated fragments attributed to Jesus by second century writers may be useful for illustration or corroboration of some aspect of the teachings, but obviously it would be unwise to depend upon them when they diverge from the presentation of Jesus' thought which the gospels contain.

Before turning to these major sources there is one non-canonical document of such special interest for our subject as to call for some discussion. In 1897 two English scholars, Grenfell and Hunt, while excavating in the dry sands of Egypt at Oxyrhynchus found a leaf of a papyrus book on which were written eight sayings ascribed to Jesus. In 1903 a second piece was found, this time from a papyrus roll. Professor Evelyn White, the

[10] See "Irenæus, *Vs. Haer,*" v. 33, 3. In the Jewish *Apocalypse of Baruch* the Messianic Age is described in almost identical language. See xxix 5.

latest editor of the fragments, has shown good reason for believing that both belonged to the same collection and were written in the third century. The second leaf is badly mutilated and the original form of the sayings can only be conjectured, but those of the leaf found first are much more complete. I quote the sayings on this leaf:

. . . And then thou shalt see clearly to cast out the mote which is in thy brother's eye.

Jesus saith: If ye fast not from the world, ye shall not find the kingdom of God; and if ye keep not Sabbath for the whole week ye shall not see the Father.

Jesus saith: I stood in the midst of the world, and in flesh appeared I unto them; and I found all men drunken and none did I find thirsting among them and my soul is afflicted for the sons of men, because they are blind in their heart and see not. . . .

(Bottom of column 1 gone.)

(Column 2, top) . . . Poverty.

Jesus saith: Wheresoever there are two, they are not without God; and where there is one alone, I say I am with him. Lift up the stone and there shalt thou find me; cleave the wood and there am I.

Jesus saith: A prophet is not acceptable in his own country, nor doth a physician do cures upon them that know him.

Jesus saith: A city built upon the top of an high mountain and established can neither fall nor be hidden.

Jesus saith: Thou hearest with (in) thy
(one) ear (but the other thou hast closed)....[11]

When these sayings were first published interest in them
was high and the thought was expressed in some circles
that a considerable addition had been made to our store
of knowledge of Jesus' teaching. The more sober judgment of scholars, however, finds in the sayings no grounds
for such complete and unhesitating acceptance. The
fragments seem to come from the third century. Some of
the sayings have a mystical turn which rather suggests an
origin within some sect or special group within Christianity rather than to have come from the main stream of
the catholic tradition. The canon expressed above must
be our guide here as elsewhere: where the sayings repeat
the words or thoughts of genuine sayings in the gospels
they may well be accepted, otherwise they are of dubious
authenticity. But though this be the case, the Oxyrhynchus
Papyri are invaluable as illustrating the way in which
short lists of words of Jesus, detached from any narrative setting, were ofttimes no doubt the prized possession
of early Christians. They also illustrate quite vividly the
fact that sayings of Jesus circulated in the early Church
in slightly divergent forms. Of this latter fact we shall
meet further illustrations within the gospels themselves.

Thus one who desires to recover for our own day the
thought of Jesus turns with eager expectancy to the evidence of the gospels. But even after so brief a survey
of extra-gospel data as the above, I think he will do so
with a deep impression of the historical reality of Jesus

[11] See James, *The Apocryphal N. T.,* pp. 25 ff. for the text of both
fragments. For conjectural restoration of the 1903 papyrus see Evelyn
White, *The Sayings of Jesus from Oxyrhynchus.*

and of the impress which he made directly and indirectly on the society of his day.

TOPICS FOR DISCUSSION AND REVIEW

1. The political and cultural situation in the first century of the Christian era.

2. The cultural contributions of various peoples toward the civilization of the Roman Empire—Greeks, Egyptians, Jews, Romans, and others.

3. Western civilization as the continuation of this Hellenistic culture.

4. The necessity of scholarship for vital and intelligent religion.

5. The respective value of testimony concerning Jesus by (a) opponents of Christianity and (b) early Christians.

6. The Talmud—its contents and its place in Judaism.

7. Parallels in the Gospels for sayings in the Oxyrhynchus Papyri.

READINGS ON RELATED TOPICS

On the Myth Theory of the Gospel story:
> Case: *The Historicity of Jesus,* especially chapters 2 and 3.
> Goguel: *Jesus the Nazarene: Myth or History?* Ch. 1, 4, and 5 especially.

On the condition of world culture at the beginning of the Christian era:
> Angus: *The Environment of Early Christianity,* Ch. 1 and 2.

On the Apocryphal Gospels:
> James: *The Apocryphal New Testament,* pp. 1-19 (where the extant fragments are collected).

On the Oxyrhynchus Papyri:
> David Smith: *Unwritten Sayings of Our Lord,* Ch. 5.

CHAPTER II

THE BEGINNINGS OF THE GOSPELS

I

WHEN one turns to a consideration of the gospels and what they tell us of the life and teachings of Jesus, there are two questions which immediately arise: Who wrote these accounts? and when were they written? In the case of imaginative works, poems like Gray's *Elegy* or novels like *Silas Marner,* such questions are perhaps of no great consequence. The *Elegy* would be equally beautiful if written at some other date, and *Silas Marner* loses little of its effectiveness even though the reader be unaware that the real name of the author was Marian Evans rather than George Eliot. The gospels, however, are historical documents whose value is determined by the faithfulness with which they have recorded the story of certain events which had transpired; and questions of authorship, date, place of origin, and the like, are therefore important.

In another respect works of history like the gospels differ from imaginative works such as those mentioned. The latter come from the author's brain and are, in the main, the product of a particular occasion. The contents of a work of history, however, are fixed and determined by events over which the writer has no control. His task is simply to describe what happened with clarity and accuracy. Xenophon, for example, was a member of the army of Cyrus when it marched against the Persians and, after Cyrus's death, was one of the generals who led the ten thousand Greek soldiers in their memorable

25

retreat. His task was merely to set down what had transpired, his own contribution to the story being primarily one of selection of material and emphasis upon phases of the history which he felt called for it. In such an instance the author was an eyewitness of the events recorded. Where, as is more usually the case, the writer of history has not himself witnessed the scenes described, he must gather his material from others who did see or hear, inquire of those who knew the original actors or observers, and read the records where records have been kept. In such cases the writer is not limited directly by the original events, but rather by the knowledge of those events preserved in writing or in the memories of men. Not having been in contact with the original events himself, he cannot get behind the various portions of knowledge preserved except by the uncertain path of inference and conjecture.

It is obvious, however, that such knowledge, preserved either in writing or in the memories of men, will already have determined to a considerable extent the character of the writer's account. In such a "tradition," if we may use that word, some events will have been entirely forgotten and thus lost permanently from the ensuing record.

Other incidents may have been given a particular turn due to the point of view of some early observer or to a special interest in some phase of the story by those who told, remembered, or wrote it down. Where translation of a story or a saying has passed from one language into another, mistranslations sometimes obscure the exact meaning of the earlier story, and of these a writer, if he be working in the second language, is likely to be the victim. Thus it is quite clear that one cannot understand or use properly a work of history without ascertaining the medium through which the author's information has come to him and the conditions which affected its transmission.

A moment's reflection will show how important this is in the case of the gospels. We shall see shortly that the evangelists—with the possible exception of one—were not themselves eyewitnesses of the events they record. The gospels were not written in Palestine, but in distant cities of the Roman Empire. They appeared first in Gentile rather than in Jewish environments. They are written in Greek, whereas Jesus and the first Christians spoke Aramaic. Before proceeding to questions of the date and authorship of the several gospels, therefore, it is necessary first to ask by what means and through whose telling the Christian story had spread from Judea and Galilee to the distant Greek-speaking Christian communities of the Empire.

The story of how this came about is one which becomes more and more fascinating the further one goes into it. It is a story not so much of apostles and church officials as of ordinary members of the Christian brotherhood who told in the utmost simplicity and naturalness, without any thought of making history or of forming sacred literature, those stories and sayings of Jesus which were of the greatest value and importance to them. Later there were short collections of sayings or stories. Finally these were used in combination with facts or sayings of general knowledge in the Church but not yet put in writing, and no doubt in connection with special information which evangelists gathered for themselves, to make up our gospels. The transmission of the gospel narrative can thus be divided into three periods, though they overlap with each other: (1) the period of oral transmission, (2) the beginning of written accounts, (3) the period of the writing of gospels. Into this story of how the gospels came about, as enticing as it is, we cannot go in detail, but certain aspects of it are so important for an understanding of the gospels that they must be mentioned. The rest of this chapter will be devoted to pointing out certain consequences of the first of these periods.

II

That the story of Jesus' life and teachings was transmitted orally at first is evident from the New Testament itself. The process began on the day of Pentecost when three thousand people were converted in Jerusalem. We are told that they "continued steadfastly in the apostles' teaching and fellowship." [1] This teaching was evidently to a considerable extent the story of Jesus' life. When Peter and John came down into Samaria they "testified and spoke the word of the Lord." [2] Such testimony of necessity concerned the events of which they had been the witnesses. Similarly those members of the Jerusalem Church who had been taught by the apostles, when they were driven from the city by persecution, "went about preaching the word." [3] Such oral testimony was the only means by which the story of Jesus could be made known. In the case of Paul there are many references in his letters to his oral instruction of his converts in the facts of Jesus' life. "I received of the Lord that which also I delivered unto you," he writes to the Corinthians, "that the Lord Jesus in the night in which he was betrayed took bread: and when he had given thanks, he brake it, and said, This is my body, which is for you." [4] In the same letter he refers to the fact that he had "delivered" unto them an

[1] Acts 2: 42.
[2] Acts 8: 25.
[3] Acts 8: 4.
[4] 1 Cor. 11: 23.

account of the resurrection appearances.[5]   That he had transmitted at least a certain amount of the teachings of Jesus is not to be doubted.   Four times in his letters and once in Luke's account of his speech to the elders of Ephesus we find him quoting sayings of Jesus in support of his instructions to his converts, while in many other passages one is reminded of the words of Jesus.[6]   Thus there are echoes in these letters of the tradition about Jesus which Paul had delivered to his Churches.   But Paul was not one of the original disciples and had never seen the Lord.   Far richer would have been the reports of individuals who had been with Jesus in Galilee or Jerusalem.   Peter, for example, worked not only in Judea and Samaria, but also visited Antioch in Syria,[7] apparently had been in Corinth after Paul established a church there,[8] and according to early tradition was one of the founders of the Church of Rome.[9]   The additions which he made to each local store of knowledge of Jesus' life would be carefully treasured.   So also in the case of other apostles and missionary travelers.   In addition to the recognized leaders there were ordinary members of the Church who changed their place of residence or traveled on business and in so doing conveyed the "good news."   Some of these no doubt were eyewitnesses of some of the events narrated.   Others like Priscilla and Aquilla, the individuals who converted Apollos,[10] had learned the story from others.

Thus Christian brotherhoods formed in Palestine and in distant cities received their first knowledge of Jesus'

[5] Cor. 15: 3 f.

[6] See above, p. 18.

[7] Gal. 2. 11.

[8] 1 Cor. 1: 12, 3: 22, and 9: 5.

[9] Eusebius, *Church History*, II, 25, 5.

[10] Acts 18: 24 ff.

life by word of mouth. To the first bare outline incidents, sayings and further details were added by traveling
Christians. Received by hearing rather than by reading,[11]
the story was retold repeatedly in meetings for worship
and instruction until a fairly definite though constantly
growing tradition became established in each Christian
community. In the Hellenistic Churches founded by Paul
and others this tradition would be in Greek. In Palestine
the story would be told and the sayings repeated in
Aramaic, the language which Jesus had spoken. These
Palestinian Churches were of course the fountainhead of
information and the source of the growing knowledge of
other Christian groups. Here were individuals who had
known Jesus in the flesh; Jerusalem was the headquarters
of the apostles; in this area Jewish customs essential for
the understanding of the story were common knowledge.

There is a striking statement which has been preserved
from one of the earliest Christian writers of the second
century, one Papias, a bishop of a church in Asia Minor,
which gives a most valuable illustration of this process
of oral transmission which has been described. In the
preface to a book which he called *Expositions of Oracles
of the Lord* Papias wrote the following: "I shall not hesitate to put down for you along with my interpretations
whatsoever things I have at any time learned carefully
from the elders and carefully remembered, guaranteeing
their truth. . . . For if anyone came who had been a follower of the elders I questioned him in regard to the words
of the elders—what Andrew or what Peter said, or what
was said by Philip, or by Thomas, or by James, or by
John, or by Matthew, or by any other of the disciples of

[11] Note Paul's words in Romans 10: 17.

the Lord, and what Aristion and the Elder John, the disciples of the Lord, say. For I did not think that what was to be gotten from the books would profit me as much as what came from the living and abiding voices." [12]

This work of instructing new converts in the facts of Jesus' life and in his teachings was too important to be left to chance, nor could the apostles do more than a small portion of what was needed. Consequently we find that from the very earliest days there was a special class of workers in the Church who were called "teachers." They were evidently very important in the life of the early Church. Paul speaks of three major groups of Christian workers who in his days had the leadership of the Church: "God hath set some in the Church, first apostles, secondly prophets, thirdly teachers." [13] In Ephesians we read again of these teachers in a statement that they were called of God to their work just as were the apostles, prophets, and evangelists.[14] It is evident from Paul's enumeration of the three leading offices, "apostles, prophets, and teachers," and from the warning in the Epistle of James, "My brethren, do not swell the ranks of the teachers," [15] that the office carried with it prestige and respect. It is interesting indeed to note that for a long while the teachers ranked above those who were called bishops. A passage from an early church-manual, called *The Teaching of the Apostles,* reads: "Appoint for yourselves bishops and deacons worthy of the Lord, men who are meek and not lovers of money. . . . Despise them not; for they are honorable men among you, along with the prophets and teachers." [16]

[12] Eusebius, *Church History,* III, 38, 3 f.
[13] 1 Cor. 12: 28.   [15] 3: 1.
[14] 4: 11.   [16] Didache 15.

No details have been preserved as to the work of these teachers, but one of their tasks evidently was the oral instruction of new members of the Church in the facts about Jesus which were felt to be most important for Christian living.   This is easier to understand when one recollects that the first Christians were Jews, and that among the Jews the most influential and necessary religious officials were the scribes whose work was to instruct the people in the law of Moses.   All of us tend to model new organizations after those with which we are familiar, and the first Christians when they separated from the synagogue created their own teachers whose work was analogous to that of the Jewish scribes.   They taught from the Old Testament and handed on orally sayings of and stories concerning Jesus, just as the scribes taught the written law and its oral counterpart, the scribal tradition. The example of the Jewish scribes in preserving so accurately their oral traditions, these Christian scribes or teachers would of course emulate.   Thus what seems strange to us, that the Church ever depended on oral instruction and memory for the preservation of the story of Jesus, was in the Jewish atmosphere of Palestine the natural and familiar way of accomplishing it.

III

I have dwelt at considerable length upon this fact of the oral transmission of the gospel narrative because to it are due certain characteristics of the story when we find it put into writing some thirty years after Jesus' death. Four such characteristics should be especially noted:

(1) During this period there were many facts, incidents, and sayings which inevitably dropped out of the story. The memory is only capable of retaining a certain amount.

Even in the case of individuals who have lived through a short period of years of unusual significance or enjoyment the memory tends to focus itself on a few outstanding incidents or memories which it retains with great clearness while the rest becomes blended into a general picture. If one will recall his years in college or high school or perhaps his service in the army during the great war, this fact will be illustrated. Thus the Christian narrative tended to drop out the less significant and to focus itself on what for the early Christians were the events of greatest importance.

(2) In this period before the story was put into writing the order of the events and the chronological connections of the sayings and incidents would tend to be obscured and forgotten. There would rarely be occasion to narrate a connected account of the entire life of Jesus. Instead a single story would be told, perhaps the story of the rich man who came to Jesus and asked what he should do to be saved, or possibly the attempt of the Sadducees to trap him with their question about the resurrection. Sometimes a problem as to Christian standards of living would arise, the problem of divorce or of a quarrel between two church members, and this would be settled by the citation of a saying of Jesus, quite apart from any setting of time or place or utterance. Many a saying or incident would lose in its constant retelling all details which seemed irrelevant and unessential. As a result of such a process the tradition came to consist to a large extent of detached sayings and episodes, each one a unit to itself, though the tendency was kept within limits by a general knowledge of the sequence of Jesus' ministry.

This is what one finds when one turns to an examination of the gospels. The teachings appear repeatedly without any recollection of when or why they were uttered and without any connection with verses which precede. What would we give, for example, to know the occasion which called forth the warning, "Give not that which is holy unto dogs nor cast your pearls before swine"? Very probably it was lost long before the gospels were written. A good illustration of successive verses which have no connection with each other and in all probability were not uttered at the same time is the section in Luke 16: 14-20 f. The lack of interest in the chronological order in which events took place may be seen by a comparison of the three first gospels. Frequently they give the same stories at quite different points in the narrative.[17]

This is no doubt the explanation why in our gospels so many of the incidents or sayings are given only an indefinite or formal setting of time and place. Note how often episodes are described indefinitely as occurring "by the seaside," [18] or "in a house," [19] or "in the way." [20] Sometimes no setting is given whatever, as in the case of the healing of the leper.[21] All of this goes back to the period when the story of Jesus' life was told by word of mouth and the insignificant, unimportant details dropped from the account. The realization of this fact prevents

[17] Note for example that Mark has the visit to Nazareth in Chapter 6, while in Luke's Gospel it is the opening act of the ministry. The Lord's Prayer is given in Matthew in Jesus's first recorded sermon (Matt. 6: 9 f.), while in Luke it appears in 11: 1 f., after the final journey to Jerusalem has begun. Other examples can easily be discovered by a comparison of the gospels.

[18] E. g., Mark 2: 13, 4: 1, 5: 21.

[19] Mark 3: 19b, 7: 17 and 24, 9: 28 and 33.

[20] Mark 10: 17, 32; 8: 27.

[21] Mark 1: 40.

one being disturbed by the differences in order in the several gospels and also serves to warn against laying too much stress on the actual sequence of verses, particularly in the case of the teachings of Jesus.

(3) A third consequence of this period of oral transmission of the gospel story was the diversity in the tradition which inevitably developed in different parts of the Church. Certain main features of the story were common of course to all of the brotherhoods, yet differences also were to be found. The narrative told by Peter in Antioch or Rome would not be identical in details or even in content with that told by Andrew or Thomas elsewhere. While all of the gospels enumerate appearances of the risen Lord, no two of the lists in the several gospels are exactly the same. It is well known that the story of Jesus' birth is told in Matthew and Luke from quite different standpoints. While some of the parables of Jesus seem to have been common property, there were others which were known to Christians in one part of the Church though yet unknown in other sections. Even in common material differences naturally developed. The Lord's Prayer is given in Matthew and in Luke in not quite identical forms.[22] Sayings translated from the original Aramaic into Greek or other languages would inevitably come to have different forms even when expressing the same thought. Illustrations of such differences of wording in the gospels are plentiful. The saying on the permanence of the law in Matthew 5: 18, for example, differs somewhat from the one in Luke 16: 17, though the two are obviously two forms of the same original saying. Thus the gospel tradition as possessed by different Christian

[22] Compare the two accounts, Matthew 6: 9 f. and Luke 11: 2 f.

groups was identical in its main outlines but different to a
certain extent in content and in form.

(4) A fourth feature of the gospels which is due to
this earliest period of its history is the predominance of
teaching material over what might be called biographical
facts. Those who told the story were evidently more
interested in sayings of Jesus, his teachings on disputed
points and difficult questions, than in incidents of historical or biographical value. One must be careful not to
overstate this point. Certain events were so vitally important to the Church that they could never be forgotten
nor neglected. Of this the best illustration is the story of
the arrest, trial, crucifixion, and resurrection of Jesus
which occupies almost a fifth of Mark and nearly an eighth
of Matthew. But aside from the story of the Passion,
even a casual examination of the gospels will show that
the greater portion of the material consists either of teachings of Jesus or of incidents which lead up to and find
their point in some saying of his. With the exception of
the Passion story the gospels for the most part are made
up of discourses or of stories like that of healing the centurion's son, the point of which was Jesus' statement, "I
have not found so great faith, no, not in Israel," or like
that of the effort of the Pharisees to trap Jesus with their
question about paying taxes to Cæsar, or like the story of
the feast in Levi's house which was the occasion of Jesus'
statement, "I came not to call the righteous, but sinners."

Several factors combined to bring about this primary
interest in the teachings of Jesus. In the first place it
must always be remembered that the interests of the first
Christians were intensely practical. They did not have
in mind gathering material for future works of history,
indeed they believed that the Lord would return very

shortly to establish his kingdom.   They were interested in
his teachings on points of dispute and his command as
to how Christians should live until his coming again.
Whereas the Law of Moses had formerly been the final
religious authority, now it was the words of the Lord.
But behind these considerations and in support of them
was the influence of the whole Jewish way of looking at
religious history and their conception of what should be
most treasured of the recollections of great leaders and
teachers.   Judaism had always emphasized the teachings
of her great leaders.   The Old Testament contains no
biography of Israel's spiritual heroes, but it contains
many books of their teachings—the laws of Moses, the
utterances of the prophets, the collections of psalms and
proverbs.   Within the Old Testament are several books of
history of the nation, but no individual biographies.
Furthermore, at the time when Christianity began, the
influence of the professional group called the scribes was
very great.   These scribes coupled to a knowledge of the
Scriptures a knowledge of what is called in the gospels
"the tradition of the elders," [23] a tradition which consisted
of the opinions and sayings of the great scribes and teachers of the past.   True, we know that they also preserved
and told ancedotes concerning these great figures, but they
were generally stories which preserved some saying worth
remembering.   Those by whom the gospel story was first
transmitted had been brought up in this Jewish way of
looking at history, and the aspects of Jesus' life which it
seemed to them natural to emphasize were his most striking sayings, parables which he had told, and incidents in
connection with which he gave some of his greatest ut-

[23] Mark 7: 5.

terances.   Later Christianity passed to gentile lands, where interests were different and where books like Plutarch's *Lives* and Tacitus' *Life of Agricola* were being written.   But by that time a selection of material in the tradition about Jesus had already taken place.

Because of this lack of much historical and biographical data which we would like to have, it has often been stated that a biography of Jesus can never be written.   It is true that much of his life is for us and always will be shrouded in mystery.   A biography in the modern sense, a complete survey of the antecedents and accomplishments, the motives and purposes of the individual studied, can never be written about Jesus.   But there are two facts which should be remembered.   In the first place this preference for and presentation of teaching material referred to above was not carried out in any complete or exclusive fashion, and a general sketch of Jesus' public ministry can be gathered from the pages of the gospels, while the most important part of the story, the final events, can be known in detail.   In the second place this practical emphasis of early Christians has resulted in a remarkable collection of sayings of Jesus and of stories which preserve his utterances on problems and issues.   From these sayings one is able to see both the ideal of life which he set forth and the character which he himself exemplified.

TOPICS FOR DISCUSSION AND REVIEW

1. Why the first Christians preferred oral testimony to written records.

2. The aspects of a story which tend to be remembered and emphasized in its repeated telling and those which tend to be forgotten. Patrick Henry's saying, "Give me liberty or give me death," or the story of Benedict Arnold's treachery will serve as good illustrations.

3. The effect of some special interest in the recollection of a story. Would this apply also to the original observation?

4. The influence of Jewish religious methods and habits of thought on the early Christian tradition.

5. The scribes, their position and work.

6. The humble and nonliterary character of the majority of early Christians. How would this affect the method by which the gospel story was preserved?

SUPPLEMENTARY READINGS

On the oral tradition of the scribes:

Moore: *Judaism,* Vol. I, pp. 251-263.

Schürer: *The History of the Jewish People in the Times of Jesus Christ,* Division II, Vol. I, pp. 317-325.

On the Christian oral tradition:

Cadbury: *The Making of Luke-Acts,* Ch. 1 and 5.

Jewish and Gentile attitudes toward biography:

Cadbury: *Op. cit.,* pp. 127-132.

CHAPTER III

THE EARLIEST GOSPEL

I

FOR some time the story of Jesus was preserved in the memories of devout men and women and transmitted to others by word of mouth. Papias, it has been noted, preferred such personal testimony even as late as the second century. But at an early date this oral tradition began to be supplemented by brief written records. When this first writing took place there is no way of knowing, but it must have begun quite early.

These first writings were of varied types, though most of them were probably brief. None of them have been preserved in their separate and original form, but there is considerable evidence for their existence. Some are referred to or quoted by early Christian writers. Others, according to the general agreement of scholars, were incorporated in whole or in part in our gospels and thus have been preserved. It will be well to note some of these. Though scholarly opinion may be wrong in some of the conclusions cited below, one may feel sure at any rate that the following represent the types of writings current in the early Church previous to our gospels:

In the first place lists were made of Old Testament passages which were believed to have been fulfilled by events in Jesus' life. How important such fulfillments of prophecy were to the first Christians is clearly indicated in the New Testament. Peter in his speeches repeatedly points out that the things which had come to pass had

40

been foretold.[1]   Stephen makes the same point in his speech of defense.[2]   Philip converted the Ethiopian eunuch by explaining to him how the fifty-third chapter of Isaiah had been fulfilled.[3]   Paul laid great emphasis on the fact that Jesus "fulfilled all the things that were written of him." [4]   But the Scriptures of that day existed in a number of separate rolls which were very difficult for the ordinary Christian to use, even when all of them were available.   Hence at an early date lists of such passages were prepared; Testimonia, they were called later, and these were very popular.

One of these early collections of proof-texts may have contributed something to the formation of the Gospel of Matthew.   This gospel, as is well known, makes a special point of quoting passages from the Old Testament which the author believed to have been fulfilled by the events narrated.[5]   It is probable that he took some of these, at any rate, from an early Christian collection rather than directly from the books of Scripture.   This is suggested by the fact that the wording of a number of his quotations differs from the Hebrew and Greek texts of the Old Testament as we now know them, and by the further fact that he attributes to Jeremiah words which are actually in Zechariah.[6]

A second type of early Christian writing seems to have consisted of lists of the genealogical descent of Jesus.

[1] Acts 2: 16 f., 25 f., 3: 18, 10: 43.

[2] Acts 7: 52.

[3] Acts 8: 32 f.

[4] Acts 13: 29, cf. Rom. 1: 2, 1 Cor. 10: 11, etc.

[5] Matt. 1: 23, 2: 5, 2: 17, 3: 2, etc.

[6] Matt. 27: 9, 10.   See Burkitt, *The Gospel History and Transmission,* pp. 124-128.

Two of these are preserved in our gospels.[7]   Both trace
Jesus' descent through Joseph.   Yet it is precisely these
gospels, Matthew and Luke, which record the virgin birth
of Jesus, thus denying that Jesus was descended from
Joseph.   The answer to this strange fact must be that
these two lists were already current in Christian circles,
serving the purpose of demonstrating Jesus' descent from
David.   It is easy to understand that the evangelists might
want to include such genealogical lists already in use, but
it is quite unlikely that they would have compiled geneal-
ogies which were not in agreement with their account of
the virgin birth.

More important from the standpoint of this book,
however, is the fact that short collections of Jesus' teachings seem to have been made.   Some of these were lists of
separate and unrelated sayings.   Others seem to have contained sayings dealing with a single theme.   Of the former
the Oxyrhynchus Papyrus quoted in the first chapter
affords a good illustration, though that particular collection may not have been put in writing until long after
the period under discussion.   But that such written collections existed previous to the gospels may be taken as
an assured fact.

Two of these collections have left some trace of their
existence.   One of them was current in the Roman Church
toward the close of the first century.   The evidence for
this is a letter written by Clement, Bishop of Rome, in
which a number of quotations of Jesus' teaching are made.
Careful comparison of these with similar sayings in the
gospels show such a variation in form between the two
records that scholars believe that Clement was using some

[7] Matt 1: 1 ff. and Luke 3: 23 ff.

collection of Jesus' teaching which has since been lost.
Streeter, for example, concludes his discussion of the
evidence with the statement that the form and content
of Clement's quotations "are evidence of the existence in
the Church of Rome of a discourse document to some extent parallel to the Great Sermon in Matthew and
Luke." [8]

The second collection referred to has left traces of its
existence by its partial reproduction in Matthew and Luke.
Much about this collection is shrouded in mystery, and
many volumes have been written in debate concerning it.
But note the following facts: Matthew and Luke were
written in widely different parts of the Church and their
accounts of Jesus' life are to a considerable extent different in content and in wording. Even quotations of Jesus'
words appear differently in the two gospels, due to the
fact that the sayings had passed from Aramaic into Greek
by independent routes. Neither evangelist had read the
other's work, and some portions of their narratives differ
so completely as to make it difficult to reconcile them at
all.[9] Now in the midst of those variations natural to two
independent accounts, one finds whole sections which
agree word for word. Much of this agreement is in
teachings of Jesus, but not all of his teaching so appears.
On the contrary some of the most important portions, the
Lord's Prayer, the Beatitudes, the teaching given at the
Last Supper, for example, show considerable differences.
Nor are the ones which are alike those which would have
been treasured most tenaciously in Christian memories.
One of the longest of the similar passages is one giving

[8] *The Four Gospels*, pp. 239 f.

[9] For the proof of the first part of this statement see the note at
the end of this chapter.

the moral injunctions of John the Baptist.[10]   In a few
cases the indentical language is to be found in narrative
portions of the story.[11]

Now why should certain portions of Jesus' teachings,
a few narratives, and portions of John the Baptist's
preaching appear in identical wording while the other
portions of the story equally as valuable be given in
wording which differs?   The conclusion to which scholars
have been led by nearly a century of study of this and
closely related problems is this: There existed previous to
the writing of the gospels a written collection chiefly of
Jesus' teachings from which Matthew and Luke, working
independently, have taken those portions of their respective stories which appear in the gospels in identical language.   Just how much of our present gospels should be
attributed to this early document and what it contained
have been extensively debated, and there is no agreement of
scholars on the point.   But that such a document (or documents) existed and is the explanation of the above facts
cannot now be doubted.   The name of the early document
is of course unknown and it has been referred to by the
symbol Q.   This is from the German word *Quelle,* meaning source, and its use is due to the fact that the early in-
vestigators of this problem were German scholars.   The
importance of this early collection of sayings and incidents
called Q will be seen later.

[10] The two passages, Matt. 3: 7-10 and Luke 3: 7-9, should be compared.   In this section of sixty-four words (in the Greek) only one
word is different.   For a section of Jesus' teaching appearing in
virtually identical wording, compare Matt. 23: 37-39 with Luke 13:
34, 35.

[11] See the account of Jesus's temptation in Matt. 4: 1-11 and Luke
4: 1-13, where the wording is virtually identical though the second
two temptations are given in reverse order.

One further illustration of early Christian writing, this time a collection of Jesus' teaching dealing with a single theme, should be noted. There is evidence that there was in circulation a discourse of Jesus foretelling the destruction of Jerusalem and giving signs which would precede the coming of the final Judgment. The importance of this topic for Christians in Palestine of the first and second generation is obvious. They saw their countrymen drifting into a final struggle with the Roman power. The attitude which they should take toward the ensuing struggle was difficult for them to determine. It is not surprising therefore that sayings of Jesus dealing with the impending fate of Jerusalem and the end of the present age should have been in circulation. Now in the Gospel of Mark there is one chapter which stands out as a unique section of the gospel, chapter thirteen. Mark contains little direct teaching of Jesus, but in this chapter we have a long discourse devoted to the single theme mentioned above. The chapter furthermore is complete within itself, has its own introduction, its climax, its final parable of warning. Its general outline and development follows the conventional form of the "apocalyptic writings," with which the Jews of that day were familiar. The literary form of the chapter is distinctly different from that of the rest of the gospel. There is general agreement therefore among scholars that this "Little Apocalypse" once circulated as a separate document. The curious injunction in verse 14, "Let him that *readeth* understand," appearing in the midst of direct words of Jesus, seems also to point to such an explanation.

There were other early writings besides these mentioned, probably a collection of Jesus' parables, a narrative of Jesus' conflicts with the Pharisees, a collection of

Jesus' injunctions to his disciples on sending them forth on their mission, and other brief writings of a similarly varied nature. The above however are sufficient to illustrate this second stage of the gospel history. If much of the above discussion has seemed to the reader conjectural and hypothetical, I would point him to the opening words of Luke's Gospel. Here in a remarkable statement the evangelist gives a summary of the way in which the gospel story had been transmitted and of the condition of the tradition when he began his work. Luke begins his gospel with these words: "Forasmuch as many have taken in hand to draw up a narrative concerning those matters which have been fulfilled among us, even as they delivered them unto us who from the beginning were eyewitnesses and ministers of the word, it seemed good unto me also, having traced the course of all things accurately from the first, to write unto thee, most excellent Theophilus, that thou mightest know the certainty concerning the things wherein thou wast instructed." [12] Here we have a picture of the process by which the gospels came to be written—the early testimony of eyewitnesses and preachers of the word, the oral instruction of converts to the faith, the numerous early written accounts, and lastly the composition of our gospels.

II

Some thirty-five or forty years after the death of Jesus the earliest of our gospels was written. The latest comes from the close of the century. The period 65-100 A.D., then, represents the third stage of the history we have been following, the period of the writing of the gospels.

[12] Luke 1: 1-4.

The first fact to grasp concerning these works is that in the beginning they were *local gospels*. Written in widely different sections of the Church, they first won local recognition and only gradually were accepted by the Church as a whole.

They were written to meet the immediate and specific needs of these local churches. The aims were evangelical and practical rather than historical. "These things are written," says the Fourth Gospel, "that ye may know that Jesus is the Christ, the Son of God, and that believing ye may have life in his name." [13] That is the motive and purpose of them all. We must not think of the writers as endeavoring to supplement one another, nor as writing with an eye to future records. In the light of this practical purpose each evangelist selected from the tradition with which he was familiar the material which he felt to be most valuable for his readers.

Naturally the same incidents reappear to a considerable extent in each of the gospels. The story of the death and resurrection formed a large part of each account. The story of the feeding of the five thousand people is in all four. The Messianic prophecies of John, the temptation of Jesus, several of the miracles of healing, a number of the parables, the account of the mission on which the Twelve were sent, and many other incidents and teachings appear in the first three. The gospels constantly overlap with each other, simply because the materials of each were chosen with a view to the needs and interests of the group for which it was written without reference to what some other writer might have recorded.

Naturally also there are differences in the accounts. It

[13] John 20: 31.

has already been remarked that the Christian tradition tended to develop differences of content and of form in different parts of the widely scattered Church. When therefore one finds in the gospels variations in wording or even differences in important points of narration one need not be surprised. It was the inevitable corollary of that process of a transmission which has been described.

The four gospels with which we are familiar were not the only ones that were written. There was a *Gospel according to the Hebrews,* a *Gospel of the Nazarenes,* a *Gospel of Peter,* and others. Some of these were written much later than our gospels, notably the last named. Others, of which *The Gospel according to the Hebrews* is the best example, were written in the same general period as the canonical gospels. Some of these other gospels were widely used by Christians. The four which are in our New Testament made their way not by some arbitrary decree or plan of selection, but due simply to their intrinsic worth and to the fact that each had become an established classic in an important section of the Church long before questions of a gospel canon arose.

III

Mark was the first of the four to be written. There is strong evidence that it began as the gospel of the church at Rome. There is an early Christian tradition to that effect and this is supported by a number of indications within the gospel, and by the absence of any effective evidence against the Roman origin. The tradition may be stated in the words of Clement of Alexandria: "The Gospel according to Mark had this occasion. As Peter had preached the word publicly at Rome, . . . many who were present requested that Mark, who had followed him for a long time and remembered his sayings, should write them out. And having composed the gospel he gave it to those who had requested it. When Peter learned of this he neither directly forbade nor encouraged it." [14] With this statement of Roman origin a number of facts in the gospel itself are in accord. It is necessary for the author to explain even the simplest Jewish customs and practices.[15] He translates also all Aramaic words and phrases which his book contains.[16] The readers apparently were ignorant of the system of coinage of Palestine and of the climate there at the time of the Passover.[17] In one case the author adapts a saying of Jesus to make it fit the conditions of life under Roman law. In 10: 11 f. the saying of Jesus prohibiting divorce is given. It reads as follows: "Whosoever shall put away his wife and marry another committeth adultery against her: and if she herself shall put away her husband and marry another, she committeth adultery." But according to Jewish law the wife could not divorce her husband, divorce being a prerogative of the husband only. The possibility of a wife divorcing her husband did not exist among the hearers of Jesus and in the saying of Jesus as given by the other gospels there is no mention of this side of the case. Roman law, on the contrary, did grant divorce to the wife as well as to the husband. It seems obvious, then, that in this instance Jesus' teaching has been interpreted and expanded for the use of readers who lived under Roman rather than Jewish law.

Other evidence for the Roman origin of Mark could be

[14] Eusebius, *Church History,* VI, 14, 6.
[15] 7: 3, 4; 15: 42.
[16] See 6: 4, 7: 11, 34, 15: 34.
[17] See 12: 42 and 11: 13.

added were it necessary. On one point, however, the tradition as quoted by Clement has to be corrected. His statement asserts that Peter knew of the work of Mark but that he had nothing directly to do with the composition of the gospel. Now there is another account of the origin of the gospel which very probably gives the true explanation and a correction of this rather curious tradition. Irenæus, who lived a generation earlier than Clement of Alexandria, and who himself had been in Rome, having mentioned Peter and Paul in a preceding sentence, makes the following statement: *"After their decease* Mark, the disciple and interpreter of Peter, also transmitted to us in writing, those things which Peter had preached." [18] These two statements of Clement and Irenæus, together with the internal evidence of the gospel, give the clue to its origin. It was written in Rome, and its story went back in part to Peter's preaching and authority; but Peter had no connection with the work, for it was not written until after his death.

This is probably the explanation, as Rawlinson has pointed out, for the attitude toward the Apostle Peter which the gospel reflects. "Peter is hardly mentioned as an individual in the pages of the gospel except in terms of rebuke or disgrace." Immediately following Peter's great confession of Jesus as the Christ he is rebuked as a tempter (8: 33 f.) ; in the story of the Transfiguration, attention is called to his foolish remark (9: 5 f.) ; in the story of the betrayal, Peter boasts of his loyalty, then falls asleep in the garden, and finally denies all knowledge of Jesus (14: 29, 37, 66 f.). "There is in fact only one reasonable explanation," concludes Rawlinson, "and it is the one involved in

[18] *Against Heresies,* III. I. i.

the acceptance of the traditional date of the gospel. When this gospel was written the character of Peter had been transfigured by martyrdom. The humiliation and shame of the past had been washed out in blood. . . . Thus the story of the past had lost its sting. Its effect was no longer to discredit St. Peter, but to serve as an encouragement to martyrdom. Those Christians who were conscious in themselves of such weakness as St. Peter had at one time displayed might nevertheless hope like St. Peter in Christ to become strong." [19]

We must not think, however, of this gospel as simply the written record of Peter's preaching. An examination of its contents disproves such a view. Though the story has many primitive characteristics it is certainly not the direct narrative of an eyewitness and actor of the events recorded. The absence of definite knowledge of place and date and the disconnected, detached character of the narratives and sayings which has previously been pointed out is quite plain in Mark. In several instances the adaptation of the account to the needs and interests of Roman Christians, as in the divorce sayings above, is to be seen. No doubt a number of the narratives go back to Peter, but they are Peter's narratives as told to and repeated in the Roman church some years later. The author must have had available also and used to a certain extent briefer written records. The apocalyptic chapter, Mark 13, is the clearest instance of this, but it is possible that there were others beside it. Not Peter's memoirs, then, though Peter contributed indirectly to it, but the work of Mark, in Rome, sometime after the death of Peter and Paul, who used in his work all the materials which were available

[19] Rawlinson, *The Gospel according to St. Mark*, p. xxviii.

—so we should describe the gospel. Since Peter was martyred in Nero's persecution of 64 A.D., the date of composition will be after that year. For the purposes of the present study we need not attempt a more exact dating than the general statement that it was written shortly before, or soon after, 70 A.D.

One last point in connection with this earliest gospel. It is singularly deficient in the teachings of Jesus. This has often been explained on the grounds that the author was a man of action and loved a vivid story. This is scarcely the explanation. The author includes two long discourses by Jesus, the apocalyptic utterances in chapter 13 and the collection of parables in chapter 4. He refers to Jesus' teaching or preaching constantly, indeed his account furnishes simply a framework for a ministry of teaching which is repeatedly mentioned, though its content is not given.[20] He speaks of the effective way in which Jesus answered his critics.[21] On the contrary the author seems much interested in Jesus' teaching. The reason why he includes in his book so little of this teaching is more probably the fact mentioned above, that there was already in circulation in Rome a written record of the teachings of Jesus. Mark's gospel was written to supplement this collection with a narrative of the chief events which had taken place. Thus understood the gospel in reality becomes one of the early writings of which so much has been said, writings which attempted to give only a part of the whole story. The full account, the combination of narrative and teaching, was the next stage in the development of Christian literature. This step was taken independently by the authors of two great

[20] Note 1: 38, 2: 2, 2: 13, 4: 1, 4: 34, 6: 2, etc.
[21] 12: 28.

works, the Gospel of Matthew and the Gospel of Luke, to which we now turn.

ADDITIONAL NOTE

It was stated on page 43 that neither of the authors of Matthew and Luke had read the other's work. The evidence for this statement is the totally different accounts which they give of the descent of Jesus, the events which preceded his birth, the resurrection appearances, the Beatitudes, the names of certain of the apostles, and other teachings and narratives which both record. It is not so much the actual difference between the two accounts which proves the point, for frequently it is possible for these differences to be reconciled, as it is the total absence of any reference by either Evangelist to other and different statements. To illustrate: In the list of the apostles in Matthew (10: 2 f.) one of the Twelve is said to have been named Thaddæus. In the list in Luke (6: 14 f.) the name of this member of the Twelve is Judas, son of James. Now the individual *may* have had both names; but if either Evangelist had read the other's list, surely we would find, "Judas, son of James, also called Thaddæus," just as in both gospels one finds "Simon, also called Peter." Such illustrations could be multiplied.

TOPICS FOR DISCUSSION AND REVIEW

1. The roll form of the Scriptures in the first century. Its effect on their use.
2. The Bible of the first Christians, its extent and its use.
3. Possible explanations of identical wording in passages in different gospels: (a) inspiration by the Holy Spirit, (b) the influence of earlier oral tradition, (c) the common use of written records.
4. The date and occasion of Mark's Gospel.
5. Special interests and characteristics of this earliest gospel.

SUPPLEMENTARY READINGS

1. On the condition of the Christian tradition when Mark wrote his gospel:
   Menzies: *The Earliest Gospel*, pp. 20-25.
2. Why the first gospel was written thirty-five years after the death of Christ:
   Streeter: *The Four Gospels*, 495-497.

3. On the originally local character of the gospels·
   Ibid., pp. 1-15.
4. On the date and authorship of Mark:
   Burkitt: *Earliest Sources for the Life of Jesus,* Ch. 4.
   McNeile: *Introduction to the New Testament,* pp. 12-14, 27-31.
   Rawlinson: *St. Mark (Westminster Commentaries),* pp. xv-
   xxiv, xxix, xxx.
5. On the historical character of Mark's Gospel:
   Burkitt: *The Gospel History and Transmission,* Ch. 3.
6. On what is known of the life of John Mark:
   Menzies: *Op. cit.,* pp. 40-51.

CHAPTER IV

THE GOSPELS ACCORDING TO MATTHEW AND LUKE

I

THE Gospel according to Mark quickly attained a widespread popularity. Rome, as Streeter remarks, "was the most convenient distributing center for the civilized world. The Christian mate of an Alexandrian grain ship, or the confidential freedman of some Antiochene merchant at Rome on his master's business, would hear a reading from the new gospel at some Sunday gathering. At once he would take steps to acquire a copy of such a treasure to take back to his fellow Christians at home.[1] Such a written narrative covering the public ministry of Jesus met an obvious need, and Christians no doubt wondered why it had not been done before. In addition to its intrinsic merits it had the backing of the influential Church at Rome and had attached to it the great name of Peter. It represented in writing the best of the Christian tradition concerning the deeds of Jesus.

But as remarked it was lacking when it came to a record of the teachings of the Lord. It contained little of his teachings on the Christian ideal of life, little about the practical duties of forgiveness and non-retaliation, very little about prayer and faith and the providential care of God, only one or two sayings on a number of important points such as the danger of riches, the sin of pride, the conduct of the Christian mission, etc. Many important

[1] *The Four Gospels,* p. 495.

55

sayings with which the Church was familiar were not included. For this material one had to go to the oral tradition or to other writings. But once a beginning had been made of a connected account of Jesus' life, the expansion of this account to include also his teachings was natural and inevitable.

The gospels of Matthew and Luke were two results of this process. For all we know there may have been other attempts to add to Mark's gospel, but, if so, the resulting works were quickly eclipsed by these two great gospels and were neglected and forgotten very soon after they were written.

That the authors of Matthew and Luke made use of Mark in constructing their works is one of the most assured results of modern Biblical scholarship. The detailed evidence in support of this conclusion cannot be presented here. It consists of many volumes of the most minute examination and comparison of the first three gospels by several generations of scholars working in different countries. But a brief summary of the leading facts which point to the conclusion may be of value, first as indicating the general character of the evidence and, secondly, as revealing the extent to which the Gospel of Mark was used by the second and third evangelists. I list six of the most striking facts:

(1) Mark begins with the public ministry of Jesus, Matthew and Luke preface this with narratives of the birth and childhood. The text of Mark ends at 16: 8.[2] Where Mark begins, Matthew and Luke begin to agree with Mark and each other in wording and general outline; where Mark ends they cease agreeing.

[2] Note the marginal comment at this point in any of the revised versions.

(2) Mark has 666 verses. Of these Matthew and Luke repeat 408 verses in more or less identical fashion. Of the remaining 258, 207 are found in Matthew but not in Luke, 21 are found in Luke but not in Matthew. This leaves only 30 verses of Mark which are not reproduced in Matthew or Luke or in both.[8]

(3) In any one section occurring in all three gospels the majority of the words of Mark will be found to appear in Matthew or in Luke or in both.

(4) The order in which the incidents are told in Matthew and Luke is generally that which is found in Mark. But where one departs from Mark's order, the other will be found to adhere to it. This is the more striking in view of the lack of early Christian attention to matters of chronological order.

(5) The way in which matter not found in Mark occurs in Marcan contexts in Matthew and Luke is such as to suggest that the authors of the latter works had before them and used as a main source the Gospel of Mark, and each interpolated additional material at what seemed appropriate points. Luke's method is to insert all non-Marcan material not definitely connected with the beginning or end of the ministry in three large blocks. Matthew rather distributes his non-Marcan material, inserting it where somewhat similar material stands in Mark.

(6) Minor verbal differences between the three gospels in parallel passages are such as to suggest that Mark is

[8] Slight variations from the above figures may be noted by the reader in different books. These variations are due to the use of different texts of Mark and to different opinions as to whether verses which show a small degree of similarity to Mark should be counted. The variations in the count, however, are not such as to affect the point involved.

the more primitive and that Matthew and Luke independently attempt to refine and improve on it.[4]

These facts, here stated in such condensed form, have to be seen in the light of their detailed proof to carry all of their cumulative weight. The general proposition which they demonstrate is of the first importance. If Mark was one of the sources used by Matthew and Luke, then Mark's account of incidents narrated in similar terms by all three will obviously be one step nearer to the original event. One is able, furthermore, to observe the special interests and methods of work of each of the later writers by observing the material they selected from Mark, the modifications they make in it, and the narratives and sayings which they felt they could omit with the least loss to their readers. Indications of date found in Mark will apply also as fixing a limit after which the other two gospels were written, and conversely indications in Matthew or Luke help to date the writing of Mark. The proposition that Mark was the earliest gospel and was used by the authors of Matthew and Luke is, in fact, the cornerstone of all modern study of the gospels.

But the authors of Matthew and Luke did not merely recopy Mark. Using that gospel as the main outline of their story, they added to it elements from other sources. In both gospels an account of Jesus' birth, told in accordance with the tradition with which each evangelist was familiar, was prefixed to Mark's story and formed the introduction to the gospel. From the important document

[4] The best short discussion of the above facts is an article by Streeter in Peake's one-volume *Commentary on the Bible,* pp. 672-678. For a longer discussion see *The Four Gospels,* Ch. VII, by the same author. The above is a summary of the argument as stated by Streeter.

referred to above by the symbol "Q" both drew a considerable body of teachings of Jesus.   Other collections and writings were available and of these use was made. A number of scholars think that Luke had another account of Jesus' trial and crucifixion besides that which Mark contains and that he even preferred it to Mark's narrative.   Luke also had at his disposal a collection of Jesus' teaching which the others seem not to have had, for in his gospel only are to be found such parables as that of the Prodigal Son, the Lost Sheep, the Lost Coin, and the Good Samaritan, as well as many sayings of Jesus.[5]   The author of Matthew, as noted above, seems to have used a collection of passages from the Old Testament.   Much more important however was another source.   In this gospel are to be found a number of sayings of Jesus which seem to enjoin obedience by Christians to the Mosaic law.   Such sayings, whatever their original meaning and intention, would have been treasured by those circles of Christians who, in contrast to Paul, maintained that the law should be kept by followers of Jesus.   This fact, in combination with certain other data, makes it likely that the Gospel of Matthew contains in part the tradition of the Jerusalem Church.   In addition to all written sources no doubt there were sayings and incidents which each evangelist had learned orally from individuals who had been eyewitnesses of the events recorded.

In this way these two great gospels took shape, present-

[5] Some scholars have recently advanced the theory that this special source of Luke had already been combined with material selected from the Q document.   Such a combination would constitute quite a lengthy document, and Streeter thinks that it was a preliminary draft of his gospel made by Luke himself.   See *The Four Gospels,* Ch. VIII.

ing to their respective sections of the Church connected accounts of the life and teaching of Jesus which were more complete and more finished than the gospel written at Rome some few years earlier. The materials out of which they were compiled were largely those available in the locality in which each was written and they were no doubt familiar in the main to local readers. But these separate and unrelated records were now brought together and the whole blended to produce two distinct portraits of the person and mind of Jesus. The various facts and sayings which the evangelists used owed their existence to the devout recollections and faithful preservation of the Church as a whole. The total impression of Jesus which emerges from each gospel was the contribution of each author, who selected, arranged, compressed, and expanded the material available.

II

The Gospel according to Matthew was very probably written in the city of Antioch in Syria.[6] The Christian group in Antioch had played an important part in the history of the Church. There, according to Acts, the gospel was first preached to Greeks.[7] It was in this city that the name Christian was first applied.[8] In Antioch Barnabas had worked with great success, and it was by the church there that he and Paul were sent out on their missionary journey.[9] The church in Antioch was in close contact with the one in Jerusalem. In Acts alone there is mention of three different delegations which came from

---

[6] For the evidence on this point the reader is referred to Streeter, *op. cit.*, pp. 500-511.

[7] 11:20.   [8] Acts 11:26.   [9] Acts 13:1 ff.

Jerusalem to Antioch and two which went from Antioch to the mother church.[10] Peter also spent some time in the church there.[11] Thus it is easy to see that its local church traditions would have been rich in content.

In another respect also Antioch is noteworthy as the place of origin of this gospel. It was here that the controversy over the observance of the Mosiac law came to a head. Due to the large Jewish population of the city [12] and to the fact that it was in such constant contact with Jerusalem, orthodox influences were strong, while on the other hand the church had enjoyed the liberal leadership of its first founders, of Barnabas and of Paul. The conflict of these two points of view is therefore not surprising. It was the church at Antioch which precipitated the conference at Jerusalem over the issue and it was at Antioch that the personal controversy on this point involved Paul, Peter, and Barnabas.[13] It is significant that the problem of the Jewish law is one of the leading themes of the Gospel of Matthew.

As to the author we are dependent on Christian tradition, for the gospel itself is completely anonymous.[14] From an early time it was attributed to Matthew, the publican, a member of the Twelve. But all of the earliest witnesses to this tradition agree that the book which Matthew wrote was in the Hebrew language (Aramaic),

[10] 11: 27, 15: 1 and 15: 22; 11: 30 and 15: 2.

[11] Gal. 2: 11.

[12] "The Jewish race densely interspersed among the native populations of every portion of the world is particularly numerous in Syria. . . . But it was at Antioch that they especially congregated."—Josephus, *The Jewish War,* VII. 3. 1.

[13] See Acts 15: 1 ff. and Gal. 2: 11 ff.

[14] It must be remembered that the headings to the books of the New Testament are not part of the original texts.

while our gospel is a Greek work. Furthermore, careful linguistic study of the gospel and comparison of it with Mark makes it certain that it is not the Greek translation of a Hebrew original. If Matthew wrote a Hebrew gospel, as all the earliest witnesses testify, this one, in its present form, is not his work.

This is borne out by the contents of the gospel. The narrative portions of Matthew are taken in the main from the Gospel of Mark, the author having virtually nothing to add to the story contained in that work. One of the original apostles would not have been so dependent upon the account of one who had not been an eyewitness. The same impression is given by his arrangement of the sayings. We shall see shortly that he grouped them into a number of lengthy discourses. He evidently had no first-hand information as to the original occasion of the sayings. Hence there is unanimous agreement among scholars that this gospel which will always bear the name of Matthew was not written by one of the originial Twelve.

How, then, did it come to have this name, for the early tradition is cited too often to be ignored, and Matthew was too insignificant a member of the Twelve to have been selected had the early writers merely been hazarding a pious guess? The most likely explanation is that Matthew, the publican, wrote one of the works which was used by the author of the gospel. Just as Peter's name was remembered in connection with Mark's Gospel, so in similar fashion the name of Matthew was associated with the great gospel of the Church at Antioch. Attempts have been made to identify this work of Matthew. Some think that it was the document Q, others the collection of proof-texts from the Old Testament. Such guesses can be neither proved nor disproved.   One must be content with the general conclusion that the gospel was written by an unknown Jewish Christian of Antioch who probably used in its compilation an earlier writing by the apostle whose name it bears.

While space does not permit an exhaustive discussion of the characteristics of the gospel, there are three features which should be noted before we proceed.

In the first place this gospel more than any other stresses the fact that Jesus was the long-awaited Messiah of his people whose life and deeds had been foretold by the ancient prophets.   Particularly does it emphasize the fact that those traits of his character and circumstances of his life which were obstacles to his acceptance by Jews had been prophesied in the Old Testament.   Thus his lowly birth in Bethlehem and residence in Galilee of the Gentiles (2: 6 and 4: 15), his acceptance of the burden of human suffering and grief (8: 17), his silence as to his Messiahship (12 16 f.), his entry into Jerusalem riding upon an ass (21: 5), his rejection by the Jews (21: 42), even his betrayal by Judas for thirty pieces of silver (27: 9)—all had been foretold.   These and other fulfillments of words of the prophets cited in the gospel indicate the essentially Jewish character of the author's thought and outlook.

A second feature of this gospel is its portrayal of Jesus as a Teacher and Lawgiver, "one greater than Moses," whose words constituted a new law superseding that which had been so long in force.   Using older materials the author has so arranged and organized them as to present this conception with force.   The sayings of Jesus given on various occasions are massed chiefly into five formal discourses, equaling in number the books of the law. The first of these discourses is delivered from a mountain as in the case of the Mosaic legislation.[15] With reference to this older law it is said that Jesus came not to destroy but to fulfill it,[16] and this is followed by a number of specific contrasts in which it is shown how his teachings supplement and complete the law "said to them of old." [17] In spite of some elements in the tradition which do not fit smoothly into the conception, the gospel thus works its way up to the closing words of the "Great Commission": "Go ye therefore and make disciples of all the nations, . . . teaching them to observe all the things whatsoever I commanded you." [18] The duty of the Church is thus to obey the words of Jesus rather than the law of Moses. This was the basis of the answer which the gospel gave to the problem of the Mosaic law which was felt so acutely by Jewish Christians. Written in a church where the two opposing points of view were both strongly maintained, the gospel utilized sayings of Jesus to present the view that the old law had not been destroyed by Jesus but rather completed or carried to its fulfillment, and that his teachings thus constituted a new law which was binding upon all Christians. This view of the matter was so satisfactory and helpful that it gradually became adopted by the Church as a whole and is probably the view of the average Christian to-day, although we shall see that Jesus never thought of his teachings as a new body of laws—taking the place of those of Moses.

A third feature of this gospel which should be noticed

[15] Note that in Luke the same Great Sermon is said to have been delivered on a level place. (Luke 6: 17.)

[16] Matt. 5: 17.   [17] Matt. 5: 21-43.   [18] Matt. 28: 19 f.

is its organization of the sayings of Jesus into formal discourses of considerable length. There are a number of these, five of which end with the same formula of conclusion. These are:

The Sermon on the Mount, Ch. 5-7.
The Mission Charge to the Disciples, Ch. 10.
The Discourse on Parables, Ch. 13.
Sayings on Offenses and Forgiveness, Ch. 18.
Sayings concerning the End of the World and the
Final Judgment, Ch. 24, 25.

These discourses, with a sixth which does not have the stereotyped formula of conclusion (Matt. 23), are a noteworthy characteristic of the gospel, and give it a tone of dignity and formality which the other gospels, with their unconnected incidents and sayings, do not have. That the discourses have been built up by the editor of the gospel by the process of collecting together sayings on the same or related topics seems clear. Each of the discourses when examined will be found to consist of sayings found in various contexts in the other gospels with some material peculiar to this gospel added. The editor of the gospel has merely organized his scattered materials, very probably for pedagogical purposes.

There are other features of the Gospel of Matthew to which one would like to call attention. The author's mathematical arrangement of much of his material in series of three, five, or seven, for example, suggests that he himself was one of the Christian teachers and was endeavoring to facilitate memorization by his readers.[19]

[19] See the long lists of these in Plummer, *Commentary on Matthew,* pp. xix-xxii, or the briefer one in Moffatt, *Introduction to the Literature of the New Testament,* p. 257.

One should also call attention to the strong universalistic outlook of the gospel. The message of Christ is to be "proclaimed to the whole world"[20] and Christian missionaries are to "make disciples of all nations."[21] But space forbids any elaboration of these points. Suffice it to say that this most Jewish of the gospels quickly attained widespread popularity and in time completely eclipsed its predecessor Mark. In the earliest lists of the gospels in use in the Church one finds Matthew first in the list, a testimony to its popularity rather than to its priority in time.

III

In contrast with Matthew, the most Jewish of the gospels, the Gospel according to Luke is the most Gentile. Its author most probably was a Gentile and it was written for Christian readers who were for the most part Gentiles. Such descriptive phrases in the gospel as "Capernaum, a city of Galilee," "a city of Galilee named Nazareth," "the country of the Gerasenes, which is over against Galilee," were not written for people who knew all about these places and their location. Incidents in Mark involving details of Jewish law, such as the controversy over eating with unwashed hands, the author omits entirely, nor is he interested in the larger question of the validity and authority of the Mosaic legislation. On the other hand, he shows an eager interest in the conversion of the Gentiles and in the rejection of Jesus by the Jewish nation. He is careful to date his story by reference to the year of the emperor and the names of the governors and tetrarchs of the political divisions in Palestine.[22] In Acts 28: 2 there

[20] Matt. 24: 14.   [21] Matt. 28: 18.   [22] Luke 3: 1.

is a phrase, "the barbarians showed us no common kindness," which seems to show that the author contrasted
himself with those who were non-Greek, "the barbarians."
None of these taken by itself would be conclusive, but
taken together and with certain other indications in the
gospel and in Acts, they indicate that the author was a
Gentile.   Indeed, it is quite likely that these two books are
the only ones in the New Testament which have come
from the hand of a Gentile.

According to tradition this Gentile was Luke the
physician.   Irenæus, whose statement about Matthew has
already been cited, states that "Luke, the attendant of
Paul recorded in a book the gospel which Paul declared." [23]   This was the common belief of the Church
by the end of the second century.   The tradition, however,
has been questioned by some scholars on the ground that
the book of Acts—written by the same hand—pictures
Paul as quite in harmony with the leaders of the church
at Jerusalem over the issue of the Mosaic law, a picture
which Paul's own letters correct.   A companion of Paul,
it is argued, would have known of these differences and
difficulties and would not have presented so harmonious
a picture as is to be found in Acts.   But Luke, it must be
remembered, was a physician, not a theologian, a Gentile,
not a Jew, a writer more concerned in emphasizing the
providential development upon which the Church looked
back than in reviving and putting on permanent record
unpleasant memories of differences among the apostles.
In view of a considerable body of internal evidence in the
book of Acts in favor of the traditional view, the objec-
tions to the Lucan authorship fall short of producing con-

[23] Eusebius, *Church History*, V, 8, 3.

viction. Irenæus, however, goes too far in stating that Luke "recorded the gospel which Paul preached." That is a deduction from the tradition, but one which the works themselves show to be unwarranted. On certain points he did not share nor even understand Paul's point of view.

As to the place of origin of the gospel nothing definite is known. Various localities are mentioned in one way or another in connection with the work. One tradition attributes it to the province of Achæa (Corinth was its chief city), Alexandria is named by another, Rome is mentioned in a third. The evidence is too vague and insufficient for a positive decision to be made. Rome is unlikely. Beyond that, all that one can say with assurance is that it was written in some great center of the Church sufficiently far from Antioch in Syria for its traditions of Jesus' birth and resurrection to be different from those that went into the Gospel of Matthew, and sufficiently in touch with Rome for a copy of the Gospel of Mark to have reached it soon after publication. It is generally agreed that it was written in the period 85-95 A.D.— twenty to thirty years after Paul's death and at a time when a serious persecution of the Church by the Roman government was either imminent or in progress.

Two special features of Luke's Gospel should be noted. The author was a man of marked literary skill and his gospel exhibits a smoothness and finish to be found in none of the others. In quoting Mark, Luke constantly improves the rough Greek of his source. In putting together incidents from different sources he takes pains to make the connections smooth and natural. Frequently he inserts questions or statements addressed to Jesus which provide a natural occasion for some saying. A good example of this is to be seen in 11 : 45 where the statement (or question), "Teacher, in saying this thou reproachest us also," put in the mouth of one of the lawyers (scribes) provides a natural transition from Jesus' rebuke of the Pharisees to that of the scribes. That such a touch is the work of Luke himself is indicated by a comparison of the account with the similar words in Matthew where no such statement is to be found.[24] For detached parables or sayings of Jesus the author frequently provides appropriate settings by referring to some current criticism of Jesus, some question of his disciples, or merely to the presence of the multitudes. Note the appropriate introduction which is provided for the three great parables of the Lost Sheep, the Lost Coin, and the Prodigal Son.[25] In some instances he introduces a dinner table conversation into the story in order to provide a striking setting for some saying.[26] In all these cases Luke is not taking unwarranted liberties with his history, but merely connects together in a smooth manner the different elements in his story by mention of situations or questions, generally those which the material itself implies. Due to these editorial modifications and improvements, the Gospel of Luke is, from a literary standpoint, the most readable of the gospels.

A second characteristic of the Third Gospel which should be mentioned has to do with its content, or rather,

---

[24] See Matt. 23 : 2 f. This is one of Matthew's discourses which he has built up by combining words from Mark, Q, and elsewhere. The saying of Luke 11 : 45 appears in verse 4.

[25] 15 : 1. For other examples see 11 : 29, 12 : 41, and 16 : 14.

[26] For example, 11 : 37. This is another one of the sayings which appears in Matthew's long rebuke to Pharisees and scribes. Had the setting given it in Luke been original it would scarcely have been dropped by Matthew.

its spirit as a whole. The gospel is pervaded by a spirit of tenderness, sympathy, and grace which even the casual reader will feel. This is due partly to the writer's skill and delicacy of touch, but even more to his special interest in certain aspects of the story. It will be possible here only to mention some of these special interests and to refer the reader to the commentaries and special studies on the gospel where these are treated at length. Luke is the gospel of the outcasts and the poor. In this gospel only do we find the statement, "The Son of Man came to seek and to save the lost," and the remarkable saying, "There shall be joy in heaven over one sinner that repenteth, more than over ninety and nine righteous persons who need no repentance." In Luke only is found the story of the woman who was a sinner who anointed Jesus' feet with ointment and wiped them with her hair (7: 36 f.). Here only is to be found the parable of the Pharisee and the publican who were praying in the temple, the parable of the Lost Coin, and that of the Prodigal Son. In this gospel only is the story of Zacchæus, who gave half of his goods to feed the poor, the sayings, "Blessed are ye poor, . . . Woe unto ye rich," and the parables of Lazarus and Dives and the Rich Fool who filled his barns with good things. The Third Gospel is also the one in which women and children and domestic scenes play a larger rôle than in any other. Here we find the stories of Mary and Martha, the mention of the women who ministered unto Jesus of their substance, the description of family relationships in the story of the Prodigal Son, and a greater interest in Jesus' presence as a dinner guest. In this gospel the religious attitudes most stressed are those of repentance, gratitude, prayer, and kindly service to one's fellows, while, correspondingly, God's gracious forgiveness and his gift of the Holy Spirit are emphasized. These special interests in the gospel go back undoubtedly to the character and spirit of the author. More than any of the other evangelists Luke possessed a sense of sympathy and understanding for the more delicate emotions of the heart as well as a skill in portraying them. If one will read in the gospel two stories only, he will not ask for further proof—the story of the woman whose sins were forgiven "because she loved much," and the parable of the profligate and prodigal son who returned to his father's house.[27]

TOPICS FOR DISCUSSION AND REVIEW

1. The importance of the discovery that the Gospel of Mark was one of the sources used in the composition of Matthew and Luke.

2. The value of identical wording as a proof of this fact. What does identical wording in two examination papers generally indicate?

3. Study in a Harmony or Synopsis the following parallel passages:

Mark 1: 40-44 = Matthew 8: 1-4 = Luke 5: 12-14.

Mark 2: 1-12 = Matthew 9: 1-8 = Luke 5: 17-26.

(a) Which of the two, Matthew or Luke, follows the wording of Mark the more exactly?

(b) What reasons can you suggest for some of the changes made by Matthew or Luke in Mark's account?

4. Discuss the respective value of the arguments against the apostolic authorship of the First Gospel. Compare Matthew with Mark as regards its connection with the original apostles.

5. In what phases of the story of Jesus' life would one expect a Gentile writer to be least interested? In what phases would he be most interested?

SUPPLEMENTARY READINGS

On the priority of Mark's Gospel:

Burkitt: *Earliest Sources for the Life of Jesus,* pp. 33-38.

On the source called Q:

Ibid., pp. 38-47.

Streeter: *The Four Gospels,* pp. 182-186.

[27] Luke 7: 36-50 and 15: 11-32.

On the authorship of Matthew:

    McNeile: *The Gospel according to St. Matthew*, pp. xxviii-xxx.

    Robinson: *The Gospel of Matthew (Moffatt's New Testament Commentary)*, pp. ix-xiii.

On the special interests and character of the Gospel of Matthew:

    McNeile: *Introduction to the New Testament*, pp. 7-12.

    Montefiore: *The Synoptic Gospels* (2d ed.), Vol. I, pp. lxxiii-lxxviii.

On what we know about Luke, the man:

    Hastings: *Dictionary of the Bible*, Art. "Luke."

On the special interests of Luke's Gospel:

    Cadbury: *The Making of Luke-Acts*, Ch. 17 and 18.

    McNeile: *Introduction to the New Testament*, pp. 14-18.

On the date of writing of the gospels:

    McNeile: *Op. cit.*, pp. 27-36.

CHAPTER V

THE GOSPEL ACCORDING TO JOHN

I

THE three gospels, Matthew, Mark, and Luke, form a group to themselves. They were written in the same period, were the product of the same process in the growth of the Christian tradition, and are related to one another by the use to a certain extent of common materials. They are called the Synoptic Gospels, a term which rests on the fact that the contents of the three are so much alike that they can be arranged in parallel columns and a synopsis made of the whole.

On the other hand the distinction and uniqueness of the Fourth Gospel has been recognized from the earliest days of the Church. Clement of Alexandria, whose words concerning the origin of Mark and Matthew have already been quoted, concludes his statements concerning the gospels with this striking sentence: "Last of all, John, perceiving that the external facts had been made plain in the gospel, being urged on by his friends and inspired by the Spirit, composed a spiritual gospel." [1] In this statement three affirmations are made concerning the Gospel of John: (a) It was the latest gospel of the four; (b) it does not attempt to present a biography or life of Jesus; and (c) it is to be understood as a "spiritual gospel"— *i. e.*, one intended to convey a definite religious message and teaching rather than to record a series of historical facts. These three phases of the gospel, with certain implications which they carry, may be considered in turn.

[1] Eusebius, *Church History*, VI, 14, 7.

(a) The Gospel of John, like so many of the other early Christian writings, contains no statement as to when or under what circumstances it was written. There are some statements which seem to look back to the events narrated as if over a long period of time,[2] but these could have been written any time after twenty-five years, let us say, had elapsed. Other indications in the book, such as the developed theology to be found in the opening words, are equally indefinite. In such a case there is only one recourse left. That is to trace back through the extant literature of the third and second centuries all references to and quotations from the gospel until all such references and quotations cease. The last one of these will give the date before which the gospel certainly was written. This method of procedure yields the following results: By 180 A.D., all four gospels were so firmly established in the Church that one finds it argued that since there are four directions, four winds, four faces to the cherubim, etc., there must have been four and only four gospels. At this date quotations from the gospel are plentiful. At 150 A.D., the quotations are but sparing. About the year 130 A.D. there are traces of its use and also very probably an indirect reference to it in a saying of Papias. The Epistles of Ignatius, written in 110 A.D., show a remarkable familiarity with the circle of ideas found in the gospel. Previous to this date there is no evidence of the existence of the gospel. On the other hand study of the Fourth Gospel itself shows it to have been familiar with two of the Synoptic Gospels, if not with all three. We have seen that these were not in existence until 85 or 90 A.D. and a few years must be al-

[2] 7: 39, 11: 13, for example.

lowed for them to have gained currency. Thus the Fourth Gospel was not written before 90 nor after 110 A.D. We may summarize these results by saying that it was written about the beginning of the second century of the Christian era.

The situation which the Church faced at the beginning of this second century was a critical one. "The first fine flush of enthusiasm" was beginning to fade. In every Christian community there were members who had been born into the Church and whose faith was inherited rather than acquired for themselves. The original apostles and founders of the Church and the eyewitnesses who had told of Jesus' deeds were virtually all gone. The mother Church at Jerusalem, which had been a unifying center in the early days, had ceased to exist after the destruction of the city by the Romans in 70 A.D. The hope of the first Christians which had centered around the expectation of an early return of Christ was giving way to skepticism. In addition to these specific difficulties the Church found itself in a new world. It was now predominantly Gentile in membership and location and its future development obviously was to be along Gentile lines. This meant that the older Jewish phrases and ideas were no longer very convincing. New theological concepts had to be faced. The thought of Jesus as the Jewish Messiah who was expected to restore the kingdom of David was not particularly impressive nor appealing to Gentiles whose thoughts had been moulded by Platonic and Stoic philosophy, nor was the term, "The Kingdom of God," which had been so central in early Christian thinking, very full of meaning. The Fourth Gospel, then, was a gospel for an age of transition, a statement of the essential elements of the Christian faith for a time of uncertainty over what these essentials were and what the older statements meant.

(b) In such a situation the need was not merely for more biographical data concerning Jesus. The tradition handed on orally, the written records of sayings and episodes and, finally, the more complete written accounts in the first three gospels provided the essential facts concerning Jesus' life. What was needed was not more information but more understanding.

John, therefore, did not set himself to write another biography. A glance at the gospel will show this immediately. He adds very few incidents to the stock of information which the Synoptic Gospels provide. The list of such new incidents to be found in the gospel is short—the story of the marriage feast at Cana, the raising of Lazarus, the healing of a blind man, a nobleman's son, and a man by the pool of Bethesda, a conversation with Nicodemus and one with a woman of Samaria, the fact of visits to Jerusalem previous to the final one—this, with the exception of small touches added to the familiar stories, is virtually all. The fact also that he repeats a number of incidents told by the other evangelists makes it plain that he did not write, as sometimes it has been suggested, simply to supply what the previous gospels had left out. John the Baptist's testimony, the feeding of the five thousand, the cleansing of the temple, the triumphal entry, Christ's walking on the water, the denial of Peter, the trial and crucifixion, all are narrated in John despite the fact that these appear in all three of the other gospels.

John thus presupposes the existence of the other gospels and wrote neither for the purpose of displacing them nor of supplementing their account of the facts. In the words of Clement, "Last of all, John . . . composed a spiritual gospel."

(c) There were two specific dangers which threatened the Church at the time the Fourth Gospel was written. On the one hand there was the danger that Christianity would lose its creative power and become simply a narrative of certain events of history coupled with a belief that Jesus would come again at some future hour. Such a conception made the religion a matter of great importance at a past and a future date, but not for the present. This loss of a sense of reality and power was due to the factors already mentioned, the passing of the original founders and eyewitnesses, the settling down process of a religious organism now in its third generation, and the fact that its hopes and beliefs were stated in terms derived from the Jewish thought world of a previous generation rather than in terms and ideas of the world in which the Church now found itself. In the second place, there was an opposite danger. Christianity was surrounded by a welter of popular religions, the majority of which were based on mythological accounts of deeds performed by angels and semi-divine beings for the redemption of mankind. There was danger that Christianity would be assimilated to this type of religion, and that the story of the life of Jesus would gradually lose its reality and become more and more a sacred myth. The inevitable result of this tendency, as was demonstrated in certain Christian circles, was the introduction of various mythological beings into the story, and the loss of the distinctive elements which Jesus himself had imparted to the religion. Thus on the one hand Christianity was in danger of becoming merely a story of great deeds once performed, while on the other hand and in other circles there was a possibility of its losing connection with the facts of history to which it owed its genius.

In this critical hour of transition the Gospel of John was written. It met the difficulties the Church was facing by interpreting the life of Christ in a new and larger fashion than had been attempted before. The essential beliefs were reworked in terms of contemporary philosophic thought. No longer is Peter's confession, "Thou art the Christ"—*i. e.*, the Messiah of Jewish expectation— the climax of the narrative. Instead, the author applies to Jesus the term "Logos" (most unfortunately translated "Word" in our English Bibles), which current Stoic and Platonic writing and discussion had made familiar to educated minds of the day.[3] Instead of beginning the gospel with the genealogy of Jesus or with the stories of his birth or childhood, the author sets forth certain great propositions which were to become the basis for future theological thinking: "In the beginning was the Word, and the Word was with God, and the Word was God. . . . All things were made by him, and without him was not anything made that hath been made. In him was life; and the life was the light of men. . . . And the Word became flesh, and dwelt among us, and we beheld his glory, the glory as of the only begotten of the Father." [4] This is very different from the concrete narratives of the Synoptic Gospels. It is a delineation of Jesus in the highest terms available in the Gentile rather than in the Jewish world.

There was a practical as well as a theological purpose behind this description. The divine "Word," which was

[3] The term "Logos" was used in philosophic thought to refer to the divine reason or mind immanent in and explaining all natural phenomena.

[4] John 1: 1, 3, 4, and 14.

in the beginning and through whom all things were made, was not limited in life and activity to the few short years of his earthly ministry. The death upon the cross had only meant the removal of the limitations of the flesh. Henceforth Christ became an invisible spiritual presence in the hearts of those who loved him. The life on earth and the death on the cross had been preliminary to an inner communion more intimate and more revealing than his intercourse with his disciples during the days of his flesh. Thus in answer to the current tendency to regard Christianity as something which had happened seventy years before, John repeated in clearer and more consistent terms the thought which Paul had emphasized, the continued presence of Christ in the hearts and lives of his followers. The expressions of this Christian mysticism are among the most beautiful in the New Testament. "It is expedient for you that I go away; for if I go not away, the Comforter will not come unto you; but if I go, I will send him unto you." [5] "I will not leave you desolate: I come unto you. Yet a little while, and the world beholdeth me no more; but ye behold me: because I live, ye shall live also." [6] "I am the vine, ye are the branches: he that abideth in me, and I in him, the same beareth much fruit; for apart from me ye can do nothing. . . . If ye abide in me, and my words abide in you, ask whatsoever ye will, and it shall be done unto you." [7] The gospel thus declared that Christianity was a present power, not a past history. Similarly, it translated the Christian belief in a future judgment and reward into present and living terms: "This is the judgment, that the light has come into the world,

[5] John 16: 7.   [6] John 14: 18 f.   [7] John 15: 5, 7.

and men loved the darkness rather than the light. . . . He
that believeth on the Son hath eternal life." [8]

Such conceptions, however, tended to encourage the
contemporary tendency to regard the earthly life of Jesus
as unimportant and to make him a purely spiritual and
supermundane being. John's answer to this danger is to
insist on the reality of Jesus' earthly life. "The Word
was *made flesh,* and dwelt among us." By means of
that earthly life we are able to know the nature and character of the invisible, indwelling Christ. Professor Scott
has suggested that it is for this reason that the author
throws his work into the form of a gospel.[9] The opening
words of the First Epistle of John, written by the same
hand, are the clue also to the gospel. "That which was
from the beginning, that which we have heard, that which
we have seen with our eyes, and our hands handled, concerning the Word of life, . . . declare we unto you also." [10]

But this life story the author does not attempt to tell
in its details. He is more interested in summing up its
essence. The specific controversies over points of the law,
the criticisms of different Jewish parties, the sayings of
Jesus on the duty of forgiveness, the dangers of wealth,
the need of humility and the other practical aspects of the
life of the kingdom of God, he leaves to the Synoptic
Gospels to tell. He is content to sum it up: "This is my
commandment, That ye love one another, even as I have
loved you." [11] In addition to this theme, which comes to
frequent expression in the discourses, there is another.
Over against the speculations which peopled the unseen
universe with various other divine and semi-divine beings,

[8] John 3: 19 and 36.
[9] *The First Age of Christianity,* p. 220.
[10] 1 John 1: 1-3.   [11] John 15: 12.

John emphasized that Christ was the "only begotten Son."
In him was to be seen completely and perfectly the mind
of the Father. In the Prologue it is stated, "The Word
was God," and this emphasis on the complete revelation
of God to be seen in Christ is carried through the
gospel.[12]

This brief sketch of the aim and purpose of the gospel
is necessarily inadequate. For the full thought of the
writer and for the unity and harmony of his ideas one
must go to the gospel itself. It is sufficient, however, to
show that the object of the gospel was *to convey a religious and spiritual message about Jesus* rather than to
record the facts of his life. One turns therefore to the
question of the materials he has used and the method
he has followed in order to present this message.

II

There are three means by which the evangelist con-
veys this religious message to the reader. In the first
place he states his own convictions quite directly. A comparison here with the Synoptic Gospels is instructive. In
the latter there is virtually no comment by the writers
themselves. The events and sayings recorded are allowed
to tell their own story. True, the author of Matthew
calls attention to the fulfillment of ancient prophecies in
the events narrated, but even in so doing the intrusion
of his own thought into the story is confined to the absolute minimum. John, on the other hand, opens his gospel
with certain statements of his own about Jesus and his
nature which occupy over a column in the average English
Bible. In the course of the gospel, furthermore, he does

[12] For example, in such passages as 10: 30 ("I and the Father are
one"), 5: 20, 10: 37, etc.

not hesitate to insert his own comments. Sometimes he does so without giving a clear indication where the words of Jesus end and his own comments begin. A clear illustration of this is in the third chapter. Up to verse 11 or 12 Jesus has been speaking and the discourse is in the first person. From verse 14 on the third person is used in referring to Christ and the words—including the familiar John 3: 16—are clearly the evangelist's own comment.

In the second place the author uses incidents from the life of Jesus to convey his thought. He tells the story of a conversation at a well with a Samaritan woman in order to present in it the thought that Jesus is the living water, and that whoever partakes thereof shall never thirst.[13] He narrates the feeding of the five thousand as an introduction to a discourse presenting Jesus as the bread of life.[14] He describes the restoration of the sight of a blind man as an illustration of the proposition, "I am the light of the world." [15] In all these and other instances the interest is not in the incidents themselves but rather in the message which they suggest. This is demonstrated by the fact that the author sometimes does not trouble even to complete the story. Was Nicodemus converted as a result of the famous interview with Christ? John does not say how the conversation concluded. What happened when the Greeks came and asked to see Jesus? We are not told; their request is mentioned only as the introduction to a discourse the point of which is the thought, "And I, if I be lifted up from the earth, will draw *all men* unto me." [16] Such facts as these show

[13] John 4: 7-14 ff.

[14] John 6: 13, 32-35.

[15] John 9: 5 ff.

[16] John 12: 32.

plainly that the gospel must be read as a work of interpretation rather than one of history.

This brings us to the third means which the writer has employed. He has constructed a number of discourses of Jesus in which the great themes of the gospel are given their clearest presentation. Are these to be regarded as the exact words of Jesus?

There are two considerations which throw further light on this question. In the first place, the teaching which these discourses contain is noticeably different from that in the Synoptic Gospels. The subject matter is not the same. In the first three gospels the sayings of Jesus deal with the practical duties of men, the specific issues which arose between Jesus and the Pharisees over the law, the nature of the kingdom of God, the impending Day of Judgment, and the necessity of repentance. In John the discourses concern themselves for the most part with the divine nature of the Son, his revelation of the Father, his gift of life to men, his abiding presence with his followers after his death, and the fulfillment of his commandments by love. In method, the teachings of the Synoptic Gospels are concrete and specific. The principle of forgiveness of one's enemy, for example, is enunciated and then applied to various specific situations, turning the other cheek, going the second mile, praying for the enemy, etc.[17] In John the teaching is for the most part in abstract and general terms. In form the teaching of the Synoptics is figurative and picturesque, full of metaphors and similes, with many of those longer illustrations which we call parables. In John there are no parables and few figures of speech. The latter are chiefly confined to terms de-

---

[17] Matt. 5: 38 ff.

scriptive of Jesus—"I am the good shepherd," "I am the vine," "I am the light of the world," etc. It is sometimes said that the explanation of these differences is to be found in the fact that the teaching in the Synoptic Gospels was addressed to the general public, while that in John was given to his intimate disciples who could understand the deeper truths. A glance at the gospels will show that this is true in neither case. Many of the most typical sayings in the Synoptic Gospels were addressed to his intimate disciples, the Mission Charge, the warning against the leaven of the Pharisees, the apocalyptic sayings, the Lord's Prayer, to mention only a few examples.[18] Conversely, a number of the most characteristic discourses in the Fourth Gospel are addressed to the multitudes and to hostile Pharisees.[19]

The second consideration mentioned above is one that is difficult for a modern reader to grasp. It is that in the Gentile literary world of John's day exact quotation of the words of some great teacher or hero was not regarded as necessary so long as one was faithful to his spirit and general ideas. In the days before printing, when no such things as quotation marks and footnotes existed, when the ideas of copyright and property values in writing were unthought of, the modern point of view in this matter simply did not exist. Illustrations of this attitude are plentiful. Thucydides, who was one of the most conscientious of all Greek historians, explains in the beginning of his history that where a speech had to be provided for any of his characters he has supplied sentiments which he felt were appropriate to the speaker and the occasion.[20] Plato, who

---

[18] Matt. 10: 5, 16: 5, Mark 13: 1, Luke 11: 1.

[19] John 6: 22-51, 10: 24-38, etc.   [20] 1: 22.

felt that he owed everything to Socrates, composed his writings in the form of dialogues in which Socrates is the principal speaker. In none of these dialogues does Plato feel under any obligation to confine himself to the exact words of Socrates, while in the later ones the thought is developed to a point considerably beyond the actual views of his teacher. Those who have read the *Agricola* of Tacitus will recall the clever satires on Roman social life and political administration which the Latin historian puts into the mouths of the British chieftains. To this point of view the Jewish literary tradition offered a striking contrast. The latter, due probably to the collection of the proverbs and maxims of the "wise men" and to the transmission of the decisions of famous rabbis concerning the oral law, preserved the actual words of great teachers of the past. It is to this Jewish practice of preserving as far as possible the exact words of a teacher that we owe the different collections of sayings of Jesus found in the Synoptic Gospels. The Gentile readers of John's gospel, however, familiar themselves with the teachings recorded in the Synoptic Gospels, would readily understand that the author did not intend the speeches in the Fourth Gospel to be a verbatim report of his utterances.[21]

In the light of these two considerations one returns to the question asked above. No doubt many of the sayings to be found in the Fourth Gospel do go back to genuine sayings of Jesus. The author knew certain facts of the life of Jesus not mentioned in the other gospels— the earlier visits to Jerusalem, for example—and it is likely that he knew additional sayings as well. But these

[21] See Streeter, *op. cit.*, 369, 370.

sayings had been meditated upon for many years in a mind of profound originality and power which sought to seize their inner meaning and deeper significance. Furthermore, the writer was a Christian prophet who believed in the guidance of the Church by the Holy Spirit. "The Spirit shall guide you into all truth," he writes in his gospel. The message which he gave to the Church in his gospel, therefore, was not simply his own. The author had reached certain conclusions concerning Christ's work and message which were not to be found in the familiar tradition of the churches, but he believed that he had reached them not by his own intellectual efforts alone but by direct revelation of the Spirit of Jesus. As Canon Streeter states it, "John knows quite well that his theology is a development of the original Apostolic teachings, but it is a development directly inspired by the Spirit." [22]

How then shall we read the discourses of the Fourth Gospel and what is their value? Written at a critical hour of change and transition they represent the greatest of all interpretations of Jesus' significance to the world. Essentially John's gospel presents a theological reinterpretation of Jesus, but one so simple, so profound, and so practical that millions of devout Christians have never thought of the gospel as stating theology but only religion in its simplest and most practical terms. For more than eighteen centuries it has been the classic definition of Christianity. One will always read the Synoptic Gospels in the light of the Fourth Gospel, and many a point of emphasis and aspect of meaning which might otherwise have been missed will be suggested by it. But since the Fourth Gospel is thus interpreting the message of Jesus,

[22] *Op. cit.*, p. 373.

the endeavor to discover first what that teaching was must be based on the records in the first three gospels. Passages from John will be used in corroboration of results reached, and as summarizing in definitive fashion the spirit and larger meaning of the whole.

This discussion of the Gospel of John has omitted all reference to the question of authorship. That it was written probably at Ephesus by John, a great figure in the Church at the close of the first century, all the evidence agrees. But whether this John was the apostle, the son of Zebedee, or whether he was an individual called John the Elder (or Presbyter) as is suggested by the opening words of the Second and Third Epistles of John, is a complicated and difficult problem on which there is still a difference of opinion. That there was another John who was held in high esteem is proven by the statement of Papias already quoted,[23] and by the statement of several early authorities that there were two tombs in Ephesus each of which bore the name of John.[24] But whichever answer be adopted, the gospel itself is not changed. Hence it is wiser to base one's view of how the gospel should be used on the indubitable facts which it supplies rather than on *a priori* deductions from a particular view as to the identity of the author.

TOPICS FOR DISCUSSION AND REVIEW

1. Would it be more convenient to have one gospel giving the complete story of Jesus's life instead of the four gospels which we now possess? Would the Church win or lose by the exchange? Give reasons for your answer.

[23] See above, p. 30 f.

[24] Eusebius, *Church History*, 3: 39; Dionysius of Alexandria (in Eusebius, 7: 25). Jerome *De Vir Illus.*, 9.

2. What did Clement of Alexandria mean when he said that John composed "a spiritual gospel"?

3. Read the Prologue to the Fourth Gospel (John 1: 1-18) and compare it with the Prologue to Luke (Luke 1: 1-4). State the difference in the purpose of the two authors which is suggested by this comparison.

4. What liberties are permitted a clergyman when citing incidents from the life of Christ in a sermon? Consider from the standpoints of chronology, fullness of detail, exact quotation of wording, etc. Does the purpose of the Fourth Gospel justify a similar liberty?

5. Jesus taught nothing about child-labor in factories nor the honest conduct of political elections. Compare our application of his teaching to such themes with the interpretation of Jesus's message and work in the Fourth Gospel.

SUPPLEMENTARY READINGS

On the differences between John and the Synoptic Gospels:

Macgregor: *The Gospel of John (Moffatt's New Testament Commentaries)*, pp. xii-xx.

On the historical value of John:

Bundy: *Our Recovery of Jesus*, pp. 40-62.

Drummond: *The Character and Authorship of the Fourth Gospel*, Ch. 4.

Macgregor: *Op. cit.*, pp. xx-xxvi.

Streeter: *The Four Gospels*, Ch. 13.

On the authorship of the Fourth Gospel:

Streeter: *Op. cit.*, Ch. 15.

Macgregor: *Op. cit.*, pp. xliv-lxviii.

McNeile: *Introduction to the New Testament*, pp. 264-275.

CHAPTER VI

WAS JESUS PRIMARILY A TEACHER?

THE sayings of Jesus preserved in our gospels embody certain great principles in such clear and striking fashion that Jesus has often been described as the world's greatest teacher. To describe him in these terms, however, or to refer to "the teachings of Jesus" is apt to leave a misimpression. One is led to think of Jesus as a philosopher and teacher something after the nature of Confucius or Socrates or some European philosopher like Kant. And one is likely to read his sayings as a body of teachings carefully prepared and organized for pedagogical purposes. Such conceptions would be far from the truth. There are a number of indications that Jesus did not regard himself primarily as a teacher and that his work of teaching was entirely subordinate to a larger objective.

In the first place it is to be noted that Jesus did not choose as his life work the profession of teaching. In Jewish society in his day this profession was a well-established and highly honored one. Its members were the scribes (also called rabbis), and their work was to study and teach to the people the comprehensive and many-sided law of Moses. This law governed the whole social and religious life of the people. It contained not only religious precepts and teachings, but also criminal laws, regulations concerning damages to property and persons, laws concerning the amount and kind of taxes to be paid, regulations as to the date, length, and character of the national festivals, laws concerning the quarantining of lepers and

certification as to their recovery, etc. As a result these
scribes or official teachers were not only religious leaders
but civil authorities as well. Being expert in the law
they were the lawyers and judges of the country. As a
class they were perhaps the most important group in the
land.

They were also a very learned class. The study of the
written law required a knowledge of the Hebrew language
which was no longer spoken by the people. A modified
form of this language was also used for the learned discussions in the scribal schools. In addition to these
linguistic requirements a minute and exact knowledge of
the Bible was necessary. More difficult still was the
mastery of the constantly expanding "oral law" or official
interpretation, application, and adjustment of the written
law to practical and changing conditions.

By his mastery of the details and exact meaning of the
law the scribe was thus the official guide of the religious
and secular life of Judaism. So important was the office
that it was carefully guarded. Unlicensed and untrained
teachers of the law were effectively opposed. "He who
profanes holy things and despised the festivals . . . and
gives interpretations of the law not in accordance with the
established rule, even though he possess the law and good
deeds, he has no portion in the world to come," is a
familiar saying of the Talmud which expresses this point
of view.[1] Nor could one become a scribe without the
training in the schools. "Betake thyself to a school for
study of the law and say not that it will come after thee
. . . and rely not upon thine own understanding," [2] formu-
lates the rule in this particular. In this way the candidate

---

[1] *Sayings of the Fathers,* 3: 15.   [2] *Ibid.,* 4: 18.

would learn the traditional rulings concerning the law and be enabled to carry on the tradition which underlay the whole fabric of Jewish culture. The training thus enjoined was most exact. "Even a moderate proficiency in it," says Professor Moore, "was not to be attained without long and patient years of learning; mastery demanded unusual capacity. The method of the schools developed not only exact and retentive memory and great mental acuteness, but an exhaustive and ever-ready knowledge of every phase and word of Scripture." [3]

As a group the scribes exemplified that exact obedience to the law which they urged upon the people. Thus they were learned, influential, and scrupulously pious. Consequently they were regarded with great respect by the people. In the synagogues they had the chief seats, at feasts they occupied the leading places, in the market places they received the salutations of their fellow citizens, by their personal disciples they were called, Rabbi, "My Master." [4] Nor were they entirely undeserving of such respect and honor. Through its leadership for many generations the scribal profession had made Judaism what it was, and to list the contributions which it had made to the religious and social life of the people would be virtually to describe the development of Jewish society from Ezra to Hillel. [5]

But with all its opportunities and honors, Jesus did not choose as his life work the career of the scribe or professional teacher. Nor did he take the training in preparation for that office. True, he had learned to read the Hebrew

---

[3] *Judaism,* Vol. I, pp. 319, 320.   [4] Matt. 23: 7.

[5] Hillel was perhaps the most famous Jewish rabbi. He died at the beginning of the first century of the Christian era.

text of Isaiah,[6] but it is plain that he had not attended the advanced scribal schools. When he spoke in Nazareth, his home town, the people were astonished and said, "Where did he get all this? . . . Is not this the carpenter?"[7] That was the trade he had practiced up until the time his public activity began, and his fellow townsmen knew of no other training which could explain to them his appearance in their synagogue.

This absence of scribal preparation and the scribal point of view is evident from other incidents in the gospels. When he spoke to the multitudes in the Galilean villages or beside the sea they were impressed with the fact that he taught in quite a different manner from that of the scribes.[8] In Jerusalem the chief priests and scribes and elders came to him and inquired, "By what authority doest thou these things?"—a question which implies that he had no proper authority according to their way of thinking.[9] In the Book of Acts we read that when the Sanhedrin "beheld the boldness of Peter and John, and had perceived that they were unlettered and ignorant men, they marveled; and they took knowledge, that they had been with Jesus."[10] The implication of the statement is that their opinion of Jesus was in similar terms—he was an untrained and unlearned person who had nevertheless arrogated to himself the right to teach the people.

Jesus then was not a professional religious official or teacher. He was an artisan, one who had quietly followed his trade in the small town of Nazareth until one day he began a public ministry to the whole of Galilee and to a certain extent to Judea. What was that ministry and what was its primary objective?

⁶ Luke 4: 17 f.   ⁸ Mark 1: 22.   ¹⁰ Acts 4: 13.
⁷ Mark 6: 1 ff.   ⁹ Mark 11: 28.

In the first place we may be quite sure that it was closely related to the work of John the Baptist. The accounts of Jesus' public ministry all begin with the story of John's preaching in the wilderness. Among the multitudes who went out to hear him was Jesus. He was baptized by John in the Jordan. This baptism was a crucial experience. Not only did he see the heavens opened, but there came a voice which said, "Thou art my beloved Son, in thee I am well pleased." [11]   Immediately following this experience came certain temptations in the wilderness. Then the account goes on, "Now after John was arrested, Jesus came into Galilee, preaching the gospel of God, and saying, The time is fulfilled, and the Kingdom of God is at hand; repent, and believe the good news"—a message almost identical with that which John had been proclaiming.[12]   Later in his ministry we find Jesus saying, "Verily I say unto you, Among those born of woman there hath not arisen a greater than John the Baptist." [13]   Thus it is evident that Jesus' work had a direct relation to that of John.

What was the work of John? His whole manner of life was calculated to recall to the people the ancient prophets who had brought messages from God in times past. He dressed in camel's hair with a leather girdle about him, as had the prophet Elijah.[14] He went out into the wilderness to do his preaching and ate the wild food which was to be found there. Prophets had not been seen in Israel for many centuries, but John took up the rôle. He declared that the kingdom of God which the prophets had proclaimed and Jewish hopes had so long

[11] Mark 1: 11.   [13] Matt. 11: 11.
[12] Mark 1: 14 f.; cp. Matt. 3: 2.   [14] Mark 1: 6; cp. 2 Kings 1: 8.

awaited was now at hand.   He declared that this great
divine event would be primarily a day of judgment and
condemnation on all men who sinned, and accordingly he
urged his hearers to repent and to bring forth the fruits
of repentance.   "Even now," he declared, "the axe lieth
at the root of the trees; every tree therefore that bringeth
not forth good fruit is hewn down and cast into the
fire." [15]   The judgment would be executed by God's
representative, the Messiah.   "He that cometh after me is
mightier than I. . . . He shall baptize you with the Holy
Spirit and with fire; whose fan is in his hand, and he
shall thoroughly cleanse his threshing floor; and he will
gather his wheat into his garners, but the chaff he will
burn up in unquenchable fire." [16]   John thus was a
prophet who proclaimed to the people the coming of the
kingdom of God and endeavored to prepare men for its
arrival by repentance and a complete moral renewal which
he symbolized by the act of baptism.

Now the message which Jesus came preaching in Galilee
after John's arrest was in its main outline the same as that
of John, "The kingdom of heaven is at hand, repent and
believe in the good news."   Jesus too was more than
merely a herald.   That he regarded his task as one of
saving the nation rather than merely proclaiming this
news, is evident from a multitude of his sayings.   "I came
not to call the righteous, but sinners," is one of the first
answers which he gave to criticisms of his manner of
life.[17]   On one occasion he defined his mission in the
statement, "The Son of Man came to save that which was
lost." [18]   He called Peter and Andrew to join him in his

[15] Matt. 3: 10.   [17] Mark 2: 17.
[16] Matt. 3: 11, 12.   [18] Luke 19: 10.

undertaking in terms which left no doubt of its positive and practical character, "Come ye after me, and I will make you to become fishers of men." [19] Later he sent out his disciples. "Go," he said, "to the lost sheep of the house of Israel; and as ye go, preach, saying, The kingdom of heaven is at hand." [20]

Jesus thus took up the burden of John's preaching, though unlike John he went where people were. He knew his countrymen and saw that they were not prepared for the coming of the kingdom of God. On the one hand there were great groups whom the scribes had failed to reach or influence in any vital way and who were dropping out of the influence of the synagogue and disregarding the precepts of the law. "When he saw the multitudes," says Matthew in one passage, paraphrasing a verse in Mark, "he was moved with compassion for them, because they were distressed and scattered, as sheep not having a shepherd." [21] Some of these were merely neglectful of the legal refinements of the scribes, others were violators of the moral codes as well, the outcasts from society, the publicans, harlots, and others. Jesus felt that these could be saved. Besides the outcasts there were others whose religion was only formal and superficial, some of them Pharisees, or even scribes themselves. To bring to these various groups a knowledge of what the establishment of God's kingdom would mean and to bring them into its ranks—this was the task that Jesus undertook. Thus instead of going into the wilderness he went throughout the villages and towns of Galilee declaring that the kingdom was at hand, and urging men to repent and believe in the good news.

[19] Mark 1: 17.

[20] Matt. 10: 6 and 7.

[21] Matt. 9: 36; cp. Mark 6: 34.

But this very undertaking involved a good deal more than merely reciting these words. When he declared that the kingdom of God was coming there were many who thought that he was announcing the recovery of the ancient glory associated with the names of David and Solomon. That was because they had a wrong conception of the reward which God would give to those who served him. There were others who had a totally misplaced idea of the kind of goodness that God wanted men to show and who needed to realize the simplicity and naturalness and goodness of the divine commandments. There were others who thought of the coming kingdom rather in terms of dread and fear. That was because they thought of God as a hard taskmaster. Back of nearly all of these problems was the fact that people had the wrong idea of God. Jesus had not been trained in the schools, but on these various themes, particularly on the last one, he had certain deep convictions. Thus he found his work of preaching becoming also one of teaching, for his task of proclaiming the kingdom involved making clear to the people the nature of that kingdom and the kind of righteousness it demanded.

Jesus' teaching thus was only incidental to his larger objective. His call was not to be a teacher but to bring his people into the kingdom of God. The objectives which stood before his mind were in terms of persons and groups of persons rather than of a complete and systematic presentation of his thought. "The harvest indeed is plenteous," he said to his disciples, "but the laborers are few; pray ye the Lord of the harvest that he send forth laborers into his harvest." "O Jerusalem, Jerusalem, . . . how often would I have gathered thy children together, even as a hen gathereth her chickens under her wings, and ye would not!" Such statements show the positive and practical task to which Jesus gave himself. Not as a teacher expounding a thesis is he to be understood, but as the prophet of the kingdom and the shepherd of the lost sheep of God's Israel.

TOPICS FOR DISCUSSION AND REVIEW

1. The scribes, their duties, their authority, their prestige.
2. Causes for the disappearance of prophets from Jewish life.
3. The education of Jesus—home, workshop, synagogue, village, countryside, the near-by city of Sepphoris.
4. Jesus, a layman, not a professional religious worker.
5. The practical task which Jesus undertook.
6. Why Jesus taught.

SUPPLEMENTARY READINGS

On the work of John the Baptist:
    Headlam: *The Life and Teaching of Jesus the Christ,* Ch. 3.
    Holtzman: *The Life of Jesus,* Ch. 5.
    Scott: *The Kingdom and the Messiah,* Ch. 3.
    Warschauer, *The Historical Life of Christ,* Ch. 2.
On Jesus' baptism and call:
    Bosworth: *The Life and Teaching of Jesus,* Ch. 6.
    Holtzman: *Op. cit.,* Ch. 6.
    Warschauer: *Op. cit.,* Ch. 3.
    Wendt: *The Teaching of Jesus,* Vol. I, pp. 96-105.
On the character of Jesus' public ministry:
    Bosworth: *Op. cit.,* Ch. 8 and 9.
    Bousset: *Jesus,* Ch. 1 and 2.

CHAPTER VII

HOW JESUS TAUGHT

THE mission of Jesus was to announce the nearness of the kingdom of God and to prepare his people for its coming. His objective was to save men rather than to teach in a formal way. But his proclamation of the kingdom involved necessarily exhortation, warning, explanation, and instruction. Teaching thus became one of the primary aspects of his work. In this chapter the manner and method of that teaching is to be considered.

In the first place one should note that in spite of Jesus' baptism at the hands of John the Baptist, and his appreciation of the greatness of the prophet of the wilderness, Jesus did not become one of John's disciples. According to the Fourth Gospel Jesus had begun an independent work of his own in Judea even before John was cast into prison by Herod Antipas.[1] Nor did Jesus imitate John in his ascetic manner of life nor in his withdrawal into the wilderness. John dressed like one of the Old Testament prophets, took up his abode in the rough country of Judea near the Jordan, and waited for the multitudes to seek him out. Jesus, on the contrary, wore no unusual garb. Instead of endeavoring to create a sensation, he charged those who acclaimed him as God's special representative to keep silent,[2] and forbade individuals whom he healed of diseases and afflictions to tell anyone of it.[3] Instead of withdrawing into the wilderness

[1] John 3: 22-24. [3] Mark 1: 44 and 7: 36.
[2] Mark 1: 24, 25, 34; 3: 12; 8: 30, etc.

98

he went wherever people were to be found and spoke to them about the kingdom of God.

Jesus, we are told, "came into Galilee, preaching the good news of God." [4] Galilee, his native land, was one of the most thickly populated regions of Palestine. Within its borders were two especially fertile sections, the great plain of Esdraelon, stretching from the Jordan valley northwest to Mount Carmel and the Mediterranean, the scene of many a stirring event in Old Testament history, and the plain of Gennesaret on the northwest of the Sea of Galilee, a region the fertility and beauty of which Josephus praises in most fulsome terms. [5] Jesus began his work in the latter section, making one of its towns, Capernaum, a sort of headquarters or center. But this was only that he might carry his message out from there to all the towns and villages which dotted Galilee so thickly. As Luke's gospel reads, "He went about through the cities and villages, preaching and bringing the good tidings of the kingdom of God." [6]

His means of reaching the people was first of all through the synagogues. Such assemblies lent themselves easily to his use. The order of service consisted primarily of certain opening prayers, readings from the law and the prophets and the exposition of the passages read. This last was no doubt usually done by some scribe who was trained in such exposition, but it is evident that others could take part. Paul, for example, on visiting the synagogues of the Jews during his missionary travels was always given an opportunity to speak, even though a stranger. [7] In the case of Jesus there is one story which

---

[4] Mark 1: 15.

[5] *The Jewish War*, III, 516-21.

[6] 8: 1.

[7] Note Acts 13: 15 especially.

describes in some detail his appearance in the synagogue. This is Luke's account of his visit to the synagogue of Nazareth. When the time came for the reading from the prophets Jesus was called on. They handed to him the book of Isaiah, he read the opening verses of the sixty-first chapter, and then having handed the book back to the attendant he proceeded to declare that these verses were being fulfilled before their eyes and to explain and interpret the message which they contained.

How constantly Jesus availed himself of this opportunity of teaching in the synagogues, the gospels give ample testimony. The Gospel of Matthew summarizes the early period of his activity in the words, "And Jesus went about in Galilee, teaching in their synagogues and preaching the good news of the kingdom, and healing all manner of disease and all manner of sickness among the people." [8] Repeatedly as the story proceeds one reads of his entering into the synagogue on the Sabbath and of some episode which happened there. To attend the synagogue on the Sabbath was, we are told, "his regular custom." [9] It is evident that he found there one of his most effective means of reaching the religious and law-abiding elements in each community.

Jesus did not confine himself however to these more or less formal assemblies. Wherever men were to be found he spoke to them of the kingdom of God. Passing by a group of fishermen mending their nets he talks to them of the far greater task of catching men for the kingdom which was coming.[10] At the boundary of the territory of Herod Antipas a tollhouse stood beside the road and in it sat Levi, the tax collector, a man whom current

<hr>

[8] 4: 23.   [9] Luke 4: 16.   [10] Mark 1: 7.

opinion regarded as hard, extortionate, and unresponsive to religious appeals. Jesus talks with him, describes what membership in the kingdom of God means, and calls him not only to enter that kingdom but to join him in his endeavor to win other men to it.[11] Through such men as Levi he met others who were notorious for their disregard of the religion of the law. It was not long before he began to be talked about, and crowds thronged around him. He taught them wherever he could find a convenient place. On a number of occasions we find him teaching on the shores of the Sea of Galilee, sometimes sitting in a little boat with the people on the land.[12] On other occasions the multitude followed him into the desert or wilderness country where he had withdrawn with his disciples for rest. Instead of sending them away or suggesting that they attend the services at the synagogue on the following Sabbath, one reads that "he had compassion on them . . . and he began to teach them many things." [13] On other occasions he taught in private homes before which or into which the people, hearing that he was present, crowded.

Nor did he regard it essential that a crowd be present to hear the teachings which he had to give. Many of the finest sayings preserved in the gospels are addressed to small groups or to individuals. His saying as to the greatest commandment was addressed to an inquiring scribe.[14] His teaching on the danger of riches was addressed to a single individual and to the Twelve who were present during the conversation.[15] To Mary sitting at his feet, he talked at length, just as he did to the Samaritan

[11] Mark 2: 14.
[12] Mark 2: 13; 3: 9; 4: 1.
[13] Mark 6: 34.
[14] Mark 12: 28.
[15] Mark 10: 17.
[16] Luke 10: 39; John 4: 7.

woman at the well near Sychar.[16] He invited himself to
visit Zacchæus in his home, and no doubt much time was
spent teaching the publican and answering his questions.[17]
Such illustrations are plentiful. They show how Jesus
carried forward his work not only by speaking in the
synagogues and to the multitudes, but to individual men
and women wherever he found opportunity.

What was the manner of this teaching? What sort of
teacher was Jesus? What was his method? The best
answer to these questions is to be gained by reading his
sayings rather than any book about them. Before going
further with this chapter I suggest to the reader that he
turn to the gospels and reread some section containing
Jesus' teachings. Though one chapter is practically as
good as another for this purpose, I suggest the fifth
chapter of Matthew or the twelfth chapter of Luke. Only
one warning, or rather reminder, is necessary. One must
recall what was said earlier as to the way in which our
gospels were compiled. The evangelists took their
material for the most part from earlier records. The first
of these records were quite evidently fragmentary, short
lists of detached sayings or brief parables or incidents,
the kernel of which was some important saying. This
material the evangelists incorporated into their works,
arranging it sometimes by topics, sometimes without any
connection between the different sayings. But it is obvious
that this arrangement does not represent Jesus' ordinary
mode of speech. A long discourse consisting of one
epigrammatic statement after another, frequently without
any connection between them, would have been highly
artificial, unnatural, and difficult to follow. As Professor

[17] Luke 19: 5.

Scott has remarked, "Far more likely are we to think of each of the sayings as a text which he expanded and illustrated. He would speak of the need of self-denial in view of the kingdom, telling parable after parable to show how a smaller object must often be sacrificed for a greater, and would finally drive home the whole discourse in a vivid sentence—'He that saves his life shall lose it.' We can understand in this way why the sayings that have come down to us are so pregnant and concise. We can understand, too, how they came to be remembered. Each of them was the summary of a discourse in which it was illustrated from many sides, and perhaps often repeated, so that it impressed itself indelibly." [18] With this reminder, however, the sayings are their own best comment. If the reader will examine them carefully, I believe that he will find that the teaching of Jesus had the following four characteristics:

(1) It was natural, not formal. In the first place the occasion of his teaching was marked by the greatest naturalness and informality. We never read of a prepared address delivered on a formal occasion. One of his greatest discourses seems to have been delivered in the open air, on the side of one of the low sloping mountains in Galilee. Repeatedly we find him speaking beside the sea. Frequently he taught in the house of friends or disciples. More than once it was in a desert place. There was nothing stilted or formal in a message that could be delivered in such places as these.

Most of his teaching seems to have been extempore, and therefore completely informal. The occasion arose and he spoke that which he had in mind. A good illustra-

[18] Scott, *The Ethical Teaching of Jesus*, p. 24 f.

tion of this is to be found in Mark's account of his return
to Capernaum after the first journey through the villages
of Galilee. "It was noised that he was in the house, and
many were gathered together, so that there was no longer
room for them, no, not even about the door: and he spake
the word unto them." [19]   Similarly, when the crowds
sought him out in the wilderness, it would be absurd to
suppose that he spent the day delivering formal addresses.
In his dealings with small groups and individuals this
informal and extempore character of his teaching is the
more obvious. Some of his greatest teaching was done
in the ordinary give and take of mealtime conversation,
or in answering questions which individuals asked. One
thinks in this latter connection of the question of the rich
ruler as to how to gain eternal life, of the riddle of the
Sadducees concerning the resurrection, of the question
concerning paying taxes to Rome, and concerning the
chief commandment. Even in the case of his teaching in
the synagogue it must not be supposed that his speaking
had the formality of our modern Church services. The
synagogue was a place for instruction in and explanation
of the law much more than it was an institution of worship.

Even when he taught crowds the tone of the gathering
was still informal and intimate. There are constant
interruptions which he utilizes again and again for the
purposes of driving home his thought. A message comes,
for example, that his mother and his brethren are without
and wish to see him; [20] he uses the statement to impress
the lesson of Christian brotherhood. On another occasion
a paralytic is brought before him and he does not hesitate

[19] Mark 2: 2.   [20] Mark 3: 31.

to turn his attention to the case in hand.[21]   Sometimes there are questions from the hearers, some of them sincere, some framed by opponents for the purpose of trapping him. He does not refuse to answer. There are instances where the hearers make their own comments upon the matter that is being discussed. Peter seems especially talkative in these discussions. Once a woman broke into the discourse with the ejaculation, "Blessed is the womb that bare thee," [22] and Jesus turns her statement into the general theme of his instruction.

In the content of what he said this same naturalness and complete absence of artificiality or formality comes out. This is one of the greatest charms of his sayings. There is never the slightest indication of a striving for rhetorical effect. His language is the speech of everyday life, his illustrations are drawn from the commonest experiences of his hearers, the subject of his teaching is the practical problem of what normal life should be like.

(2) It was popular, not logical. Jesus apparently never aimed at a systematic and logical presentation of his teaching. He did not speak to the crowds of fisherfolk and peasants in the logical manner of a professor lecturing a classroom. Nowhere do you find definitions of terms used, premises laid down, deductions drawn. He did not attempt to transform men by syllogisms. These things are the mechanics of speech; they are difficult to follow and almost inevitably convey a sense of artificiality. Certainly the deepest things of life are not determined by argument. That is probably due to two things. On the one hand, the ordinary person always feels that if clever enough he might find a flaw in the argument. There is

[21] Mark 2: 3.   [22] Luke 11: 27.

a vague general feeling that one cannot believe everything that one may not be able to answer. But there is, I think, a deeper reason than this. Logic divides a subject into its parts, dissects its different phases, and deals with them separately. Never the whole is before the eyes. Analysis —with the average man at least—is not the method by which people are stirred to great decisions.

Jesus' method was fundamentally different. He appealed to the intellect—note the controversies with the Pharisees in particular—but so far as our records go he never set himself to present his view of God and man and duty in a systematic theology. Instead, what he does is to present a very few central and basic truths, in such fashion that men may see them whole and feel their drawing power. In the longer discourses which are recorded he takes some basic principle of conduct, presents it now from this side, now from that, illustrates it by a parable, shows its application to life in a concrete example, returning thus ever again and again to the main thought with which he is dealing.

Of this manner of teaching the Sermon on the Mount in Matthew is the clearest illustration. The theme is the nature of Christian righteousness. First it is pictured in the character of those who are truly blessed; then we have it set forth by way of contrast with the Jewish ideal; next Jesus shows what it actually means in practice, taking such familiar illustrations as almsgiving, prayer, fasting, the laying up of riches, and criticizing others; there then follows a section on the complete trust in God which is characteristic of the righteous individual; and finally it is closed with parables of warning and exhortation. This is not a logical or piecemeal treatment: the whole subject is constantly before the mind and is exemplified by various means. Several times one finds verses which seem to state the whole Christian ideal with such completeness as to seem to leave nothing further to be said, only to pass on to further illustrations and presentations. That was always Jesus' method. He did not divide his subject into its proper divisions and present his views systematically. Instead he constantly holds up before his hearers the ideal of the good life in all its completeness and perfection.

(3) It was picturesque, not literal. Many people have made mistakes in trying to understand Jesus because they have failed to take this fact into consideration. Jesus was in the best sense of the word a popular teacher. His thought was picturesque, full of figures, illustrations, striking expressions, all of which made the meaning so clear that even the most ignorant could understand. "I send you as sheep amid wolves." "Be ye wise as serpents, and harmless as doves." "I saw Satan fallen as lightning from heaven." "O, Jerusalem, Jerusalem, . . . how often would I have gathered thy children together, even as a hen gathereth her chickens under her wings." "Ye are the salt of the earth." One could go on and on with such striking similes and metaphors. It was his method of speaking and teaching.

"Without a parable spake he not unto them," says Mark. And if one would understand him one must read his teaching in this light. Yet how many times Christian people have refused to recognize this, and instead of seeking the thought behind the vivid, picturesque expression or illustration have insisted on an exact obedience to the letter of the command. "Carry no purse, no wallet, no shoes" [23]—and I saw on the street corner of a Southern

[23] Luke 10: 4.

city a man who goes barefoot the year round with the thought of obedience to this command. One denomination employs symbolical rites based on the literal acceptance of the saying, "If I then, the Lord and Master, have washed your feet, ye also ought to wash one another's feet." [24] "It is easier for a camel to go through a needle's eye than for a rich man to enter into the kingdom of God," [25] and many people have felt it necessary to adopt a quite unjustifiable translation of the Greek word so as to make it a small gate instead of a needle. "When they deliver you up, be not anxious how or what ye shall speak, for it shall be given you in that hour what ye shall speak," [26] and one finds a preacher every now and then who boasts that he makes no preparation. All such interpretations are unfair to Jesus. He refused to let the fear of possible criticism shackle him into the exact language of a legal document. He taught in strong, fearless, and unforgettable utterances that swept away all obstacles and won their way directly to the human heart.

(4) It was clear, not hidden or abstruse. This is implied in all that was said above. In the best sense of the word Jesus was a popular teacher. Crowds of ordinary people would stay all day listening to him, even forgetting their lunch in the eagerness with which they hung upon his words. From that fact alone we might infer that what he said was lucid and clear, easy to understand. The recorded teaching bears this out. What could be simpler or clearer than Jesus' statement of the chief commandment? Or the summary of Christian duty which is called the Golden Rule? Or the parable of the Good Samaritan?

And yet the very opposite has ofttimes been assumed.

[24] John 13: 14.   [25] Mark 10: 25.   [26] Matt. 10: 19.

Many people have tried to interpret Jesus on the assumption that his utterances contain a meaning hidden to the average reader, which must be elicited by systems of symbolism and a network of Scriptural cross references. I have in mind, for example, an interpretation of the parable of the mustard seed in a pamphlet which has had wide circulation. The parable declares quite simply that the kingdom of God is like a mustard seed, which is the smallest of all the seeds when it is planted, but when it is grown up becomes a tree great enough to shelter the birds and to give shade to the beasts of the field. The interpretation referred to declares that Jesus meant by the field to refer to the world, within which the kingdom of God or the Church has grown to be a very large affair. Since leaves of the mustard seed are mentioned, but no fruit, it is alleged that Christ thus prophesied that the Church would become worldly. And the birds and beasts who are sheltered by the tree then are said to represent the infidels and the worldly-minded who have come into the Church in these modern days. Thus the moral is drawn that the Church should return to a small state more like its original condition. Ingenious? Yes, indeed, but quite opposite to the plain meaning of the parable, the meaning which certainly the hearers drew from it, that the kingdom of God, though in its beginning a most insignificant movement, would expand and grow unto a great consummation, just as does the mustard seed.

His teaching was natural, it was popular, it was clear. And if we would interpret him aright we will take the natural meaning of his words. Jesus came to reveal truth, and reveal it he did, so clearly and so naturally that the common people heard him gladly. Of course this does not mean that one will not compare a passage with another upon a similar topic, nor seek to get the setting of a saying to understand its point, nor fail to remember the vivid and picturesque fashion in which Jesus spoke. These things have been emphasized. But it does mean that we will not conceive of Jesus' teaching as conveying one impression to his hearers while actually having a hidden meaning that was quite different.

As one looks back over these four characteristics which have been enumerated, the realization emerges that what Jesus actually did was to teach men and women, rather than a message. He adapted his words to their ideas and their experiences. He taught in such a way that they could not forget. He taught them and trusted them to transmit that truth to succeeding generations.

TOPICS FOR DISCUSSION AND REVIEW

1. The types of individuals whom Jesus reached by preaching in the synagogues. The way in which he reached other types. Would these differences in the audiences tend to disappear after he became known?

2. The synagogue as an institution primarily for religious education. Where does the emphasis fall in the average modern Church service?

3. Compare Jesus and John the Baptist as regards their use of sensational methods of appeal.

4. Illustrate the way in which Jesus framed his message for his immediate hearers rather than for some future generation.

5. In the light of the material thus far presented as to the nature of the gospels and the characteristics of Jesus' teaching, draw up a list of principles which should be followed in the interpretation of Jesus' sayings.

SUPPLEMENTARY READINGS

On Galilee, the character of the country, the leading occupations, etc.:

Grant: *The Economic Background of the Gospels*, pp. 54-111.
Hastings: *Dictionary of the Bible*, article "Galilee."

On the order of service in the synagogue:

    Schürer: *The History of the Jewish People in the Time of Jesus Christ*, Div. II, Vol. 2, pp. 75-83.

On religion as Jesus found it:

    Bosworth: *The Life and Teaching of Jesus*, Ch. 3 and 4.

    Klausner: *Jesus of Nazareth*, pp. 193-228.

    Scott: *The First Age of Christianity*, pp. 23-30.

On the popular and forceful character of Jesus' teaching:

    Bousset: *Jesus*, pp. 36-46.

    Robinson: *The Sayings of Jesus*, Ch. XV.

    Wendt: *The Teaching of Jesus*, Vol. I, pp. 106-151.

On the poetic form of much of Jesus' teaching:

    Burney: *The Poetry of Our Lord*, Ch. 1-3.

On the parables of Jesus:

    Hastings: *Dictionary of the Bible*, Article "Parable."

On the interpretation of Jesus' parables:

    Russell: *The Parables of Jesus*, Ch. 2.

CHAPTER VIII

THE THEME OF THE TEACHING

JESUS began his work, says Mark, by going through Galilee preaching, "The kingdom of God is at hand. Repent and believe in the good news." Quite obviously he preached a good deal more than just those phrases, but this is the way that Mark sums it up. If one will examine the teaching that has been preserved, Mark's statement will be verified. It deals constantly with God's "kingdom." The parables begin, "The kingdom of God is like . . ." The Beatitudes speak of people who are blessed because "theirs is the kingdom of God." The true aim of life is that men should "seek first his (God's) kingdom and his righteousness." And as his ministry began so it ended—Jesus' last saying to his disciples before he led them out into the garden was a confident reference to this same kingdom of God.[1]

Why this unusual phrase? It is surprising to find Jesus speaking so constantly about a kingdom. He despised arbitrary authority and had a contempt for the trappings and cheap pomp characteristic of the petty Palestinian courts. He said on one occasion, "They who are accounted to rule over the Gentiles lord it over them, and their great ones exercise authority over them. But it is not so among you."[2] The regal robes of Solomon were not so beautiful in his eyes as one perfect lily.[3] "The kingdoms of this world and the glory of them" he had once for all put behind him[4] and had chosen instead

[1] Mark 14: 25.

[2] Mark 10: 42.

[3] Matt. 6: 29.

[4] Matt. 4: 8-10; Luke 4: 5.

poverty and obscurity. Why, then, does he speak so much about a "kingdom"?

The answer is in the fact that there was no break between Jesus and the religious revelation which his people had given to the world. He was bred in the Old Testament Scriptures. For him no other foundation could be laid than that which was laid by the prophets and the law. In the forms of his thought he made no fresh start, but built upon the ideas and the ideals that were Israel's contribution to the world. His hearers found no difficulty in acclaiming him a "Son of David" or "one of the prophets." And this sacred tradition of the fathers had talked about a kingdom that was to come.

The matter can be approached from another side. Jesus was not interested in giving abstract truth. He taught men and women. Furthermore he spoke to the particular men and women who were before him, not to those of some century to come after. He must have been a marvelous teacher, for the crowds would stay all day listening to him. It is only what we should expect, then, to find that he put his message in terms that were clear to them and full of meaning. This phrase, "the kingdom of God," summed up to their minds their deepest social and religious yearnings. And so he spoke of that, changing as he spoke the content of much that they had in mind.

I

The conception goes back to the idea, fundamental in all Hebrew religion, that God was Israel's ruler and protector. This was true from the earliest days of the nation. The laws of Moses were authoritative because they were regarded as the commands of Jehovah. Gideon, the hero of the deliverance from the invasion of the Midianites and Amalekites, is described as refusing a crown with the words, "I will not rule over you, neither shall my son rule over you; the Lord shall rule over you." [5]   When Saul was made king over the protest of Samuel, Jehovah said to the prophet, "They have not rejected thee, but they have rejected me, that I should not be king over them." [6] When kings came to the throne who did not worship Jehovah but went after the Baal-gods of the Canaanites, the prophets insisted that Jehovah alone must be king over Israel and his commands only must be obeyed.   An Ahab or a Manasseh who did not rule in accordance with that divine will had no claim to the loyalty and obedience of the nation.

As the religious ideas of the people enlarged under the teaching of the prophets the earlier polytheism of the people began to be replaced by a belief in monotheism and God's universal supremacy.   The thought of God's kingship was now enlarged.   He was not king over Israel alone, but over all the earth.   Israel, however, was the only nation who acknowledged his sovereignty.   The prophets and psalmists break into magnificent stanzas when they speak of the universal power and majesty of their God:

"Jehovah hath his way in the whirlwind and the storm, and the clouds are the dust of his feet. He rebuketh the sea and maketh it dry, and drieth up all the rivers. . . . The mountains quake at him and melt, and the earth is upheaved at his presence, yea, the world and all that dwell therein." (Nahum 1: 4-6.)

"Thus saith Jehovah, who stretched forth the heavens, and layeth the foundation of the earth, and formeth the spirit of man within him: Behold, I will make Jerusalem a cup of reeling unto all the peoples round about." (Zech. 12: 1 f.)

[5] Judges 8: 23.   [6] 1 Sam. 8: 7.

"God is the King of all the earth: . . .
God reigneth over the nations." (Ps. 47: 7 f.)
"The Lord is a great God,
And a great King above all gods." (Ps. 95: 3.)
"The Lord has established his throne in the heavens
And his kingdom over all." (Ps. 103: 19.)

From such concepts the greater prophets drew the lesson that Jehovah had an interest in all peoples and that Israel was to be a medium of the divine revelation. But the prophetic vision was above that of the ordinary people. For them monotheism meant simply an assurance of Israel's future unique glory.

The downfall of the Jewish state and the captivity which followed shook the faith at first. Not only was it true that these great pagan powers refused to acknowledge the kingship of Jehovah, but under the tutelage of false gods they had taken captive and were exacting tribute from Jehovah's people. It seemed as if Jehovah were impotent rather than omnipotent. But the prophets had foretold punishment to fall upon the nation, and under the guidance of the prophetic writings and the living voice of prophets of the Exile the faith of the people emerged with renewed vigor. God was king over all peoples and some day he would establish his kingdom and make actual and visible upon the earth that which was implicit. A day would come, as Isaiah had said, "when the lofty looks of men shall be brought low and the haughtiness of men shall be bowed down: and the Lord alone shall be exalted in that day." [7] God reigns now in part, but in that day he shall reign completely. In Zechariah the thought is put in specific terms: "Behold a day of the Lord cometh. . . . For I will gather all nations

[7] Isa. 2: 11 f.

against Jerusalem to battle. . . . Then shall the Lord go forth, and fight against those nations. . . . And the Lord shall be king over all the earth: in that day shall the Lord be one, and his name one." [8] In similar words Obadiah prophesied the destruction of Israel's enemies: "For the day of the Lord is near upon all the nations: as thou hast done, it shall be done unto thee; thy dealing shall return upon thine own head. . . . And the kingdom shall be the Lord's." [9] Or note the following quotation from the Psalms:

> "The Lord Most High is terrible;
> He is a great King over all the earth.
> He shall subdue the peoples under us,
> And the nations under our feet.
> Sing praises to God, sing praises.
> For God is the King over all the earth:
> Sing ye praises with understanding."
> (Ps. 47: 2, 3, 6-8.)

The day when God's sovereignty would be established was to be the day of Israel's vindication and reward. Not only would the nation's enemies be destroyed or subjected, but the faithful dreamed also of a golden age which God would bring about as a recompense to his people for all that they had endured. Pestilence and violence would exist no more, the earth would bring forth its fruits with bounty, the scattered tribes of Israel would be gathered out of the various lands into which they had been carried, and would live in peace and blessedness under a series of kings of David's lineage. Among the most beautiful passages in all literature are some of those in the prophetic books which picture that age to come. "And

[8] Zech. 14: 1-9.   [9] Obad., verses 15-21.

it shall come to pass in that day," writes Joel, "that the mountains shall drop down sweet wine, and the hills shall flow with milk, and all the brooks of Judah shall flow with waters. . . . And Judah shall abide forever, and Jerusalem from generation to generation." [10] The book of Amos closes with a similar prophecy: "In that day will I raise up the tabernacle of David that is fallen, and close up the breaches thereof; and I will raise up its ruins, and I will build it as in the days of old. . . . Behold, the days come, saith Jehovah, that the plowman shall overtake the reaper, and the treader of grapes him that soweth seed; and the mountains shall drop sweet wine, and all the hills shall melt. And I will bring back the captivity of my people Israel, and they shall build the waste cities and inhabit them; and they shall plant vineyards and drink the wine thereof; and they shall also make gardens, and eat the fruit of them. And I will plant them upon their land, and they shall no more be plucked up out of their land which I have given them, saith Jehovah thy God." [11] Even more beautiful is Isaiah's description of that new age: "And the wolf shall dwell with the lamb, and the leopard lie down with the kid; and the calf and the young lion together; and a little child shall lead them. . . . And the suckling child shall play on the hole of the asp, and the weaned child shall put his hand on the adder's den. They shall not hurt nor destroy in all my holy mountain." [12]

Such poetic descriptions of national vindication and material blessedness were part of the vision which the prophets, in the midst of recurrent pessimism and despair, held before the eyes of the people. For many it was all

[10] Joel 3: 18-20.   [11] Amos 9: 11-15.   [12] Isa. 11: 6-9.

of the picture. Besides victory, glory, and plenty, what else was there to want? But the greatest of the prophets saw another aspect of the picture which to them was of even greater value. That coming kingdom of God would be characterized not only by the possession of peace and plenty, but also by complete obedience to God's will and by the consciousness of the divine presence. "The earth shall be full of the knowledge of the Lord as the waters cover the sea," is the conclusion to the great passage just quoted from Isaiah. Ezekiel's description of the moral renewal of the people in that day is the heart of his prophecy: "For I will take you from among the nations and gather you out of all countries, and bring you into your own land. . . . And a new heart also will I give you and a new spirit will I put into you. And I will put my spirit within you, and cause you to walk in my statutes, and ye shall keep my judgments, and do them. . . . And I will save you from your uncleanness." [13] The same thought comes to expression in Jeremiah: "This is the covenant that I will make with the house of Israel after those days, saith Jehovah: I will put my law in their inward parts, and in their heart will I write it; and I will be their God, and they shall be my people: and they shall teach no more every man his neighbor and every man his brothers, saying, Know Jehovah: for they shall all know me, from the least of them unto the greatest of them, saith Jehovah: for I will forgive their iniquity, and their sin will I remember no more." [14] This religious aspect of the kingdom to come was, for these great prophets, the heart of it.

These are the basic ideas which the religious genius

[13] Ezek. 36: 24-30.   [14] Jer. 31: 33 f.

of the Hebrew people had brought to expression in their thought of the kingdom of God to come. God is King now, but his kingship is acknowledged by only the righteous few. The great majority of mankind has either spurned him or given his law a superficial service. But God will not bear with evil always, neither will he leave his servants without their reward. His power will be revealed, his rule established. And the establishment of this rule would mean destruction for the wicked, and for the righteous complete obedience to his will and enjoyment of his highest blessings.

II

At this point it will be well to recall some of the facts of Jewish history. The reader will remember that after the division of the kingdom of David and Solomon into two parts, the kingdom of Judah outlasted the northern half by more than a century. In 586 B.C., however, Judah fell before the armies of Nebuchadrezzar, king of Babylon, and a large number of its leading citizens were taken away as captives. These captives seem to have been allowed to settle in fertile sections near the city and to carry on their own manner of life. When some two generations later the Babylonian Empire was overthrown by Cyrus, king of the Medes and Persians, and a decree was issued permitting the Jews to return to their native land, only a small number took advantage of the opportunity. A century or more later one finds Nehemiah and Ezra lamenting the ruined state of Jerusalem and urging Babylonian Jews to give up their more comfortable life in Babylon in order to help rebuild the fallen fortunes of their native land. With the walls rebuilt and the temple repaired, and with the inducement afforded by patriotic

and vigorous leadership, there seems to have taken place
a steady movement of return to Jerusalem and its en-
virons. In the minds of those who returned there were
no doubt hopes of the glorious kingdom which the prophets had declared that God would give to his people after
the trials of exile and captivity. But these hopes were
doomed to disappointment. Palestine lay prone under
Persian domination for over two centuries (538-330
B.C.), in spite of certain disastrous endeavors to throw
off the yoke. Finally the Persian Empire crumbled and
fell before the eastward advance of the all-conquering
Alexander the Great; but instead of freedom, the Jews
only gained an exchange of masters. For about a century
and a quarter they were under the rule of the Ptolemies
of Egypt (320-198 B.C.). Then they passed as the spoils
of war to Syria, whose kings, Greek by descent, ruled
from Antioch. Instead of finding relief, conditions soon
became intolerable and an organized effort was made by
King Antiochus Epiphanes to stamp out the Jewish faith.
A successful rebellion led by Judas Maccabeus and carried on by his brothers achieved independence, and Jewish
hopes now were high. After centuries of subjection independence had been regained! Alas, the hopes were
short-lived. The successors of the first generation of the
Maccabees proved ambitious, inefficient, cruel, and even
indifferent to the Jewish religion, and independence gave
way to civil war and civil war to the intervention and
domination of the invincible power of Rome. In 63 B.C.
Jerusalem was captured by the Romans after a desperate
resistance, and from then on the Roman grip on the country was never broken. In 70 A.D. a vain effort at
rebellion led to the destruction of Jerusalem, and sixty
years later, in 132-135 A.D., a second desperate outbreak

led to the destruction of the Jewish state and the dispersion of the remnants of the nation.

This brief survey of the tragic history of the Jews during the centuries which preceded and immediately followed the birth of Christ serves to call to mind two facts which are significant for the subject in hand. In the first place one is reminded of the continuous domination of the Jews by pagan powers. Each empire which held the Jews in subjection crumbled in time, but only to give way to another equally powerful and equally tyrannical. It was inevitable that the Jewish world outlook should become pessimistic. God's kingdom seemed far off. This world appeared to be ruled not by God but by evil forces of which the great heathen empires of Assyria, Babylon, Persia, Egypt, Syria, and Rome, with their idolatry and their cruelty, were but the earthly and visible representatives and embodiments. The second fact of significance is the long and continuous contact of the Jews with Babylon and the religion of the Persians. This was Zoroastrianism, and it supplied a view as to the nature of the universe which seemed demanded by Jewish experience. According to this view the world is the battleground of two opposing spiritual forces. The evil in the world is due to the activity of the spiritual or demonic forces of evil at the head of which stands the god of evil. At some day in the future, said the Persian magi or priests, God will destroy these evil forces and eliminate them from the world. Freed from the malevolent activities of the god of evil, the world will then be a good and happy place. Following the destruction of the devil and his angels, the sacred books of Zoroastrianism taught that the dead would be raised and judged, the wicked would receive punishment, while the righteous would be revived to enter into the enjoyment of the new age.

As pious Jews meditated on their national fortunes, more and more this world view seemed to supply the explanation which they sought. Though remaining faithful Jews, reading with faith and hope the promises of the prophets and endeavoring to build anew the Jewish community on the basis of obedience to the law, they gradually adopted this central idea of the religion of the Persians. This world was under the domination of evil spirits. The postponement of the day of deliverance was not due merely to God's delay in punishing Babylon or Persia or Syria. The conflict was deeper than that. Behind visible phenomena there was a conflict between the righteous God and the foul spirits of evil under the leadership of Satan. The present age was the age of Satan, but at the predestined time God would destroy him, and then would come the day of deliverance and reward.

> "His kingdom shall appear throughout all creation:
> Then Satan shall be no more,
> And all sorrow shall depart with him." [15]

The period just before that great deliverance would be one of special trial and calamity, for the forces of evil would be making their last stand and wreaking in one final outburst their malevolent rage against God and those who serve him.

This development of Jewish thought about the kingdom of God under the influence of Persian dualism is known as the apocalyptic development. The essential changes which it brought in the older doctrine or belief were three in number:

[15] Assumption of Moses, 10: 1.

(a) In the first place, it transferred the struggle from this world to the world of spirits. Instead of thinking in terms of the defeat of Egypt or Babylon and the vindication of the people of Israel before the eyes of the surrounding pagan nations, the thought now moves in circles which are supramundane and speaks of the overthrow of Satan and his elimination from the control of the world.

(b) In consequence of this the conception of the kingdom which will result becomes more supernatural and more comprehensive. The older view thought in terms of the restoration of the kingdom of David in Palestine; and while the picture of that kingdom was painted in poetic terms, and it was declared that the seasons would be propitious and the land fruitful and the wild beasts would do no harm, nevertheless the conception dealt essentially with the land of Palestine and neither the course of nature nor the condition of the rest of the world was regarded as changed. But according to the apocalyptic thought the coming of the kingdom is an event of cosmic and supernatural character. It is preceded by a world judgment, the righteous dead rise to share the kingdom, and the very nature of the universe is changed through the overthrow of Satan.

(c) In the third place the world outlook of Jewish apocalyptic thought becomes definitely pessimistic. The present age is given over to the forces of evil. For its amelioration no hope is held out. On the contrary conditions are expected to grow from bad to worse and the hour is darkest just before deliverance.

Side by side with these new apocalyptic ideas the older conceptions no doubt lingered. That Jews in the days of

Jesus still thought in terms of a victory over Rome and a recovery of an earthly political kingdom is abundantly clear from the pages of the New Testament. Various combinations of the older beliefs and the newer ideas appear in the literature from 200 B.C. to 100 A.D. The earthly kingdom would come first and would last five hundred or a thousand years, then would come the great Judgment and the New Age. Other combinations along similar lines are to be found. On the various details of the hope there was a variety of opinion. What will be the lot of the Gentiles on the Day of Judgment? Will the kingdom be on this earth or in heaven? Will God establish his kingdom directly or through an intermediary figure, the Messiah, as the older hope had expected? On these and other questions different answers are given. The phrase used to describe the kingdom differs. But amid all these differences and confusions of detail the basic belief still appears: God is king, though his complete sovereignty has not yet been established. At a time in accordance with his good pleasure he will establish his kingdom over all men. That means judgment upon and destruction of all wickedness, and a state of society in which the righteous will receive God's fullest blessings and do his will completely.

III

We can see now why Jesus spoke of the kingdom of God as he went throught Galilee preaching the good news. This hope of the coming kingdom had in the course of the centuries become the basic conception of Jewish piety. It embodied the world outlook of the Jews. As they looked backward over the history of the past or contemplated what the future held in store, their thoughts fell inevitably into the mold of this basic belief. It had become the center and core of Jewish faith. Prayer for the speedy coming of the kingdom of God was one of the most constant elements in the liturgy of the synagogue.[16] Rabbi Johanan declared that a "prayer in which there is no mention of the kingdom ["kingship"] is no prayer." [17] It was as impossible for a Jew of the first century to think in other terms as for a modern American to believe in the divine right of kings. Jesus spoke of the kingdom of God because as a man of his age it was the center of his intellectual and religious outlook.

But while this must be clearly recognized, it should also be remembered that this hope of the kingdom of God contained certain vital religious conceptions which formed the basis and foundation for Jesus' teachings. Three of these may be singled out for special mention:

(1) The proclamation of the kingdom recalled to the mind the supremacy of God over all earthly powers and forces. God is King over all the earth. He is absolute sovereign and ruler. Against him no opposition can stand, whether of rebellious human wills, hostile pagan governments, or demonic forces of the spirit world. Belief in the coming kingdom meant faith in the supremacy of God and his will over all other facts of life. Beside God and his law, this world and its processes are ephemeral. Heaven and earth shall pass away, but God's will shall be established—that was the core of the Jewish doctrine of the kingdom.

(2) The proclamation of the kingdom revived the longing for and belief in a perfect day to come. All signs to

[16] See Moore, *Judaism*, Vol. II, p. 373.   [17] *Ibid*.

the contrary, blessedness and glory will yet be given to men. Hope for the kingdom to come was an affirmation of discontent with careless, sinful Israel. It pictured the ideal before the eyes of men—the ideal Israel, the perfect earth—and it declared that this ideal was attainable through the power of God.

(3) The thought of the kingdom embodied the conception that there could be no perfect or complete righteousness apart from association with other righteous individuals. The word "kingdom" is a social concept—*i. e.*, a group of people having a common allegiance. It was a legacy to Judaism from the days of the nation's early life when people thought in terms of the tribe or nation and of individuals only as units in that larger group. Jesus was perhaps the world's greatest exponent of the rights of the individual, but he took over from the early thinking of his people this assertion of social solidarity. The perfect rule of God is not over a series of unrelated individuals, but over a fellowship. There is no ideal goodness for one individual off by himself. Jesus did not have to give directions for the formation of a Church. It grew naturally out of his conception of the kingdom of God.

Fundamentally the phrase, "the kingdom of God," means simply God's kingship. But it appears repeatedly in the gospels in certain derived senses. It is used many times from the standpoint of those who "enter" the kingdom or are its members. So used, it might be defined thus: a group of individuals bound together by a common allegiance to God, who do his will and receive his blessings and await the manifestation of his righteous judgment in the world. We shall see that the phrase is also used repeatedly to refer to the cataclysmic event in the future when God shall establish his kingship or rule over all the world, rewarding the righteous and punishing sinners. Such variations in usage are only on the surface. The vital concept beneath is the same, being regarded now from one aspect, now from another.

Thus when Jesus appeared in Galilee preaching, "The kingdom of God is at hand," it is not surprising that he stirred the masses to eager attention. A new prophet had appeared, declaring that God was ready to establish his reign. No longer need men be perplexed over the divine delay, no longer cry, "How long, O Lord, how long?" Thronging about Jesus the multitudes cried out on one occasion, "Blessed is the kingdom that cometh, the kingdom of our Father, David: Hosanna in the highest." [18] From their standpoint that was the "good news." But to show, as Jesus had to show, that men were not ready for that complete rule of God, that many of those who talked most about it were really unwilling that God should rule, and to make clear what was involved in the kingship of God—this was a long and heartbreaking task.

TOPICS FOR DISCUSSION AND REVIEW

1. The geographical factors responsible for the unhappy national fortunes of the Jews.

2. The basic element in the Jewish hope of the coming kingdom of God.

3. The changed world outlook of the apocalyptic school of writers.

4. Is the apocalyptic outlook pessimistic or optimistic?

5. The religious values contained in the apocalyptic expectation. Its dangers.

6. Discuss the fact that Jesus addressed his teachings to the particular men and women of his day from the standpoint of (a) its vividness, (b) its interpretation, (c) its permanent value.

7. Discuss the proposition that theology is the expression of men's deepest hopes and values.

[18] Mark 11: 10.

SUPPLEMENTARY READINGS

On Jewish apocalyptic belief:
  Fairweather: *The Background of the Gospels*, Ch. 7.
  Porter: *The Message of the Apocalyptic Writers*, pp. 49-64.
  Scott: *The Kingdom and the Messiah*, Ch. 2.
On Zoroastrianism:
  Emmett, in Streeter: *Immortality*, pp. 183-185.
  Moore: *History of Religions*, Vol. I, Ch. 15, 16.
On the Relation of Apocalyptic Literature to Old Testament
      Prophecy:
  Hastings: *Dictionary of the Bible*, Art. "Apocalyptic Litera-
      ture."
  Porter: *Op. cit.*, pp. 20-27.
On the reasons for pseudonymous authorship of the apocalypses:
  Porter: *Op. cit.*, pp. 27-34.
On the permanent value of the apocalyptic theology:
  Bevan: *Hellenism and Christianity*, Ch. XI.
  Porter: *Op. cit.*, pp. 64-75.
On the double aspect of Jewish thought of the kingdom of God:
  Schechter: *Some Aspects of Rabbinic Judaism*, Ch. V-VII.

CHAPTER IX

THE KINGDOM OF GOD IN JESUS' TEACHING

In the last chapter it was shown that for many centuries faith in God led the Hebrew people to look forward to a day when the injustices and wrongs of this life would be rectified and good would reign supreme. At a certain period due to their unhappy experiences their world outlook had become pessimistic. So far as this world was concerned a belief in God's direct rule and activity was virtually abandoned. The more this took place the more sharply was the age to come contrasted with it, and the more supernatural and miraculous its advent became. Apocalyptic thought looked to God and to the future; but because it could not see God's hand in the world's order or course of events, it must needs think of the divine manifestation as a cataclysmic supernatural event. Thus from the Jewish standpoint all history was divided into two periods, the present age and the age to come, the latter being the period when evil would be destroyed and the kingdom of God would be established.

Did Jesus hold such views? When he taught the multitudes on the hillsides and beside the sea or spoke in the synagogues about the kingdom of God, was he referring to a future supernatural event which was to mark the end of this present age and the beginning of a new world order? Did Jesus, in other words, share the apocalyptic world outlook? The question is of prime importance. For there is no doubt that it was about the kingdom of God that Jesus preached, for its coming he prayed and taught his disciples to pray, and for it he gave his life. Consequently if one would hope to understand Jesus at all one must have a clear understanding of what he meant when he used that phrase.

Different answers have been given to this question. There are those who maintain that Jesus shared the apocalyptic point of view to the fullest, that he declared that this world is hopelessly bad and doomed to destruction, and that men should live only with the purpose of gaining admission to the supernatural kingdom to come. Others have argued that when Jesus spoke of the kingdom of God he meant a group of people who would do God's will—*i. e.*, the Christian Church, which he taught would grow from small beginnings to become a great body. The difficulty with both of these views is that they base themselves on certain sayings in the gospels and ignore or interpret away all passages which run counter to their respective points of view. Both of them are guilty to a certain extent of making Jesus speak according to our preferences and prejudices. The task of the reverent reader of the gospels, however, must be always to recover the mind and thought of the actual Jesus, not some figure of our own creating. Only thus can we hope to find for our day the inspiration which he gave to those who knew him in the flesh. With these preliminary remarks let us turn to the gospels for the answer to the problem, What did Jesus mean when he spoke of the kingdom of God?

I

The gospels show that Jesus used the term in the basic sense in which it was current in his day—namely, the "kingship" or perfect rule of God. There are two aspects, however, of his teaching about that rule of God.

In the first place the evidence is overwhelming that Jesus accepted the belief which his people had held for many generations that God was going to bring about a new age or condition of things in which evil would be destroyed and good would be supreme. The evidence that he did accept this belief is as follows:

(1) This was the primary connotation of the phrase to his hearers. For many centuries the Hebrew people had believed in such a manifestation of God's power and righteousness, the greatest of the prophets had proclaimed it, and prayer for its coming was regularly offered in the synagogue and by individuals. That this was thought of as a supernatural divine intervention in the course of the world's affairs has been indicated above. Jesus could scarcely have used a phrase which had so definite and well-established a meaning if his thought was of something quite different and new.

(2) Jesus' public ministry began as a continuation of that of John the Baptist. The gospels make it clear that John shared the apocalyptic expectations of his time. His preaching dealt with the imminence of the great Day of Judgment. "Already," he declared, "the ax lies at the root of the trees; every tree which does not bring forth good fruit is hewn down and cast into the fire." [1] He asserted that after him would come the One who would execute this judgment. "He who comes after me is mightier than I am, . . . whose fan is in his hand, and he will thoroughly cleanse his threshing floor, and will gather his wheat into the garner, but the chaff he will burn up with unquenchable fire." [2] Such words show that John's warning, "Repent, for the kingdom of heaven is at hand," [3]

---

[1] Matt. 3: 10 and Luke 3: 9.   [3] Matt. 3: 2.
[2] Matt. 3: 11 f. and Luke 3: 16 f.

referred to the imminence of that divine and supernatural kingdom which was to be inaugurated by the Great Judgment. The facts that Jesus was baptized by John, that he spoke of John in terms of the highest praise, and that his own initial preaching is summed up by the evangelists in terms identical with the preaching of John, "Repent, for the kingdom of heaven is at hand," [4] would indicate that his thought of the kingdom was not out of line with that of John.

(3) The early church was deeply imbued with the expectation of the end of the present age and the imminence of the supernatural kingdom, at which time it was believed that Christ would return in glory. The evidence of this is abundant. In Acts we read that Jesus' own intimate disciples asked after the resurrection, "Lord, dost thou at this time restore the kingdom of Israel?" [5] Paul speaks of how certain passages in the Old Testament were written for "our admonition, upon whom the ends of the ages are come," [6] and indicates to one of his churches that he expected to be alive at the dawn of the new age.[7] In 1 Peter one finds the plain statement, "The end of all things is at hand." [8] James writes, "Murmur not, brethren, one against another, that ye be not judged; behold, the judge standeth before the doors." [9] The First Epistle of John warns its readers, "Little children, it is the last hour." [10] The Revelation of St. John is filled with the thought. Thus there can be no doubt that the early church was thoroughly imbued with the apocalyptic expectation. While the first Christians no doubt magnified and developed this hope, the unquestioned acceptance of this point of view

[4] Matt. 4: 17; cf. Mark 1: 15.   [5] Acts 1: 6.   [6] 1 Cor. 10: 11.
[7] 1 Thess. 4: 13-18.   [8] 4: 7.   [9] 5: 9.   [10] 2: 18.

strongly suggests that Jesus, who spoke much about the kingdom, did not deny its validity. Thus Jesus' predecessor and his followers thought of a supernatural change in the world's order which was to come. The fact constitutes strong evidence that Jesus, whose thought was the connecting link between the two, did not deny this ancient hope and belief of his people.

(4) These considerations, however, only raise certain presumptions. In the light of them one turns to an examination of Jesus' own sayings. His statements concerning the kingdom are so numerous and so varied that one cannot cite and examine them all. The best method perhaps will be to organize the sayings into groups, citing a certain number as illustrations of each group.

a. There are a number of sayings of Jesus which show that the division of history into two worlds or ages, this present age and the age to come, was axiomatic with Jesus as with others of his day. "The sons of this world [or age—note the marginal reading of the Revised Version] marry and are given in marriage: but they that are accounted worthy to attain to that world [or age] and the resurrection from the dead neither marry nor are given in marriage." [11] He speaks of the "sons of this age who are wiser for their generation than the sons of light," [12] of the reward of eternal life which shall be given to the righteous in the world [or age] to come,[13] of a sin against the Holy Spirit which shall be forgiven "neither in this world nor the world to come," [14] and of the judgment which shall take place "at the consummation of the

[11] Luke 20: 35.   [13] Mark 10: 30.
[12] Luke 16: 8.   [14] Matt. 12: 32.

age." [15]   All such expressions are indications of Jesus' world outlook.

b. There are a number of sayings or parables in which the kingdom of God is identified with the coming of the Day of Judgment.   One of the most striking of these is the parable of the dragnet.   "The kingdom of heaven is like a net that was cast into the sea and took in fish of every kind.   And when it was filled the fishermen threw it upon the beach and sat down and gathered the good into vessels, but threw the bad away.   So shall it be at the completion of the age." [16]   Similarly the kingdom is compared to the separation of the tares from the wheat,[17] to the reward and punishment given to the wise and foolish virgins,[18] and to the account which the lord demanded of the servants with whom the talents had been intrusted.[19] In Mark 9: 47 "to enter into the kingdom of God" is the opposite of being "cast into Gehenna."   In these and other passages Jesus warns his hearers that the kingdom of God will be a time of reckoning and judgment.

c. There are many passages in which the kingdom of God is referred to as a future event.   Under this heading should be placed those sayings in which Jesus spoke of entering the kingdom as an event of the future.   Thus one finds the following: "Not every one who says unto me, Lord, Lord, will enter the kingdom of heaven;" [20]   "I tell you that the publicans and harlots shall go into the kingdom of heaven before you;" [21] "How hard will it be for those that have riches to enter the kingdom of God!" [22]   There are others in which Jesus announced or

[15] Matt. 13: 39.

[16] Matt. 14: 47 ff.

[17] Matt. 13: 24 ff. and 40 ff.

[18] Matt. 25: 1 ff.

[19] Matt. 25: 14 ff.

[20] Matt. 7: 21.

[21] Matt. 21: 31.

[22] Mark 10: 23.

instructed his disciples to announce that the kingdom was "near" or "at hand." [23]   At the Last Supper he speaks to his disciples of the day when the kingdom will come.[24] There is the prayer which he taught his disciples to utter, "May thy kingdom come." [25]   There are references to the future punishment of the unrepentant nation in words such as these: "I tell you, The kingdom of God shall be taken away from you, and be given to a nation bringing forth its fruits." [26]

d. Lastly there are two passages in which this conception of the kingdom as that supernatural state which God had reserved for those who serve him is stated in a way that is especially striking.   There is the significant saying which seems to have come to the evangelists from the document Q: "And I say unto you, that many shall come from the east and the west, and shall recline with Abraham, Isaac, and Jacob, in the kingdom of heaven; but the sons of the kingdom shall be cast forth into the outer darkness." [27]   The other is a passage in the parable of the Great Judgment.   To those upon his right hand the king shall say, "Come, ye blessed of my Father, inherit the kingdom prepared for you from the foundation of the world." [28]

The evidence of these sayings is cumulative, and taken together with the general considerations first mentioned, they make it clear that Jesus shared the belief of his countrymen—the basis of which was to be found in many a passage in the Scriptures—that God would shortly establish his "kingship" in complete and sweeping fashion. For many centuries the nation had prayed for the coming

[23] Mark 1: 15, Matt. 10: 7.
[24] Mark 14: 25.
[25] Luke 11: 2 and Matt. 6: 10.
[26] Matt. 21: 43.
[27] Matt. 8: 11 and Luke 13: 29.
[28] Matt. 25: 34.

of that complete rule of God, and now the prophet John had appeared in the wilderness, proclaiming that the Day was near at hand and urging men to prepare for its coming. Not only the multitudes were excited at his preaching, but Pharisees and even the sedate Sadducees went out into the wilderness to hear him. In the midst of this situation Jesus began his public ministry. He saw with keen and penetrating eyes that his countrymen for the most part were unprepared for that divine visitation whenever it should appear. Whole groups of individuals were not only indifferent and irreligious, but were neglected and ostracized by the religious leaders of the people. He saw furthermore how misguided were the expectations and ideas of the people as to what they should expect at God's hands, what God's rule really meant, and what sort of blessings it would bring. Hoping for national glory and dreaming of material blessings—how little they realized what true blessings God had to give and how blessed it would be to order their hitherto misguided and ineffectual lives by his will. "When he saw the multitudes he was moved with compassion for them, because they were distressed and scattered, as sheep not having a shepherd." [29] Thus he took up the burden of John's preaching, speaking to the people of that kingdom of God to come, urging men to repent that they might be prepared for its coming and explaining by many a parable and illustration the supreme desirability of that kingdom and the kind of lives that God demanded of its members.

II

Now the thought of the kingdom of God contained, as we have seen, a number of different elements, and differ-

[29] Matt. 9: 36.

ent minds laid the emphasis on different aspects of the hoped-for kingdom. There was a party in existence in the first century, called the Zealots, which thought mostly of the overthrow of the hated Romans. One recalls the request of James and John to sit one on the right hand and the other on the left hand of Jesus when he should come in the glory of the expected kingdom. Certain minds dwelt, as the extant literature shows, on the supernatural fertility of the soil and fruitfulness of the vine and olive tree in the day of God's kingdom. But Jesus was indifferent to these aspects of the familiar picture. The elements in the thought of the kingdom which he regarded as the important ones and which constituted the subject of those marvelous discourses of his were the religious aspects of the kingdom. God's will to be done as in heaven so on earth, God's fatherly goodness to be enjoyed, God's loving character to be reflected by a society of loving individuals—these were the elements on which Jesus placed his emphasis. The rest were relatively unimportant. To dwell upon ideas of national vengeance was not only wrong in itself, but was to think of the kingdom of God in terms of this world's institutions and organizations. To dream about wealth and comfort when the great and lasting blessings were those of the inner spirit, was misleading. To puzzle about the time of the great consummation and to put the emphasis on the hour of its arrival was to show a lack of trust in God who would give the kingdom in his own good time.

This deep and unwavering emphasis on the religious and spiritual elements in the thought of the kingdom led to a second aspect of Jesus' teaching about God's rule. The religious aspects of the kingdom of God, he taught, need not be postponed until the end of this present age.

Each individual could enter the kingdom here and now. Instead of waiting for that "far-off divine event" one could take upon oneself now the "yoke of the kingdom," to use a phrase of that day, and make God's rule actual and present in one's own life. By so doing he would be prepared for that Day when it came, and could begin immediately the enjoyment of a large part of the rewards and blessings of the kingdom. Thus Jesus endeavored not only to proclaim the coming of the kingdom, but also to bring men into the kingdom, to create a brotherhood of individuals who would show on this earth the life of the kingdom. He was not only the herald of the kingdom, but its founder as well. Furthermore, by his confidence in men and his faith in God he saw beginning in his ministry that victory over the powers of evil which would consummate in the kingdom. The beginnings of the kingdom were to be seen already.

With this in mind various passages in the gospels which speak of the kingdom of God as a present reality become clear. When his critics accused him of doing good deeds by the power of Satan, he replied: "If I by the Spirit of God cast out devils, then is the kingdom of God come upon you." [30] When some Pharisees, dissatisfied with his teaching about the character of the kingdom, wanted specific information as to when it would come, he turned their attention to the practical and immediate challenge of the kingdom in the words, "The kingdom of God does not come with watching for it . . . for lo, the kingdom of God is within you." [31] To the scribe who answered wisely concerning the chief commandment, he declared, "Thou

[30] Matt. 12: 28 and Luke 11: 20. [31] Luke 17: 20.

art not far from the kingdom of God." [32]   In Matthew and Luke there is a saying, taken perhaps from the Q document, the full import of which is uncertain, but which expresses specifically this thought of the beginning of the kingdom: "From the days of John until now the kingdom of heaven suffereth violence, and men of violence take it by force." [33]

Several of the most familiar of Jesus' parables express the thought of the kingdom as something which begins in a small way but grows or develops to be a great thing. It is in the sense of which I have been speaking that they must be taken. "How shall we liken the kingdom of God, or in what parable shall we set it forth? It is like a grain of mustard seed, which, when it is sown upon the earth, though it be less than all the seeds that are upon the earth, yet when it is sown, groweth up and becometh greater than all the herbs, and putteth out great branches; so that the birds of the heaven can lodge under the shadow thereof." [34]   Similarly the kingdom is described as being like the corn which grows without man knowing how, and like the leaven which a woman put in three measures of meal until it leavens it all. [35]

This thought of the present beginnings of the kingdom rests on or has its roots in two characteristics of Jesus' thought. In the first place, it goes back, as we have seen, to his sense of the religious aspects of the kingdom as the core and the heart of it. God's rule over the human heart was the central thing, and this was independent of the supernatural conditions of time and life which constituted the framework of the Jewish hope. In the second

[32] Mark 12: 34.   [33] Matt. 11: 12 and Luke 16: 16.   [34] Mark 4: 30 ff.
[35] Mark 4: 26 ff., and Matt. 13: 33 = Luke 13: 21.

place Jesus was not a pessimist.   He did not regard this world as hopelessly bad with no regenerative, saving forces in it.   Instead he saw God at work in it, active and effective of good.   It was here that he differed from the people who wrote the apocalyptic books.   They hoped for another age in which God would show himself; Jesus saw God at work saving men and destroying evil of all sorts. When his disciples returned from the first missionary journey on which Jesus had sent them and recounted with enthusiasm their success, he said in reply, "I beheld Satan fallen as lightning from heaven." [36]   Jesus had faith in men, even in publicans and harlots whom the official leaders regarded as incorrigible.   But he had greater faith in God.   "Ask," he said to his disciples, "and it shall be given unto you; seek, and ye shall find; knock, and it shall be opened unto you."   Because of this faith in God he was confident that the forces for good which he saw already at work would not be defeated, but would lead on to the realization of the kingdom.

III

But when will be the day of that ultimate divine manifestation?   That question had disturbed men from the beginning.   Paul found it necessary to write to the Thessalonian Christians on the subject.   Many are the apocalypses that have been written declaring that the predestined hour is just before us.   Many fanatics have disturbed the Church throughout the centuries, proclaiming the fulfillment of prophecy.   The missionary programs of the church, the endeavors to make our own institutions righteous, the tasks of social service have frequently lagged through such distraction of the interest of devout

[36] Luke 10: 18.

Christians. What did Jesus say about the date of the end?

Nothing shows better the spiritual genius of Jesus. He said that the kingdom was near, near enough for men to prepare to meet it, but beyond that he did not go. Whatever interpretation may be put on the thirteenth chapter of Mark or the twenty-sixth chapter of Matthew, we may be sure that Jesus never told his disciples when that day would be. Once the Pharisees put the question and he answered, as we have seen, by declaring that his questioners should cease saying, "Lo here, lo there," but should turn their attention to the kingdom of the heart. A second occasion is given in Mark 13. The disciples, resting on a hill overlooking Jerusalem, asked him specifically about times and seasons. And what was his reply? He warned them of many things—of the difficulties they would meet, of the certain fall of Jerusalem—but refused to name the day of the great consummation. Why? For the simple reason, he declared, that he did not know: "But of that day or that hour knoweth no one, not even the angels in heaven, neither the Son, but the Father." [37]

That one verse should be a challenge and a warning to his followers. If Jesus gave his life in the service of the kingdom of God, uncertain when the final consummation would be, and saying plainly to his disciples that he did not know, can we do less than follow his example? Is it not mockery for Christian people to spend their time and attention and zeal in endeavors to find out from the Scriptures how long our age shall last? Jesus has shown the way. Our duty is to work for the kingdom, to pro-

[37] Mark 13: 32.

mote its growth, to enter into its privileges and joys. To God belongs the consummation in his own good time.

IV

To all of this the objection may be raised that nearly two thousand years have elapsed since those days when Jesus taught the multitudes in Palestine and no such miraculous intervention in human affairs as described above has taken place. While that supernatural kingdom may yet appear, there are no grounds, it is argued, for expecting it. The only kingdom that one has any right to trust in is that one which we build painfully and gradually from day to day.

The answer to this is twofold. In the first place it must be recognized that the value of Jesus to the Christian conscience does not rest upon a belief that he was endowed with an infallible and detailed knowledge of future events. The gospels themselves emphatically deny any claim to such supernatural knowledge on his part. He "advanced in wisdom and in stature, and in favor with God and man," says Luke's gospel.[38] He asked questions, apparently for information, endeavored with zeal and sincerity to bring to repentance such towns as Bethsaida and Chorazin and Jerusalem, but in vain, and prayed that last night in Gethsemane in terms that make it clear that he did not possess final knowledge as to the path which God would have him tread.[39] We have his own statement that he did not know the hour of the coming of the kingdom. Jesus no more than his followers possessed divine foreknowledge of all that was to take place. Had it been otherwise, his life would have been merely the acting of a

[38] Luke 2: 52.   [39] Mark 14: 35 f.

part in a play and his endeavor to win his people to the kingdom an insincere parade. The issues of his life he decided by courage and faith, not by foreknowledge. Only thus could they possess moral values. The uniqueness of Jesus is to be found in his spiritual insight, rather than in any ability as a soothsayer. The belief which the church has always held in the divinity of Christ is a conviction that in his own character and in his insight into the realm of spiritual values Jesus reveals to us the character of God and his purposes for life.

From his ancestors Jesus inherited this belief in the supernatural kingdom of God to come just as he inherited other ideas of his day. He accepted the concept, and it furnished the form or framework for his teachings. But the materialistic and purely national elements he eliminated and the ethical and the religious he brought to the fore. He taught that the rule of God over men's lives was possible here and now, and he discerned the beginnings of that future kingdom. The full consummation would come in the future. And this leads to the second phase of that answer suggested above. The kingdom of God in so far as it is already present upon earth struggles against ignorance, greed, and cruelty. Looking back over the centuries one can see progress, a gain here, a victory there. But how slow is that advance! All around one sees vice organized for gain, selfishness despoiling the helpless, indifference betraying the cause of the good. After nearly two thousand years of endeavors to bring in the kingdom the ordinary slum of an American city is almost enough to make one lose heart. Can we keep faith after the desolations of 1914-1918? Must not one modify one's hopes for the future and recognize, as many thinkers have concluded, that after all evil is ineradicable?

In such hours of discouragement Jesus' teaching that the kingdom will come in all its goodness and its beauty comes with ringing challenge. We fight not in our own strength alone. There is no possibility of failure. Ultimately God's rule will be universally established. God is king and he will establish his sovereignty. "Fear not, little flock; it is your Father's good pleasure to give you the kingdom." [40] Through God's power the leaven will yet leaven the whole lump. "The Son of Man shall send forth his angels, and they shall gather out of his kingdom all things that cause stumbling and all them that do iniquity. . . . Then shall the righteous shine forth as the sun in the kingdom of their Father." [41] That is the assurance of Jesus' faith. When the Christian church gives up that vision of the future kingdom—though men may vary as to the mode of its coming—we shall become in prophetic language "a people of relaxed hands and trembling knees."

TOPICS FOR DISCUSSION AND REVIEW

1. Summarize the evidence that Jesus accepted the belief in the supernatural kingdom of God to come.

2. What was the difference between Jesus' world outlook and that of the apocalyptic writers?

3. The sense in which Jesus spoke of the kingdom as a present reality.

4. The limitations which marked Jesus' earthly life.

5. Would Jesus' life be more or less inspiring on the assumption that he was gifted with complete foreknowledge?

6. Discuss the moral value of the belief (a) that the Golden Age lies in the distant past, and (b) that it lies in the future.

[40] Luke 12: 32.   [41] Matt. 13: 41, 43.

SUPPLEMENTARY READINGS

On the idea of the coming kingdom as the center of Jesus' thought:
  Bundy: *The Religion of Jesus*, pp. 104-128.

On Jesus' conception of the coming kingdom:
  Bosworth: *The Life and Teaching of Jesus*, Ch. 23.
  Bousset: *Jesus*, Ch. 5.
  Scott: *The First Age of Christianity*, pp. 58-66, 89-94.
  Warschauser: *The Historical Life of Christ*, Ch. 5.

On whether Jesus' apocalyptic beliefs invalidate his ethical teachings:
  Rashdall: *Conscience and Christ*, pp. 55-67.

On the divinity of Jesus:
  Fosdick: *The Modern Use of the Bible*, Ch. 7 and 8.
  Macintosh: *The Reasonableness of Christianity*, Ch. 10.
  Soper: *What May I Believe?* Ch. 10 and 11.
  Streeter: *Reality*, Ch. VII.

CHAPTER X

JESUS' TEACHING ABOUT GOD

THE theme of Jesus' preaching to his countrymen was the kingdom or rule of God. The nature of that kingdom will be determined obviously by the character of the king. Thus we are brought to the question, What was Jesus' conception of God?

It has sometimes been argued that Jesus' teaching dealt primarily with duties and obligations which men owe their fellow men, and that the theological side to it was secondary and unimportant—an accident due to the fact that in that day everything was in some way or other related to religion. The ethical teaching, it is maintained, is still valid and useful, though the theology is outworn and must be stripped away from the practical teachings to which it was attached. The fact is, however, that Jesus taught primarily a certain religious view of life. The ethical and the moral elements flow directly from the religious teaching. The more we study the records the clearer this becomes. Everything he did and said springs from a religious basis, his sense of God's presence and God's character. When he taught that men should love their enemies he gave as his reason that God was like that.[1] If they asked him about divorce, he replied, "Male and female created he them," and tried to show God's purpose in the creation of sex life.[2] When he speaks of the reward of goodness, it is in terms of "seeing God," of being "sons of God," of being clothed and fed by God. Mark gives

[1] Matt. 5: 45. [2] Mark 10: 6.

the right clue to this teaching when he says at the very beginning of his work that Jesus came into Galilee preaching the "good news of God." [3]

I

Yet it was not a new set of theological ideas that Jesus brought. The God of whom he speaks had in main outline been revealed by the writers of the Old Testament. He was, as Jesus described him in the quotation, "The God of Abraham, Isaac, and Jacob." [4] Of course there were expressions in the Old Testament that Jesus would not have used, and there is a new unity and emphasis in Jesus' thought of God; but nevertheless the teaching of the Old Testament lies at the basis of his thought. This teaching of the Scriptures he took seriously. The reality and constant presence of God became the basis of his life. Therefore when he spoke of God what he said was real. He did not repeat theological maxims, but spoke from the fullness of his own experience.

The God of Jesus was the God of the Jewish Scriptures. The attributes of Jehovah most emphasized in the Old Testament were his uniqueness, his majesty above all that is finite or limited, his irresistible power, his creative activity, and his righteous will.

> "O give thanks unto the Lord, for he is good: . . .
> To him that by understanding made the heavens; . . .
> That spread forth the earth above the waters; . . .
> The sun to rule by day; . . .
> The moon and stars to rule by night." [5]

"Fear ye not me? saith the Lord: will ye not tremble at my presence, which hath placed the sand for the bound

---

[3] Mark 1: 14.   [4] Matt. 22: 32.   [5] Psalm 136: 1-9.

of the sea?" [6] "Can any hide himself in secret places
that I shall not see him? saith the Lord. Do not I fill
heaven and earth?" [7] Such passages are typical of the
thought of the Old Testament. Jesus' sayings indicate
the same exalted belief. "The Lord our God, the Lord
is one," said Jesus, citing the daily Jewish confession of
faith.[8] He was the Creator of all things—"Male and female created he them." [9] "From the beginning of creation
which God created." [10] "He maketh his sun to rise on
the evil and the good, and sendeth rain on the just and the
unjust." [11] Yet it is only by culling the pages with care
that one can find sayings which refer to such subjects as
these. Jesus said practically nothing about God's meta-
physical attributes, or the history of creation. He kept
constantly before him the real problems which men and
women had to face. Abstract speculations or theological
problems as such do not seem to have interested him.

But in the actual concrete world Jesus saw God everywhere. He walked at home in a universe which a heavenly
Father had fashioned for his children. Consider the lilies
dotting the fields with color and bordering the dusty road
in their purity—their garments came from the hands of
God! The birds that never sow nor reap nor gather into
barns are nourished by the daily care of God. In the
natural processes of the heavens he saw God's constant
activity. He makes each sun to shine. The fresh rain is
his gift to good and bad alike. Jesus never relegated
God's activity simply to one long past divine act of creation. He gave thanks to his Father at the beginning of
each meal.[12] He told his disciples to pray, "Give us this

---

[6] Jer. 5: 22.	[8] Mark 12: 29.	[10] Mark 13: 19.
[7] Jer. 23: 24.	[9] Mark 10: 6.	[11] Matt. 5: 45.
[12] Mark 6: 41, 8: 7, and 14: 22.		

day our daily bread." [13]   He saw in all those natural processes which we call physical laws simply the direct expression of God's active will.

Two things we need especially to notice about this view of Jesus.   In the first place, nothing is so small or so insignificant as to escape God's attention and care.   He knows when each small sparrow falls to the ground and ends its little chapter of life.   He sees to it that the birds are fed and the lilies clothed.   He is like a shepherd who is aware of the absence of even one sheep from the flock. [14] Or like a woman who sweeps the whole house to recover a coin that has been lost. [15]   Even the processes of each person's growth lie in God's thought—"Which of you by being anxious can add one cubit unto his stature?" [16] And, more amazing still, in God's omniscience even the hairs of our heads are numbered! [17]

In the second place, notice that God does all this directly.   The history of religions has always shown a tendency to remove God from direct contact with men and things and to believe in intermediaries, angels or spirits. This is due chiefly to the emphasis on God's holiness and exaltation, which makes men hesitate to feel themselves directly in the presence of the Almighty.   Hence the archangels, the patron saints, the prayers to the Virgin, all doctrines of mediators and intercessors.   No justification for such beliefs can be found in the teaching of Jesus. For him the elaborate angelology of Judaism is secondary and conventional.   "Pray to thy Father in secret, and thy Father which seeth in secret shall reward thee openly." "Shall he not much more clothe you, O ye of little faith?"

---

[13] Matt. 6: 11.   [15] Luke 15: 8 f.   [17] Matt. 10: 30.
[14] Luke 15: 4 f.   [16] Matt. 6: 27.

Such words show that Jesus dispensed with intermediaries and angelic agencies in the central aspects of his thought.

But this thought of God's presence and activity in all the world of nature was never to become weak or sentimental. Nor was Jesus' belief to any degree an impersonal pantheism. He was trained in the Jewish Scriptures and the God of those Scriptures stands clearly distinguished from the world and is a Being of majesty and glory before whom every man must be fearful. Isaiah, for example, speaks of "a day of the Lord . . . when the loftiness of man shall be bowed down, and the haughtiness of men shall be brought low, . . . when men shall go into the caves of the rocks, and into the holes of the earth, from before the terror of the Lord, and from the glory of his majesty, when he ariseth to shake mightily the earth." [18] That passage is typical of the prophets; and while Jesus, as we have seen, emphasized other aspects of the kingdom, that side of God's nature is never lost from his thought. He is "the Lord of heaven and earth," even in the address of prayer.[19] He holds all things in his hands. "All things are possible with thee," we find Jesus repeatedly saying.[20] There are legions of angels ready to do his bidding.[21] His majesty must not be taken lightly. "I will warn you whom you shall fear. Fear him who after he hath killed has the power to cast into Gehenna. Yea, I say unto you, Fear him." [22] The whole earth is but "the footstool of his feet." [23] Jerusalem is "the city of the great King." [23] The expanse of heaven

[18] Isa. 2: 12-19.   [20] Mark 14: 36; 10: 27.   [22] Luke 12: 5.

[19] Matt. 11: 25.   [21] Matt. 26: 53.   [23] Matt. 5: 35.

is "the throne of God." [24]   He is omniscient.   He knows
men's hearts and the events of the future.[25]

Closely associated with this characteristically Old Testament emphasis on the power of God is the thought of his
holiness.   This element Judaism had greatly emphasized,
giving to the word "holiness" a meaning which had some
unfortunate consequences; but to that holiness of moral
perfection which it was the great work of the prophets to
declare, Jesus held fast.   "Ye shall be perfect," he enjoined his disciples, "as your heavenly Father is perfect." [26]   The prayer, "Hallowed be thy name," has the
same ultimate meaning.   But even clearer than these was
Jesus' refusal to have the adjective "good" applied even
to his own person.   "Why callest thou me good?" he replied to the wealthy ruler; "none is good save one, that is,
God." [27]   Nothing could make plainer Jesus' sense of the
unapproachable transcendence of God above all that is
finite and human.

II

It is because God is perfect goodness that he is unalter-
ably opposed to evil and will destroy it.   The message of
warning which John the Baptist had delivered, "Repent,
for the kingdom of heaven is at hand," Jesus repeated.
In thus proclaiming that the coming of the kingdom would
be a day of gloom and not of rejoicing unless the nation
repented, Jesus stood in the line of succession of the
ancient prophets.   "The kingdom of heaven is like unto
a net, that was cast into the sea, and gathered of every
kind: which, when it was filled, they drew up on the

[24] Matt. 23: 22.
[25] Matt. 6: 18; 6: 32; 7: 2, etc.; 24: 36.
[26] Matt. 5: 48.   [27] Mark 10: 18.

beach; and they sat down, and gathered the good into vessels, but the bad they cast away. So shall it be at the end of the age." [28] At the time of the harvest the wheat shall be gathered into barns, but the tares shall be bound into bundles to be burned.[29] In the parable of the talents, the parable of the ten virgins waiting for the marriage feast, the parable of the Great Judgment before the King sitting on his throne, and in many another utterance, Jesus drove home to his hearers the necessity of repentance and a new life. With God, he declared, there is no minimizing of evil, no toleration of wrong such as men show so constantly. This is not to say that Jesus did not teach that there are different degrees of responsibility for sins committed, and that God takes into account all those factors of environment, etc., which enter into and are largely responsible for the life one lives. There is a significant saying in Luke, "That servant who knew his lord's will, and made not ready, nor did according to his will, shall be beaten with many stripes; but he that knew not . . . shall be beaten with few stripes." [30] But at the same time the sharpness of the distinction between good and evil was never dulled in Jesus' portrayal of God's attitude. God is primarily a being of righteous will who will not compromise with sin and iniquity. Before him we shall have to give answer at the final day. Our obligations to God are more pressing than duty to Cæsar or any earthly power before which men stand in awe.[31] "Not every one that saith unto me, Lord, Lord, shall enter into the kingdom of heaven; but he that doeth the will of my Father which is in heaven." [32] The man who deliberately sets

---

[28] Matt. 13: 47-49.   [30] Luke 12: 47.   [32] Matt. 7: 21.

[29] Matt. 13: 30.   [31] Matt. 22: 21.

himself against that divine will, who knows the right but spurns it, who refuses the divine forgiveness and fellowship, for that individual Jesus preaches—just as uncompromisingly as had the ancient prophets of Israel—the certainty of punishment. "Every one that heareth my words, and doeth them not, shall be likened unto a foolish man, who built his house upon the sand." [33]   The scribes who devour widows' houses and "make long prayers for a pretense" shall receive "greater condemnation." [34] There are two ways, one leading to life, the other to destruction.[35] There are many who choose this latter path, and Jesus never flinched from the prophetic judgment that all such could expect no divine compassion to rescue them from their own wills. There must be occasions of stumbling, "but woe to that man through whom the occasion cometh." [36]   "Be not afraid of them that kill the body. . . . But I will warn you whom ye shall fear : Fear him which after he hath killed hath power to cast into Gehenna; yea, I say unto you, Fear him." [37] "Ye offspring of vipers, how shall ye escape the judgment of Gehenna?" [38]   It is true that the picture of this future punishment is presented more severely in the Gospel of Matthew than it is in either Mark or Luke, but it is futile to try to read out of Jesus' mind the thought of God as a judge who condemns moral evil unsparingly and forever removes it from his presence. The God of Jesus is a God of uncompromising righteousness, and we miss the strength of Jesus if we try to interpret him as in any way seeing a future truce with evil or the admission of it to the kingdom of God.

[33] Matt. 7: 26.   [35] Matt. 7: 13.   [37] Luke 12: 5.
[34] Mark 12: 40.   [36] Matt. 18: 7.   [38] Matt. 23: 33.

III

Before that unapproachable power and holiness Ezekiel is said in his prophecies always to have fallen upon his face,[39] and Isaiah cried out in his vision, "Woe is me, for I am undone!" [40]   Jesus realizes just as fully the overwhelming majesty and holiness of God, and there flowed from this consciousness an element of reverence and worship which must not be overlooked. "My Father is greater than I," we read in the Fourth Gospel, but this thought runs all through the Synoptic story as well. It lies back of the whole worship life of Jesus, the lonely vigils on the mountain side, the prayers for strength and support, the complete confidence in God for strength and help. But no such feeling of God's unapproachableness as we see in Ezekiel and Isaiah exhibits itself in Jesus' thought. For he realized more strongly than did they another side of God's nature. Not only was he above all human limitations and removed from stain and sin, but his goodness consisted in an infinite activity of love. Jesus combined in closest unity that which was primary with the prophets and that which was the special contribution of the Psalms. "The Lord is my shepherd; I shall not want." "Like as a father pitieth his children, so the Lord pitieth them that fear him." "The Lord is full of compassion and gracious, slow to anger, and plenteous in mercy." This is the other side of God's character as portrayed by Jesus.

God's goodness is active love. In some religions the divine being has been portrayed as content and satisfied, engaged only in self-contemplation. There are some splendid pieces of religious literature which develop the thought that God is absolutely passive. He wants nothing.

[39] Ezek. 1: 28; 3: 23, etc.   [40] Isa. 6: 1-5.

He needs nothing. His activity is concerned only with that which is perfect. *Jesus said that God cares.* He cares for men and women, each of whom is invaluable in his eyes. How obvious that should be! For God cares for poor sparrows, and "ye are of more value than many sparrows." [41]   Indeed, in God's sight man is of more value than even the most sacred institution in the world, the Sabbath day, for "the Sabbath was made for man, and not man for the Sabbath." [42]   Furthermore, this love is not merely abstract and general, a sort of divine humanitarianism. God loves each individual. He is like the shepherd who knows each time that a sheep gets out of the fold and is ready to go into the night to bring him back. [43] He is like the woman who will not let the coin stay lost, even though she may have others. "Even so it is not the will of your Father in heaven that one of these little ones should perish." [44]   Each individual has a unique and personal value in God's sight, a value because he is just that person and not another. Herein was one of the great contributions that Jesus made to the religious and moral thought of the world. In this phase of Jesus' teaching has lain the dynamic of all Christian efforts toward social change. It contains in germ all of our modern ideas about the supreme value of personality. Society has always tended to neglect the outcast and the enslaved and to feel that consequences to them do not matter in comparison with the interests of the established classes. People who call themselves Christian have, for example, doubted whether the black man has a soul. The great slums of our cities contain just so many "hands," and industry

[41] Matt. 10: 31.   [43] Luke 15: 1-7.

[12] Mark 2: 27.   [44] Matt. 18: 14.

need take no further account of them. But if Jesus' view be right, God cares for each of these persons individually. As Immanuel Kant said, you can't think of people any longer as means to an end, they are all ends in themselves. They are such for God. Nor can we simply think in terms of masses or classes. It is because he kept saying this and living it out that Jesus was not a "safe" man to the ruling classes. And his followers who have really caught his spirit have never been "safe" to those who wish to preserve some phase of the established order which starves or crushes the personal development of human beings.

Realizing so clearly this side of God's character, Jesus did not fall down in fear at the thought of God as had many of the prophets. Instead, he called him "Father." This term had of course been applied to God long before Jesus used it. (See Isaiah 64: 8; Malachi 1: 6, 2: 10, etc.) But it had never been central in the Old Testament conception of God, the primary thought there being that of Israel's King. Jesus took the term and made it his address of intimate approach. The prayer in Gethsemane is "Abba, Father, . . . remove this cup from me." [45] In the great thanksgiving passage it is, "I thank thee, Father, that thou . . . didst reveal these things unto babes." [46] When his disciples asked him to teach them how to pray, he told them always to begin, "Our Father, who art in heaven." [47] One should forgive, he said, "that your Father in heaven may forgive you your trespasses." [48] In giving alms one should not let the left

---

[45] Mark 14: 36.   [47] Matt. 6: 9 = Luke 11: 2.

[46] Matt. 11: 25.   [48] Mark 11: 25.

hand know what the right hand doeth, that recompense may be from "thy Father who seeth in secret." [49]

One result of this loving character of God is his readiness to bestow his blessings freely. We must rid our minds of the idea that God withholds certain gifts which we may induce him to bestow. He is ready to give even before we ask—that is Jesus' thought. It is his delight to give. By many a parable and many a figure Jesus drove home this thought. "If ye, being evil, know how to give good gifts, . . . how much more shall your Father in heaven give good things to them that ask him?" [50] "Ask, and it shall be given you; seek, and ye shall find; knock, and it shall be opened unto you." [51] Instead of having to earn the blessings of God, they may be had for the mere asking! "Fear not, little flock; for it is your Father's good pleasure to give you the kingdom." [52] Notice the tone of that statement, "your Father's good pleasure." Hence why should men be fretted and fearful because of simple needs like food and apparel? "Your heavenly Father knoweth that ye have need of all these things." [53]

The parable of the workers in the vineyard, all of whom are given the same wage, is a good illustration of how Jesus taught this lesson. To those who had labored for only one hour the lord of the vineyard bestowed out of his gracious nature the reward of a full day's service. And when the other workmen protest, the landlord of the story replies, "Is it not lawful for me to do what I will with mine own? Is thine eye evil (or niggardly) because I am good?" [54] God is like that. He does not give on the

[49] Matt. 6: 4.   [51] Matt. 7: 7.   [53] Matt. 6: 32.
[50] Matt. 7: 11.   [52] Luke 12: 32.   [54] Matt. 20: 15.

basis of merit, but from the overflowing goodness of his divine grace.

Jesus taught with special emphasis a second characteristic of this loving character of God. His good will extends even to those who are opposed to his rule and refuse his fellowship. Matthew 5: 44, 45 is one of the central passages in the gospels. "I say unto you, Love your enemies, and pray for them that persecute you; that ye may be the sons of your Father which is in heaven; for he maketh his sun to rise on the evil and the good, and sendeth rain on the just and the unjust."

It follows obviously from this last that a readiness to forgive is characteristic of him. The father who loves his wayward son will not close his door when the prodigal appears upon the threshold. God is like that father, said Jesus—a father who ran out to greet his son and whose only reproof was the best robe in the house and a feast of rejoicing. "There is more joy in heaven over one sinner that repents than over ninety-nine righteous persons who need no repentance." [55]   The publican who cried, "God be merciful to me a sinner," went down to his house justified, not because of any list of righteous deeds, but simply through his penitent cry. [56]   And that Jesus thought of God's willingness to forgive as inexhaustible, is shown by his injunction to Peter to forgive seventy times seven times; for forgiveness in the case of men is but imitation of God.

It is against the background of this belief in God which has been described that we must view the deep confidence and joy which marked the life of Jesus. He met one disappointment after another. The people listened to him

[55] Luke 15: 7.   [56] Luke 18: 10 f.

gladly and hailed him as a prophet, but no mass movement of repentance followed from his work. The religious leaders who ought to have been first to leap to his aid hardened themselves into a vindictive opposition. Herod began watching him with suspicion, and from Roman officials he could expect at best only a hard cynicism. Yet never once did he lose confidence. "Blessed are those who are persecuted for righteousness' sake." Every earthly sign to the contrary, "the meek . . . shall inherit the earth." He taught his disciples to pray expecting an answer, "Thy will be done on earth as in heaven." He saw in his own and the disciples' work, "Satan fallen as lightning from heaven" [57] and signs that the kingdom of God had begun to dawn.[58] To Jerusalem, standing in all her pride and cruelty, he declared at the close of his life, "Behold, your house is left unto you desolate." [59] And, even though death in its most cruel form stood facing him, he declared to his followers that his very death would be a ransom for many,[60] and that they who had remained with him should judge the twelve tribes of Israel.[61]

Back of all this is Jesus' belief in God. If God be the "Lord of heaven and earth," with whom "all things are possible," then truly blessed are the meek, the peacemakers, the pure in heart, those persecuted for righteousness' sake. With such assurance, why be afraid? On the contrary one should be joyous. If God be like the father of the prodigal son, constantly ready to forget the sins of the past, if with loving care he knows the things we really need and it is his good pleasure to bestow of his bounty, if his love is for every individual as that person and no

[57] Luke 10: 18.   [59] Matt. 23: 38.   [61] Matt. 19: 28.
[58] Matt. 12: 28.   [60] Mark 10: 45.

other, then no wonder Jesus declared, "When ye fast, . . . be not of sad countenance, but anoint thy head and wash thy face";[62] for worship has become a joy and service a devotion. When Paul writes his outburst of Christian joy, "Rejoice in the Lord alway; again I say unto you, Rejoice," [63] he was following in this joyous belief in God which Jesus taught.

From this conception of God it follows logically that God desires in turn the love of his children. This is the implication of practically all that Jesus taught. It is this which is presented with such perfect grace in the parables of the prodigal son and the lost sheep. But we do not need to seek for implications or interpret parables. Jesus was once asked the direct question, "What is the chief commandment?"—*i. e.*, What is the primary thing that God desires of men? And his answer came without hesitation, "Thou shalt love the Lord thy God with all thy heart, and with all thy soul, and with all thy strength, and with all thy mind." [64]

But this love of God, as Jesus conceived of it, was not simply or even primarily an emotional experience. Its center and core was devotion to the purposes of God, coöperation with his will. There is a great deal more said by Jesus about doing the will of God than there is about love for him. To love God means first of all to serve him. A saying in Matthew illustrates this natural direction of Jesus' thought: "No man can serve two masters: for either he will *hate* the one and *love* the other; or else he will hold to one and despise the other. Ye cannot *serve* God and Mammon." [65] Fellowship with God is primarily

[62] Matt. 6: 16 f.

[63] Phil. 4: 4.

[64] Mark 12: 30.

[65] Matt. 6: 24.

fellowship with his purposes and coöperation with his beneficent will. But it is clear, not only from Jesus' teachings but from his own life as well, that the basis and support for this service should be a deep sense of trust, confidence, and gratitude toward a God whose dealings with men show him to be like a father.

Thus Jesus taught that love lies at the heart of the universe and directs its processes; that God calls men into fellowship with and likeness to himself; that the divine blessings are given to men freely, not on the basis of their deserts but because of God's nature; but that the results of continued moral refusal are inexorable. The rest of this study will be but the elaboration of this conception and the consequences for the life of man which Jesus drew from it.

TOPICS FOR DISCUSSION AND REVIEW

1. Explain the statement, "Jesus had the most joyous idea of God that was ever thought of."

2. What lessons as to the character of God did Jesus draw from the world of nature? Are there any aspects of God's character as Jesus conceived it which are not demonstrated in the physical order?

3. In the light of Jesus' statement that God knows the things we have need of and is ready to bestow them, what should be the primary purpose of prayer?

4. Compare the aspects of God's character on which John the Baptist laid the emphasis (Luke 3: 7-17) with those which Jesus emphasized.

5. Show how the love and service of mankind are implied in the acceptance of Jesus' conception of God.

6. What practical difference does it make whether or not God is love?

7. The meaning of Christian belief in the divinity of Christ.

SUPPLEMENTARY READINGS

On Jesus' conception of God:
    Bousset: *Jesus*, Ch. 6.

Bundy: *The Religion of Jesus,* Ch. 2.
Glover: *The Jesus of History,* Ch. 5.
Wendt: *The Teaching of Jesus,* Vol. I, pp. 184-203.
On the greater severity of the teaching in Matthew on God's punishment of sinners over that in the other gospels:
Emmett, in Streeter: *Immortality,* pp. 187-190, 194-198.
On Jesus' prayers:
Bundy: *Our Recovery of Jesus,* Ch. 6.
On the Holy Spirit in Jesus' thought:
Scott: *The Spirit in the New Testament,* pp. 71-80.
On the meaning of love for God:
Moffatt: *Love in the New Testament,* pp. 83-96.

CHAPTER XI

THE RIGHTEOUSNESS OF THE KINGDOM

I

"The kingdom of heaven," said Jesus, "is like a treasure hid in a field which a man found and hid; and in his joy he went and sold all that he had and bought it." "Seek ye first the kingdom of God and its righteousness," he urged his hearers. To gain the kingdom is the most important thing in life; it is worth the sacrifice of a hand, an eye, all of one's possessions, anything else that stands in the way. It is, indeed, the supreme good, the *summum bonum* of life.

To enter the kingdom one must do the will of God. On that all the great teachers of Israel had agreed, and that was admitted by all of Jesus' hearers. But what was the will of God? In that question lies the crux of religion and morality. It is easy to talk of doing God's will—all the bigots and fanatics of history have claimed to be doing that. The priests who led out the children from their homes to die in foreign lands on the terrible Children's Crusade, the leaders of the Inquisition in Holland, the witch burners of New England, the Mormon leaders— they all claimed to be simply doing God's will.

Jesus knew that trait of human nature. According to John's gospel he warned his disciples, "The hour cometh that whosoever killeth you will think that he offereth service unto God." [1] He knew that trait because he himself had encountered it. His opponents had declared that he

[1] John 16: 2.

163

did wonders because he was in league with Beelzebub and thus posed as representatives of God as they plotted to destroy him. They denounced his freedom from restraint, his originality, his spiritual genius, on the grounds that he differed from the Mosaic Law and hence was a dangerous iconoclast. There is little doubt that the people who crucified Jesus thought themselves exponents and defenders of the divine will.

So when one speaks of obedience to God one is thrown back on the question, What is God's will? In Jesus' answer to this question will be found the positive side of his teaching. Thus on closer examination one sees that the subject of the kingdom, or the rule of God, is the framework within which will be found the content of Jesus' real message. The thought of the kingdom—obedience to God and enjoyment of his blessings—is the scheme of presentation, so to speak, carrying within the vital, powerful, moral message which Jesus gave.

To understand Jesus' teaching of righteousness, if one may use that word instead of the longer phrase, it will be well to compare it with the ideal of righteousness which the rabbis were holding up to the people of his day. God's will, they declared, was to be found in the sacred books of the law, and to a lesser degree in the prophets. The law gave definite precepts and rules of action. These rules of action were of course the divine will, and righteousness consisted of obedience of them. Judaism was thus always a way of life, a code of action much more than it was a system of belief or a philosophy. Pharisees and Sadducees, Essenes and proselytes, might differ and did differ on matters of belief, but in action there could be no deviations. The Torah (or Law) must be kept. Specific obedience to its precepts was righteousness.

Of course the various teachers went deeper than this and insisted on motives and attitudes as well as acts. There are some splendid sayings preserved from the Rabbis of Judaism. But the primary emphasis fell upon the correct performance of the requirements of the law.

Obviously such a system is most admirable for certain purposes. It emphasizes deeds, not passing sentiments, acceptance of a creed, or outward professions. It demands actual conduct, and Judaism produced the highest moral standard of any ancient people. The principle of actual performance of deeds is the one upon which all our law codes are built. A law code frankly says that it is the deed which counts, not the thought or desire. No amount of malice in the heart brings one within the pale of the law until the intention has issued in action.

But as a religion a system of legal obedience is external and superficial. It fails to get beneath the surface. It encourages casuistry, one precept being played off against the other. It makes or tends to make all duties of equal value since all are commanded by the law—the tithing of mint on a moral level with "justice, mercy, and faith"; the stealing of a pin an equal wrong with stealing a horse. It limits and defines the moral ideal in terms of one set of acts and one set of restraints. It hardens religion into the duties of one particular period or state of culture. Such a definition of righteousness in terms of legal obedience Jesus repudiated.

Jesus declared, in the first place, that righteousness is something more inclusive than any set of rules or prescriptions. It goes beyond the act itself and demands a certain state of the heart as well. In the Sermon on the Mount he shows this in a very striking way. He takes those cases in which no one ever questioned the validity of the written precept, those cases of law at its strongest, and declares that the act of abstention alone is not sufficient. "Ye have heard that it was said to them of old, Thou shalt not kill; but I say unto you, That every one of you who is angry with his brother is in danger of the judgment." [2] "Ye have heard that it was said, Thou shalt not commit adultery; but I say unto you, That every one that looketh on a woman to lust after her hath committed adultery with her already in his heart." [3] "Ye have heard that it was said, Thou shalt not forswear thyself, but shalt perform unto the Lord thine oaths; but I say unto you" . . . let truth so dwell in the heart that your yea will mean yea and your nay, nay.[4] The mere outward conformity in all these cases is not enough.

This thought is basic with Jesus. Goodness demands something within the life as well. The rich men cast much into the treasury, but their gifts, although externally more valuable, he declared to be less than the offering by a poor widow of two small coins worth about a penny.[5] For there was something which she added to those two small coins that was lacking in large contributions. He declared in a crucial case which will be discussed later that nothing from without could make a man unclean, but only that which comes from within, a saying which carries all goodness back to the inner life from which it springs.[6] When the scribe asked him which was the chief commandment, he went behind all external performances and declared that simple love of God and man was the essential thing.[7] He declared that the primary moral issue did not concern itself with details of behavior, but rather with the question

---

[2] Matt. 5: 21, 22. [4] Matt. 5: 33, 37. [6] Mark 7: 15.
[3] Matt. 5: 27, 28. [5] Mark 12: 41 f.
[7] Mark 12: 28 and Matt. 12: 35 f.

whether there existed within the soul a light which would illuminate all the body. "Look therefore whether the light that is in thee be not darkness!" [8]

II

Thus goodness is within, said Jesus. But he did not mean by that a vapid sentiment or emotion. His demands in regard to conduct were as rigorous as any of those of the ancient prophets. "By their fruits ye shall know them." [9] "Each tree is known by its fruits." [10] "Not every one that saith unto me, Lord, Lord, shall enter into the kingdom of heaven, but he that *doeth* the will of my Father in heaven." [11] In the magnificent parable of the great judgment[12] "the kingdom prepared from the foundation of the world" was for those who fed the hungry, clothed the naked, and visited those who were sick and in prison. The parable of the house that was built upon the sand was Jesus' picture of those who hear the teachings and no doubt assent, but who "do them not." [13] The goodness within must flow into concrete expression.

The truth of the matter is that Jesus' ideal of righteousness claimed the whole man. He demanded an entire devotion. He refused to divide the nature of man into thoughts and motives on the one hand and deeds on the other. Man is a unit. Jesus did not want new acts or new motives, but new men. He called for good men, not good thoughts or good deeds. His own words here are better than any commentary: "The good man," he says in Matthew 12: 35, "out of his good treasure bringeth forth good things; and the evil man out of his evil treasure

[8] Luke 11: 35; cf. Matt. 6: 22, 23.

[9] Matt. 7: 17.   [11] Matt. 7: 21.   [13] Matt. 7: 26.

[10] Luke 6: 44.   [12] Matt. 25: 31 f.

bringeth forth evil things." "Ye generation of vipers, how can ye, being evil, speak good things?" [14]

This thought of wholeness receives a splendid illustration in some words which follow the above quotation about the good man. "Every idle word which men shall speak, they shall give an account thereof in the day of judgment." [15] That seems indeed a hard saying. But when one thinks of it, is it not just the idle word that expresses the real self, the nature within freed from all social restraints and formal requirements? The idle word, the chance act—such things are the clue to the real character of the person, a principle which every good playwright makes constant use of. What Jesus is saying is that the really righteous man is one who can stand judgment even on his idle words, when untrammeled expression is given to the self within: "The good man out of his good treasure bringeth forth good things."

III

But Jesus went further. This whole self to be righteous must have a positive and active character. Goodness is not negative. It is not a colorless abstention from certain vices, nor is it the performance of a round of stated duties. In his hands it comes much nearer being an inspired passion. Most of Jesus' teaching deals not with prohibitions, but with positive commands. He had no word of praise for passive morality. The young man who had kept all the law is commanded to do something—to sell his goods and give to the poor. One of the most striking of the beatitudes is the seventh, which declares that it is the peacemakers—not the peace keepers—that are especially blessed. The climax and close of the beatitudes is one

[14] Matt. 12: 34.   [15] Matt. 12: 36.

twice pronounced upon those "who are persecuted for righteousness' sake"—that is, those who are in the very forefront of the struggle and are suffering for the cause. He significantly told his disciples that they were "the salt of the earth," which did not mean that they were merely good people, but that a great task difficult of accomplishment awaited them, the seasoning and saving of the world.

Notice too the type of sinners we find Jesus most often denouncing. They are people who have done nothing. In the parable of the Great Judgment the condemnation is because "I was hungered and ye gave me no meat, I was thirsty and ye gave me no drink, naked and ye clothed me not, sick and in prison and ye did not visit me." [16] What had they done?—nothing at all. So in the other parables. The priest and the Levite broke no moral law, they merely passed by on the other side. Of the rich man, "clothed in purple and faring sumptuously every day," there is recorded no evil except that a beggar named Lazarus lay at his gate full of sores and sick of hunger and he stirred not to help him.[17] The unprofitable servant cast into outer darkness was one to whom a talent had been given, but who was content to hide it in the earth.[18] There is a positive self-motivating quality about goodness. It is a thing of enterprise and initiative.

Perhaps the clearest presentation of this positive outlook on life is Jesus' saying about the devil who went out of a man and later returned. He came back because the house from which he had gone stood "empty, swept, and garnished." "Then taketh he seven other spirits more evil than himself; and they enter in and dwell there: and the

[16] Matt. 25: 42 f.   [17] Luke 16: 19 f.   [18] Matt. 25: 14 f.

last state of that man becometh worse than the first." [19]
Whatever one may think about details of the parable, one
must not miss the main thought. The elimination of evil
is not enough. One's life will be filled, if not by a new
spirit and attitude, then with the old inhabitants. The
renunciation of old ideals will avail nothing unless new
aims and objectives are set before one. Honesty that
merely will not steal, purity that commits no overt act,
humanity that simply takes no "undue advantage," these
sorts of virtues fall far short of Jesus' definition of goodness.

IV

But what is the nature of that active creative disposition
which Jesus called goodness? What is to be active in
doing? The answer is too well known to require demonstration. It can be put quite simply—it is an active life
of loving service.

He summed it up in several utterances which are the
heart of the New Testament. Certain of the greatest of
these were quite extempore, arising out of questions asked
him by some listener. Without undertaking to make an
extensive list, I will cite three of these great passages which
describe the nature of the righteousness of the kingdom.

The first is the familiar answer to the question of the
scribe as to which commandment was the first. "Jesus
answered, Hear, O Israel, . . . Thou shalt love the Lord
thy God with all thy heart, and with all thy soul, and with
all thy mind, and with all thy strength. The second is this,
Thou shalt love thy neighbor as thyself." [20] In Matthew

---

[19] Matt. 12: 43 f. and Luke 11: 24 f.

[20] Mark 12: 28 f. = Matt. 22: 34 f. In Luke 10: 25 f. this quotation
from the law is made by a scribe and Jesus commends his choice.

there are added the words, "On these two commandments hangeth the whole law, and the prophets."

Side by side with this great saying should be put the so-called Golden Rule: "As ye would that men should do to you, do ye also to them likewise." [21]

And then we must add that saying which Jesus apparently uttered a number of times, judging from the variety of forms and occasions in which we find it in the gospels —"Whosoever would become great among you shall be your minister," "He that is greatest among you shall be your servant." [22]

These sayings, to which others almost as clear and conclusive could be added, are the heart of Jesus' teaching. Goodness, the righteousness of the kingdom, is just that, the complete devotion of the self in loving service. To love God and one's neighbor as oneself, to do unto others as you would have them do unto you, to become the minister and servant of all—this simple but comprehensive ideal Jesus declared to be the will of God for men.

V

The implications and significance of such an ideal of righteousness will be discussed in a succeeding chapter. But there is still another quality of goodness as Jesus thought of it that we must not overlook. The good life is one of constant growth and progress. It never is satisfied or content. It is always attaining, it has never attained. The really religious man never becomes self-complacent. This is one of Jesus' most striking, and at the same time one of his most characteristic ideas.

This comes out with unequivocal clearness in Jesus'

[21] Luke 6: 31 = Matt. 7: 12.
[22] Mark 10: 43, Matt. 23: 11, 20: 26, Luke 9: 48, 22: 26.

criticism of certain of the Pharisees. The latter were the respectable leaders of the community, noteworthy for their public rectitude and scrupulous morality. They were good people according to the general judgment of their neighbors. Now Jesus gives a parable in Luke 18: 9 f. about one of these Pharisees who went up into the temple to pray. There was also in the temple that day a publican—a moral outcast. The Pharisee stood up and prayed, "God, I thank thee that I am not as the rest of men, greedy, dishonest, or adulterous, like that tax collector. I fast twice in the week, I pay tithes on everything I get." [23] Now notice that Jesus does not suggest that this claim was not warranted. "But the tax collector stood at a distance and would not even raise his eyes to heaven, but struck his breast and said, O God, have mercy on a sinner like me. I tell you, it was he who went back with God's approval, and not the other."

That story needs little comment. Goodness of character is not so many good deeds, be they ever so valuable. It is an ongoing process of the soul. It does not mean character that is fixed, hardened into a mold, but life that is ever growing and reshaping itself to higher ends.

Much of Jesus' denunciation of the Pharisees goes back to this point. According to the conventions, they were undoubtedly the righteous of Israel. But the temper of the lives of many of them lacked a basic element. There was in these cases no sense of personal inadequacy; they wanted no nobler life. They were conscious of their goodness and remembered their virtues. They saw nothing wrong with themselves nor with a society that had so many good people in it. And so they had stopped the

[23] Luke 18: 10 f. as in Goodspeed, *An American Translation.*

fountains of growth in goodness. Jesus would not have people continually repeating the publican's experience, beating their breasts and not daring to look up to heaven, but unhesitatingly he declared that a life that was stained and marred, even like that publican's, but which had such an outlook on life, receives God's approval rather than the self-sufficient piety of Pharisaism.

Let us turn to other evidence of this attitude of Jesus. We need go no further than the beatitudes, strikingly placed by Matthew as a sort of title-page to the teaching of Jesus. These verses taken together picture the kind of character that Jesus said would be shown by those in the kingdom. It is remarkable that three out of the first four have to do with this thought of a constant moral progress and enrichment.

The first one as usually translated reads, "Blessed are the poor in spirit: for theirs is the kingdom of God." This phrase "poor in spirit" is the gospel equivalent for a very old Hebrew term. In certain Psalms, in passages like Isaiah 61: 1 and elsewhere in the prophets, the term "poor" is used frequently in the sense of those faithful Israelites whose trust and hope is in God alone. It describes "the man who has a deep sense of his deficiency and dependence upon God. Ethically characterized, the poor in spirit are the humble, the teachable, the open-minded. . . . They are to be contrasted with those who are filled with pride, conceit, self-satisfaction, and self-will." [24] In view of this real meaning of the term an American scholar of profound insight as well as learning has recently translated the first beatitude with the words, "Blessed are those who feel their spiritual need, for the

[24] H. C. King, *The Ethics of Jesus*, p. 207.

kingdom of heaven belongs to them." [25]   The chief corner stone of the ideal character, then, is humble teachable-
ness, a constant openness toward God for grace and
strength.   This is the quality that attends all growth,
whether of mind or of heart.

The third beatitude, "Blessed are the meek," repeats
the lesson, though in slightly different form.   The meek
are to be contrasted with the type of individual sure of
his own rights, confident as to the infallibility of his own
opinion, bellicose wherever his own interests are concerned.   But it is in the fourth beatitude that this thought
of Jesus comes out most simply and strongly: "Blessed
are those who hunger and thirst after righteousness."
Here we have held out as typical of the good man a permanent yearning of the soul for the ideal of life.   We
have been accustomed to pass off rather glibly this saying
as applicable to those who are not Christians, but "hunger
and thirst to become so," forgetting that these sayings
describe the life of the kingdom.   Jesus does not speak
here of a momentary state just previous to a conversion
experience.   It is a constant state of soul which he says
should mark every man striving to do God's will.

And it is a familiar fact that the great saints of the earth
have been men and women with just this quality, people
like St. Francis of Assisi, St. Augustine, John Wesley.
The Apostle Paul is a good case in point.   Here was a
man who gave up everything for the sake of his mission
and who almost alone spread the religion of Jesus over
the known world.   And yet he wrote of himself, "I am
the least of the apostles, that am not worthy to be called
an apostle," [26] or even more emphatically in a letter to-

[25] Goodspeed, *An American Translation.*
[26] 1 Cor. 15: 9.

ward the close of his life, "who am less than the least of the saints." [27]   Indeed, our best comment on this whole aspect of Jesus' teaching might be Paul's own words written from prison with his extraordinary life behind him, "I count not myself yet to have apprehended; but one thing I do, forgetting the things which are behind, and stretching forward to things which are before, I press on toward the goal." [28]

The sayings of Jesus which have been surveyed in this chapter present different sides of his conception of the goodness which God desires. In a way such a presentation tends to mislead. For Jesus did not think of goodness under the various partial categories which have been our guide. In his thought goodness is one thing, indivisible into parts. It is not simply a combination of virtues. It is rather a new spirit dominating the whole of one's life. Many times men have endeavored to define goodness in terms of particular deeds or specific performances, and indeed it would be easier if religion could be relegated to a part of life, this set of deeds, this part of the week, this habitual behavior. To Jesus all such was hypocrisy. Righteousness is no less than the whole man giving himself in loving service. And he insisted that the self which should be so dedicated must never become fixed and hardened by self-complacency and pride.

A word of comment on this ideal of life may be permitted. It is clear that Jesus' thought puts a premium on three things. The first is a completely unified life. Halfway measures will not avail. The whole self must be organized around a central principle of life. "Ye cannot serve God and Mammon" is one of the keys, he said, to

[27] Eph. 3: 8.   [28] Phil. 3: 13 f.

the problem of living. "When the eye is single, thy whole body is full of light." The religious impulse must be a unifying principle of living or it is nothing at all. In the second place, it puts a premium on activity, initiative, the inner life expressed in deeds. There is an emphasis on concrete reality throughout. In the third place it puts a premium on individuality. The fact that religion and conventionality are in many places almost synonymous terms shows that religious people have woefully missed Jesus' ideal. He emphasized in character growth, change, flux, development. The Christian ought to be ever stimulating, with new appreciations, new depths of conviction, new enlargements of personality.

But what is the basis of such a transcendent thought of goodness? The answer sweeps us away from all thoughts of practical ethics. It was not a theory of ethics that Jesus taught to the crowds of fishermen and peasants who gathered to hear him. The basis of it all was his thought of God. This is righteousness and this only, because righteousness is in its essence entering into a fellowship with God, and God is like that—completely loving, active in good will, perfect in all ways.

We are dealing here with the most central thing in the teaching of Jesus. From his thought of God radiates all else that he said. God is all loving and all perfect. His rule or kingdom is not over subjects, but children. Being like a father, he seeks love and fellowship from his children instead of servile obedience. Such fellowship must be based on likeness of character. Love is the most characteristic quality of the Divine Nature, a love of all men and all creatures. Hence he who would do God's will as a member of the kingdom will love God and his fellow men. Goodness is Godlikeness. Hence it must be a constant growth and progress—else it denies its essential character.

This final thought is simply and naturally stated in the words found in Matthew 5 : 43-48 : "I say unto you, Love your enemies, and pray for them that persecute you; that ye may be sons of your Father which is in heaven: for he maketh his sun to rise on the evil and the good, and sendeth the rain on the just and the unjust." And then a little later—"Ye therefore shall be perfect, as your heavenly Father is perfect."

We used to hear more of godliness than we do now. It has rather gone out of style, it seems. People said it was otherworldly. Unfortunately, too, the word seems to have acquired something of a passive note. But it was godliness that Jesus demanded. The greatest teacher of the pagan world, Plato, approached the same conception when he closed his great book, *The Republic,* with the injunction that we must walk on earth with our eye on heaven. Jesus went far beyond that. Yet nothing could be more simple or more clear than this teaching, a teaching that applies the character of God to even the details of ordinary experience. "And if you salute your brethren only, what do ye more than others? Do not even the Gentiles the same? Be ye therefore perfect, even as your heavenly Father is perfect."

TOPICS FOR DISCUSSION

1. In the light of the various misconceptions which men have had as to the will of God, should the standard of behavior be one's own conscience or should it be the public judgment? What are the difficulties in the latter position?

2. Modern versions of "legalism" in religion. The dangers of "legalism." The proper place of laws or rules in religious conduct and guidance.

3. The meaning of "divided personality" and the unhappiness attend-

ant on such a state. The energy and power that come from inner unity of purpose and belief.

4. Is the ethical standard of the Church to-day predominantly "negative" or "positive"?

5. The relation between Jesus' conception of goodness and his conception of the character of God.

6. The permanent validity of Jesus' ideal of goodness.

A WRITTEN ASSIGNMENT

Write a comment on the passage Matthew 5: 3-11, explaining the meaning of each verse and pointing out which phase of Jesus' conception of goodness each saying illustrates.

SUPPLEMENTARY READINGS

On the positive character of Jesus' conception of goodness:
Seeley: *Ecce Homo*, Ch. XIV and XVI.

On the new type of character delineated by Jesus:
Scott: *The Ethical Teaching of Jesus*, Ch. XVI.

On the alleged impossibility of universal love:
Rashdall: *Conscience and Christ*, pp. 189-194.

On the Divided Self:
James: *Varieties of Religious Experience*, Ch. VIII.

CHAPTER XII

THE MEANING OF THE LAW OF LOVE

JESUS went about calling men to enter into the kingdom of God. As he spoke about the coming of the kingdom he also taught what the righteousness of the kingdom meant. Love, he said, must be the central and dominant element in the life of those who would do the will of God.

One must grasp clearly the all-embracing character of this disposition of love. It cannot be confined to any portion of life. It is not, on the one hand, identical with any set of deeds or habits which we may label as good works. Nor, on the other hand, must we think of it as a general, practical life of "service." It is a light which shines from within. It is an inner attitude finding natural expression in concrete activities. The good deed, the life of service, is simply the mirror of the spirit within. In practice Christians have tended to weaken the completeness of Jesus' vision because his ideal is so far above the standards of ordinary life.

I

But once that character of love is clearly grasped, several elements in Jesus' teaching, at first obscure, become luminous. In the first place one understands why he condemned not only the wrong act but the very desire out of which it springs. "Ye have heard that it was said unto them of old, Thou shalt not kill; . . . but I say unto you, that every one who is angry with his brother shall be in danger of the judgment." [1] "Ye have heard that it was

[1] Matt. 5: 21.

179

said, Thou shalt not commit adultery: but I say unto you, that every one that looketh on a woman to lust after her hath committed adultery with her already in his heart." [2] "Ye have heard that it was said, Thou shalt love thy neighbor, and hate thine enemy: but I say unto you, Love your enemies, and pray for them that persecute you." [3] These precepts have been frequently criticized as absolutely impossible of obedience and unfair in their judgment. No man can control his thoughts, it is objected. All that one can ask is that the individual suddenly inflamed by anger shall restrain himself from committing an act of injury, that the man who is persecuted shall not retaliate. The person who locks his evil impulses within his own breast there to die for lack of expression deserves, it is asserted, not criticism, but the highest praise.

But this objection overlooks that fundamental conception of Jesus that we have stated. Lust and anger and resentment are wrong because a very different spirit should dwell in the inner life. It cannot be too often repeated that Jesus did not intend for men merely to refrain from murder and its like, but he wanted them to become loving individuals. Such an overpowering emotion of love should exist within as to eliminate contrary impulses. The whole man given in love—that, it was shown in the last chapter, was Jesus' ideal of goodness. Against that background it becomes clear why he declared that anger and lust and a vindictive spirit were absolutely and unequivocally wrong in themselves, quite apart from the question of their expression in deed.

The illustration in the last chapter of how men shall give an account for their idle words makes this principle

[2] Matt. 5: 27.   [3] Matt. 5: 43, 44.

clear. All of us realize that much of our virtue is forced upon us by environment and circumstances, but that is not the kind of goodness that Jesus demanded. The essential thing is the sort of real self one is, back of the restraints and inhibitions placed upon us. Jesus had in mind individuals who had become innately good, whose idle words would carry sweetness and good will, whose inner character would be creative of good.

In the next place, when one understands this conception of righteousness, one sees why it was that Jesus never gave rules of conduct. For if the essence of goodness be the activity of love, the moral criterion or guide ceases to be an external standard and becomes an inner light. The Christian who has love in his heart becomes his own moral guide. This is implicit in the whole of Jesus' teaching. The chief commandment was the general one, to love God and men with one's whole soul.[4] His ethical rule was, "All things whatsoever ye would that men should do unto you, do ye even so unto them.[5] His standard of the right course of action was whether or not the deed in question met human needs.[6] What further need of detailed rules? Does the loving individual need a catalogue of prohibitions? Or, putting it the other way around, could any catalogue of duties exhaust the forms of his service? In some cases love drives one to the heart of Africa, in others one's task is at the door. In some situations it is the soft answer that turneth away wrath, in others it is the voice of a prophet demanding justice in the land. Love needs no list of rules; it creates its own program to meet the needs of place and hour.

This is why Paul, when he discovered the "riches of the

[4] Matt. 22: 37-40. [5] Matt. 7: 12.
[6] See Mark 2: 17, 2: 25, 3: 4, etc.

graciousness of Christ Jesus," declared that the law was no longer binding upon the Christian converts. That was a very daring thing for him to say, for one must remember that the center of that Jewish law was the Ten Commandments and that the legal system of Judaism was the highest moral code that the world had known. We usually say that Paul rejected the "ceremonial law" but kept the moral code, but that is only because we have not understood the apostle. Paul dared to say: "In Christ Jesus neither circumcision availeth anything, nor uncircumcision; but faith working through love"; [7] "If ye are led by the Spirit, ye are not under the law"; [8] "For the whole law is fulfilled in one word, Thou shalt love thy neighbor as thyself." [9] For Paul had grasped this truth that Jesus taught—that love spontaneously performs that which commandments seek in vain. Four centuries later the great Latin scholar and Christian, Augustine, discovered the principle anew. The rule of Christian morality, he said, was this: "Love, and do anything you want to."

This self-direction of Christian righteousness gives to it a freshness ever new. It can never become hardened into a code destined in time to be outgrown. It becomes a permanent rule of righteousness. This is why the Christian ethic claims for itself an absolute finality. So long as love and service remain the need of the world, just so long will Jesus remain its moral leader.

II

But one will best understand this teaching of love by asking specifically as to its applications. What does this teaching of Jesus mean in actual practice?

[7] Gal. 5: 6.   [8] Gal. 5: 18.   [9] Gal. 5: 14.

1. First it means *forgiveness*. In ordinary conversation, when one speaks of showing a Christian spirit it is usually a forgiving spirit that is meant. In everyday life to "act like a Christian" means, for the average person, to forgive injuries done us. There is much in Jesus' teaching beside the requirement of forgiveness, but it has produced this general impression for two reasons: the rarity of such teaching in the ancient world, and the force and strength of the language in which Jesus enjoined it. Consider some of these sayings. "How oft shall my brother sin against me, and I forgive him?" asked Peter. "Until seven times? Jesus saith unto him, I say not unto thee, Until seven times; but, Until seventy times seven." [10] In the corresponding passage in Luke the injunction is "seven times per day." "Forgive us our debts as we also have forgiven our debtors. . . . For if ye forgive not men their trespasses, neither will your Father forgive your trespasses." [11] "Whosoever smitest thee on thy right cheek, turn to him the other also. And if any man would go to law with thee, and take away thy coat, let him have thy cloak also." [12] The parable of the ungrateful servant who, having received remittance of his debt, was extortionate toward him that owed a hundred pence leads up to the warning, "So shall also my heavenly Father do unto you if ye forgive not every one his brother from your hearts." [13]

Why is this teaching on forgiveness so outstanding? There seem to be two very clear ideas in the general thought of Jesus which come to a focus in the spirit of forgiveness. In the first place, situations which call for

[10] Matt. 18: 21 f.
[11] Matt. 6: 12-15.
[12] Matt. 5: 39, 40.
[13] Matt. 18: 35.

the exercise of forgiveness are the test cases, so to speak, of whether one thinks in unselfish terms. Love, every one admits, is a most commendable virtue; and a generous, hospitable, helpful disposition is admired by all. That one should be amiable toward ones' neighbors, serviceable in the community, kind to stray dogs and the grateful poor—that much of Jesus' teaching is accepted by everybody and requires no special depth of moral conviction. "If ye do good to them that do good to you, what thank have ye? For even sinners do the same," [14] as Jesus said. But this natural kindly impulse is in ordinary life reserved for those whom we say "deserve it"; that is, those who have shown no contrary spirit toward ourselves. But what happens when we have been injured, clearly wronged, as we see it? It is then and only then that anger flames up, that retaliation in the most effective way dominates the thought, and sentiments such as love and benevolence are thrust aside in the rush of passion. He who can love only those who are generously disposed themselves or those who appeal to his natural instincts of sympathy and pity is only playing at the game of Christian living. The real test is when injury has been done. Then, if one really loves, comes the great opportunity. Only then can the deepest, truest love be seen. That is the acid test which will show whether one values selfish interests above one's brethren. And if one cannot forgive, if selfish concerns do really dominate the thought and action, and love is exercised only where these are not involved, what a farce it is to pretend to the righteousness which Jesus commanded!

In the second place, it must be observed that this mat-

---

[14] Luke 6: 33.

ter of forgiveness is a clear example of the fact, pointed
out at the close of the last chapter, that with Jesus all
goodness was grounded in the character of God. "Love
your enemies and pray for those who persecute you; that
ye may be sons of your Father in heaven: for he maketh
his sun to rise on the evil and the good." [15] Jesus emphasized forgiveness because he saw it in God's dealing
with men. In the processes of nature Jesus said there
was no favoritism. The sun shines equally upon the
wicked and the good. No person, however reprobate, is
beyond the divine fellowship. God's forgiveness is universal and infinite if only men will turn away from their
sin. And so a readiness to forgive is essential to the Christian spirit because that is a characteristic of God's nature.

This is the first great application of the Christian teachings of love. Before going on to the second field of application, it will probably be well to pause long enough to
consider a question closely related to the above, over which
there has been much discussion and doubt—the question
of resistance of evil and punishment of wrongdoers.

How far did Jesus take this teaching of forgiveness?
Did he mean that wrong was never to be resisted? Tolstoy, after long dissatisfaction, felt that he had found the
center of the Christian ethic in that one phrase, "Resist
not evil." This in literal form he exalted into the cardinal
rule of life.[16] Nor does this passage stand alone in Jesus'
teachings; there are the injunctions to turn the other cheek
when struck upon the face, to give up one's cloak to an
extortioner who would take away the coat, to go the second mile with him who impresses one into service.[17]

[15] Matt. 5: 44, 45.   [17] Matt. 5: 38-41.

[16] See *My Religion,* Ch. 1-3.

Does all this mean that the police are unchristian and that aggressors should be allowed to run their course unmolested? What did Jesus actually mean in this doctrine of forgiveness?

There are a number of arguments which could be used to show that Jesus was not laying down a hard and fast rule of conduct, but was trying to teach a great principle which Christians themselves would have to apply to various situations. It could be pointed out, for example, that the Sermon on the Mount deals throughout with principles and not with rules. The teaching about praying in one's closet is surely not to be taken as a rule to be invariably followed. Nor the one about agreeing with thy adversary quickly while on the way to court. Nor do we consider it necessary nowadays always to anoint one's head when fasting. Throughout the Sermon Jesus is enunciating great principles instead of laying down exact and literal rules. In the next place, one could point out that Jesus himself used force when he cleansed the temple; and, more important still, that on the one occasion when the gospels record that he was actually struck upon the cheek he did not turn the other, but only made a calm and dignified reply.[18] But the most effective way to consider this teaching and its real meaning is to ask the question which Jesus repeatedly declared to be at the base of all moral problems: What is the course of action which love would dictate?

Now there are two phases of this answer, both of which point in the same direction. In the first place, love for the aggressor himself might sometimes mean the use of force. The policeman who prevents a murder is the would-be

[18] John 18: 22.

murderer's best friend. Discipline is frequently the highest expression of love. Waiving the debate as to the value of spanking children, one might point out that it is a poor parent who would not prevent, by force if necessary, his child from injuring another child. But, in the second place, it is a very weak form of piety which in cases of wrongdoing is interested only in the moral state of the offender. The law of love must take into consideration his victims as well. Surely that man is no follower of Jesus who would calmly stand by and see innocent lives starved and maimed because of a special interpretation of the great injunction to resist not evil. The policemen who protect a sleeping city are doing a service that Jesus would commend.

All this surely goes to show that in some circumstances love may involve compulsion. But the danger is not in this direction. For every pacifist among us there are ten who use arguments like these to cover all sorts of retaliation and revenge. Because of the need of social restraint on wrongdoers we allow penal systems that are purely punitive and vindictive. They can be justified from a Christian standpoint only if they are reformatory and educative as well as protective. Because it appears that force sometimes may be right, we go to war and preach hatred of the enemy—hatred which Jesus said no Christian in any circumstances can ever entertain. Actually we have very nearly denied this whole application of Jesus' teaching of love and forgiveness. No phase of his teaching needs more emphasis to-day in the Christian Church than this simple thought, "Thou shalt love thine enemy." Instead of resistance and retaliation when one is injured, he declared that we should love our enemies and pray for those who despitefully use us. Love—and no action not controlled by love—what a revolution that would mean in personal and social dealings! Is it unreasonable to demand that? Then the whole Christian message is unreasonable, for non-retaliation is but another way of expressing real forgiveness, and forgiveness is simply the heart of Jesus' command of love.

There is a second objection frequently brought against Jesus' teaching of forgiveness which we can only touch upon. It is charged that this whole thought of non-retaliation is weak, contemptible, and even wrong, because it feeds and encourages evil. The virtue needed in this world, it is urged, is resistance of wrong and suppression of evil. Such criticisms of Christianity are best known in the writings of the German philosopher of a generation ago, Friedrich Nietzsche, whose doctrine of the "superman" was so influential, but they are also present in much popular thinking of the present.

To all this there is one clear and convincing reply. The criticism overlooks part of Jesus' teaching. It was not merely passive, merely submissive. On the contrary, no one ever called men to a conquest and elimination of evil so vigorously as did he. Only—and here is the vital point—Jesus believed that there was just one way to overcome evil and that was by goodness. Hate, he said, cannot be destroyed by revenge, even the sort of revenge that claims the adjective "righteous." The wrong heart is only transformed by goodness, a goodness which, we must always remember, goes to the point of real forgiving. "If a man take away thy coat"—Jesus did not say, "let him have it." He said, "Give him thy cloak as well"—*i. e.,* destroy that evil will by creative goodness. If a man impress you into service to carry his goods one mile, go a second mile. If you are struck on the cheek, do not slink away in shamefaced endurance, but turn the other cheek. Such conduct as that is not weak submission, but calls for the strongest natures. It does not accept but sets out to destroy the evil from which it has suffered, and to destroy it by the only effective weapons. It calls for strength, determination, heroism; not for cowardice and weakness.

2. I turn now to the second great field in which Jesus said love should be applied. The first was forgiveness of enemies; the second is humanitarian *service*. True and genuine love of men and women seeks to minister to their needs. The accident of race, the social status of the unfortunate one, the religious affiliation of the person—these things have nothing to do with Christian service. No religion can claim Jesus as its leader that does not set itself to minister, and this, not in order to make converts, but to help life. It is a waste of space to give evidence of this thought of Jesus. It is found on practically every page of the gospel story. He constantly exhorted his hearers to give alms, this being the primary channel of helpfulness in the simple conditions of Palestinian life. Indeed, so important is this loving ministry to the unfortunate that in Matthew 6: 1, 2, almsgiving seems to be the meaning which the term "righteousness" carries. It is a righteousness which he repeatedly said receives reward from the Father that seeth in secret. The story of the Good Samaritan, plus Jesus' own example, has made care of the sick one of the special objects of Christian ministry. Notice that in Jesus' thought all such ministry is good for its own sake, simply because it makes happier living. It needs no other justification. True love in the heart finds no other course possible. Deeds of service—these are the true "Church History" far more than the record of creedal debates and changes in organization.

But it is not enough merely to perform acts of philanthropy on occasions when the distress of fellow humans thrusts itself on the attention.   Love—the love of Jesus —is positive, seeks the good of others, is a passion for human joy and happiness.   One with such an outlook on life will not be content to alleviate human misery when it is possible in so many cases to anticipate and avert it. Prevention is better than cure.   It was good to help a slave, but better to abolish slavery.   It was splendid to minister to a woman whom society regarded as the property of a brutal husband, but better to denounce and destroy the whole system which makes women chattels. Christian love is not negative, mending the broken humanity left beside the road by the rapacious.   It includes others besides the particular individual the Samaritan helped, and it will rid the road of those thieves.   Herein is the dynamic of Christian statesmanship, that would save so much of life by changing the way in which our social machine operates.   It will be no less anxious to remedy evils that ought not to have happened, to visit the sick and the imprisoned, to feed the hungry and clothe the naked, but it will show its deepest love for humanity in removing the conditions which make men sick or drive them into crime, and in insuring enough for proper clothing and food to those who labor with their hands.

In our highly complex modern life it has come about that much of such work has to be done by special organizations skilled in their particular tasks.   We cannot always serve best with our own hands or through church organizations.   The multiplication of such special agencies is likely to make one feel that activities of famine relief, or medical assistance, or the education of backward communities, is outside the scope of the specifically Christian task. Let us not allow ourselves to be deluded, but claim all such activities that are genuinely serving the needs of the world as specific applications of the Christian spirit and practical means of carrying out Jesus' task. For they serve humanity, and Christian love rejoices in and claims as its own every endeavor to make life better.

3. There is a third field in which Christian love will show itself—namely, in *evangelism* in its truest sense. The Christian view of life would not be entirely satisfied if some philanthropic scheme should succeed in banishing physical pain entirely from the earth. It would rejoice in such a result, it would do all it could to further such a cause, it would never take the position of offering an opposite ideal of endeavor or perpetuating the existence of suffering. But while Jesus fed the poor, his aim was not merely to make full stomachs. He healed disease, but he was interested in something higher than developing athletes. He even called men to persecution, suffering, and death—not for the value of these things, but for the sake of something higher than mere contentment and ease.

A wise parent realizes that there are greater things than physical comfort and will sometimes sacrifice this for higher objects. Affection that pets and pampers is either feeble or unintelligent. Jesus' love for humanity made him sensitive to the highest values of life, and these are generally achieved only by means of stern self-discipline and sacrifice of lesser values. It is not enough that men should be made contented; they should also be made loving and courageous. It is better for men to be good than to be prosperous. To provoke others to love is a greater task for the Christian spirit than to minister to their physical wants. That inner state which Jesus called "life" he was accustomed to declare of more value than all temporal blessings and more to be sought than these. To save men from being ensnared in the petty details of life and enslaved to its material elements is the highest gift of all. Hence the place of primary importance that true evangelism has always had in the Christian Church.

Only it must be remembered that true evangelization consists in the vital transformation of the inner life of the person. It is not identical with church membership. It may require a long process of education to produce in the heart of the individual the flower of Christian love. It may require the combined influence of many factors and many experiences. In the case of foreign missions, for example, it will certainly demand a new type of foreign policy on the part of the Christian governments of the world, one that will show forth the finest Christian tolerance and charity.

And here again, just as in the case of humane service, positive Christian love will be interested in obviating the growth of evil as well as in converting it. Just as Christians must study how to prevent sickness and poverty, so they should study the conditions most favorable to goodness and try to make them reign in the world. For surely, if we have learned anything, it is the power of environment for evil and for good. The hindrances to kindly feeling in any community ought to be of primary interest to evangelical Churches. Those hindrances are usually easily recognizable; frequently they are known in advance, memories of injustices and wrongs, resentments over unfairness in social dealings, commercialization of the community's amusement, the presence of houses of gambling and vice. The destructive work of these is obvious. Surely evangelization involves the removal of such corrupting influences.

But while these and other efforts are part of the process, they must not make one lose sight of the real objective. The highest and final task of religion is a transformation of the inner being by which one is released from all bondage to the world. To walk amid circumstances and yet be above them, to live in the midst of change and destruction and yet be conscious of a destiny, to be at home in the world and yet find one's true kinship with God who is a Spirit, that is the real meaning of religion. "Blessed are the pure in heart: for they shall see God," "Blessed are the peacemakers: for they shall be called the sons of God" —such sayings point to the goal. To create this inner life of fellowship with God is the final task of the loving spirit.

All this is but the practical application of Jesus' teaching of love.

TOPICS FOR DISCUSSION

1. Which is the better person, one who is good from a sense of duty or one who acts right naturally or instinctively?
2. Should punishment ever be punitive?
3. Should there be any limit set on the extent of one's forgiveness of personal enemies?
4. The differences between war and the action of a police force.
5. Should the Church itself engage in social service activities?
6. The meaning of evangelism. Is religious education evangelism?

A WRITTEN ASSIGNMENT

Write a comment on the passage Matthew 5: 38–6: 4, explaining and interpreting each verse.

SUPPLEMENTARY READINGS

On Jesus' teaching of forgiveness:
  Seeley: *Ecce Homo*, Ch. XXII and XXIII.
  Scott: *The Ethical Teaching of Jesus*, Ch. X.
  Rashdall: *Conscience and Christ*, pp. 143-150.
On Tolstoy's Conception of Christianity:
  Tolstoy: *My Religion*, Ch. 1-3.

On Jesus' attitude toward war:
 Simkhovitch: *Toward the Understanding of Jesus*, pp. 26-48.
 Dickey: *The Constructive Revolution of Jesus*, Ch. IV.
 Scott: *Op. cit.*, Ch. XI.
 Cadoux: *The Early Church and the World*, pp. 51-57.
On the Church and Social Service:
 Ellwood: *Christianity and Social Science*, Ch. VI.
 Seeley: *Op. cit.*, Ch. XVII.

On why the Church has been slow in undertaking social reconstruction:
 Rauschenbusch: *Christianity and the Social Crisis*, Ch. IV.
On the punishment of criminals:
 Wines: *Punishment and Reformation*, Ch. 3, 6, and 7.
On an inclusive conception of evangelism:
 Seeley: *Op. cit.*, Ch. XVIII.

CHAPTER XIII

HUMILITY, SINCERITY, COURAGE

THE life of the kingdom of God will be characterized by love: that was the thought that ran through the last chapter. There are, however, certain other traits which Jesus so stressed that they demand separate treatment, even though they are implications of, or closely related to, the spirit of love.

I

First there is humility. To-day humility is not greatly admired. The word calls to mind monks in hair shirts performing acts of penance. Or else one thinks of Dickens' Uriah Heep. Supermen who dominate the scene are the ones who have the admiration of modern Western civilization. Accordingly this is one of the elements in Jesus' teaching which is consistently minimized, or at any rate confined purely to the religious sphere.

But Jesus did admire the humble spirit. The parable of the Pharisee and the publican has already been mentioned.[1] If he had given nothing else but that one story, there would be no doubt as to his attitude in this respect. But there are numerous other sayings or parables which convey the same thought.

There is the parable given in Luke 17: 7 f. of the servants who, after a day of plowing in the fields, are not invited to sit down and eat, but who must labor further, preparing and serving the meat to their lord. It leads up

[1] Luke 18: 9 ff.

195

to the verse at its close. "Even so ye also, when ye shall have done all the things that are commanded you, say, We are unprofitable servants." Quite evidently the point of this parable was the same as the one above, that Jesus' hearers should forget their accomplishments and their virtues and continue to serve in humbleness of spirit.

Again there is a saying which Luke warns must not be taken literally, for it is a parable: "And he spake a parable unto them. . . . When thou art bidden of any man to a marriage feast, sit not down in the chief seat, . . . but go and sit down in the lowest place; that when he that hath bidden thee cometh, he may say to thee, Friend, go up higher: then thou shalt have glory in the presence of all that sit at meat with thee." [2] That is deft but kindly satire on the forward, pushing, self-assertive spirit.

The injunction, "Whosoever shall exalt himself shall be humbled, and whosoever shall humble himself shall be exalted," occurs three times in the gospel records.[3] The fourth time one finds, "Whosoever shall humble himself as this little child, the same is the greatest in the kingdom of God." [4] The similar statement, "Behold, many of the first shall be last, and the last shall be first," occurs four times. These were evidently habitual phrases with which Jesus kept emphasizing this thought which he felt so important. In the beatitudes one finds, "Blessed are the meek" and "Blessed are the poor in spirit," in both of which this quality is praised. And toward the close of the Sermon on the Mount he exhorts men to humility in one of the strongest of all his figures of speech: "Judge not, that ye be not judged. . . . For why beholdest thou the

[2] Luke 14: 7 f.
[3] Matt. 23: 12; Luke 14: 11 and 18: 14.
[4] Matt. 18: 4.

mote that is in thy brother's eye, but considerest not the beam that is in thine own eye? Thou hypocrite!" [5]

In the light of all this (and other passages of like import) we are driven to ask, Why does Jesus so emphasize humility? We have not generally regarded it as so important.

The answer goes back in part, no doubt, to historical factors.[6] The religion of the Pharisees with which Jesus was surrounded seems to have produced in too many cases a kind of spiritual pride. The piety to which his listeners were accustomed lacked too frequently the elements of meekness and modesty. One recalls Jesus' pointed injunction to the disciples, "Take heed that ye do not your righteousness before men, to be seen of them." [7] Accordingly when he spoke of the goodness which was requisite for entering into the kingdom, he had to insist that what he meant was *not* like that. We may well suppose that had not the religious leaders of the day been of this type, it would not have been necessary for Jesus to keep insisting on this particular virtue.

Yet, while this may be true as a matter of emphasis, it must not be carried to the point of denying the vital place that humility plays in Jesus' thought. It needs nothing external to support it. The humble spirit he declared to be one of life's basic qualities.

This was in the first place simply because of the innate fineness of Jesus' own spirit. He himself shrank from all ostentation and pretense. When a woman of the multitude shouted out an extravagant compliment to him, he

[5] Matt. 7: 1-5.

[6] Cp. the discussion of Humility in Scott, *The Ethical Teaching of Jesus.*

[7] Matt. 6: 1.

deftly turned it off to all those who do the will of God.[8]
He refused on one occasion to be called good, declaring
that only God was good.[9]   He made no open claim to
Messiahship, but waited for the disciples to come to their
own conclusions concerning him.[10]   The self-assertive attitude of the man in the parable who seized the chief place
at the feast was repugnant to the whole disposition of
Jesus. I am not sure that he was "meek and mild," as
the familiar hymn would say, but in him there was absolutely nothing of that unblushing braggadocio which we
see so frequently posing as self-confidence. His teaching
against self-exaltation goes back first of all to this fine
quality in his own nature. He could not think in any
other terms.

But in the second place Jesus insisted on humility because, as has been pointed out, he thought of goodness as
necessarily progressive and there can be no progress without the humble spirit. A spirit of inadequacy and a consciousness of one's need—without such there is no desire
for better things. The principle is true in the realm of the
intellect as well as that of morals. One doesn't ordinarily
think of Jesus' teaching about humility when quoting the
proverb that necessity is the mother of invention, but the
principle is the same. One must realize one's deficiencies,
else the way is barred. And especially is this true in the
moral realm. The person sure of his own excellence is
not likely to hunger and thirst after righteousness. This
was one of the lessons that Paul learned in his missionary
work, and it accounts for his constantly reiterated exhortation to his converts not to think of themselves more highly
than they ought to think.[11]

[8] Luke 11: 27 f.   [9] Mark 10: 18.   [10] Mark 8: 29.
[11] Rom. 12: 3, 12: 16, 11: 20, etc.

Closely related to this is a second fundamental principle of Jesus' thought which has already been touched upon. He said that the goal of life is nothing less than to be perfect, even as God is perfect. With that idea flung out before one, no other attitude is possible. Before that divine standard, humility is simply honesty with oneself, for in the sight of such an ideal even the noblest characters recognize their own poverty. To live in the sight of God, to seek his approval instead of the admiration of men—there follows from such a life and such a standard that unassuming spirit that we associate with the idea of saintliness. I mentioned in an earlier chapter that paradox of the Christian life, that the finest spirits are always farthest from self-appreciation and self-praise. The reason is this of which I am now speaking, that they look forward to the possibilities of life and not backward to what they have done. In the light of such an ideal as Jesus set forth, why boast our slight superiority over our neighbors? Are we not all sinners, even as the Galileans whom Pilate killed, or the men in Siloam upon whom the tower fell? [12]

So examined, one sees that Jesus' teaching on humility is not a demand for self-abasement, but a challenge of greatness of life. It is because he enjoined his hearers, "Be ye perfect, even as your heavenly Father is perfect," that he said, "Blessed are the meek." Christian humility is based on aspiration rather than despair—aspiration combined with honesty. The eye is on ahead. It does not say, "I abase myself," but rather with St. Paul, "I have not yet apprehended." It is the foil to a deep, true self-respect. It knows in the personal realm not to cast that

[12] Luke 13: 2-5.

which is holy unto the dogs. It does not give the pearls of one's inner life unto the irreverent and brutal, lest they trample them underfoot. But it sees clearly one's shortcomings and feels deeply one's personal need. From the root of such humility there comes the loveliest flowers, modesty, sympathy, charity of spirit, aspiration for the ideal, constant gratitude for the goodness of God.

II

The second of these traits is *sincerity*. This is also primary with Jesus. The idea conveyed by the word appears and reappears in almost every phase of his teaching. Absolute honesty of life, conformity of the outer deed with the inner spirit—that is to Jesus essential for the life of God's kingdom. In the above pages attention has already been called to the vital place that sincerity occupies in his thought. Thus he taught that an act which does not fully represent the intent of the heart has no claim to righteousness. Or, to say the same thing in other words, sincerity is an element that enters into all goodness. So also two paragraphs above it was pointed out that Christ's emphasis on humility could be traced back in part to this thought, honesty with oneself in the face of an absolute ideal. Everywhere, in his dealings, this demand for frankness, candor, sincerity comes out. "Take heed that ye do not your righteousness before men, to be seen of them, else ye have no reward." [13] "When thou doest alms, let not thy left hand see what thy right hand doeth" [14]—lest ever an insincere motive creep in to spoil the goodness of the deed. "When thou prayest, enter into thy inner chamber," [15] and, "When thou fastest, anoint

---

[13] Matt. 6: 1.　　　　[14] Matt. 6: 3.　　　　[15] Matt. 6: 6.

thy head, and wash thy face; that thou may not be seen of men to fast, but of thy Father which is in secret." [16] In such specific and even extreme illustrations he tried to make his hearers catch his own contempt for insincerity of act as well as of word. His worst epithet was the terrible, "Thou hypocrite!"

He expressed the idea in all sorts of ways that his disciples and the attending multitude might get the meaning and feel its charm. Sometimes it was in figures from nature insisting upon this conformity of the inner and outer life: "Make the tree good, and its fruit good; or make the tree corrupt, and its fruit corrupt; for the tree is known by its fruit." [17] Sometimes it was in concrete application to problems of everyday life.

One of the most interesting of these was the occasion when Jesus spoke about swearing. "Ye have heard that it was said to them of old, Thou shalt not forswear thyself, but shall perform unto the Lord thy oaths: but I say unto you, Swear not at all; . . . but let your speech be, Yea, yea; Nay, nay; for whatsoever is more than these is evil." [18] What was wrong with swearing? That it used certain syllables of religious speech? Not at all, said Jesus. Swearing is wrong whether it be done with the words "heaven" or "earth" or "Jerusalem" or even your own "head." The wrong was in the whole system of degrees of truthfulness implied by oaths. That the plain statement was not to be trusted, that the assertion backed by an oath was more trustworthy, that the use of certain more sacred terms would make the utterance more dependable, this was what Jesus wanted to sweep away. Oriental bargaining, like Western bargain driving, daily

[16] Matt. 6: 17.   [17] Matt. 12: 33.   [18] Matt. 5: 33 f.

would illustrate this loose attitude toward truth. On the contrary, said Jesus, let all speech be the very truth. The distinction currently recognized between statements sworn to and those not so supported should be absolutely abolished. Simple yea should mean yea, for deceit and hypocrisy are basic sins.

One does not need to elaborate the constituent character of this principle of honesty in any attempt at high character. There are two or three points which might well be stressed, however. In the first place one should note that sincerity with Jesus is not so much telling the truth about facts of experience as it is candidly expressing in speech and deed our own real self. Remember that it is not the "common liar" whom Jesus condemns so frequently, but the dissembler, the hypocrite, the man who pretends to be other than he really is. This kind of dishonesty he regarded as the grossest and most dangerous sin; for it strikes at the possibility of repentance and reformation. That is the vicious thing about pretense; it is so very self-deceptive. Take, for example, the case that Jesus once spoke of, the hypocrites who sound a trumpet before themselves in the synagogues or in the streets preparatory to giving alms, "that they may have glory of men." [19] There was no love of mankind in their hearts; they suffered no intensity of sympathy on seeing the helpless and the needy. Nothing in the inner life corresponded to this show of philanthropy, and hence it was far from winning the approval and reward of the "Father who seeth in secret." But it did win public applause and commendation. Men said of such a man that he was worthy and noble and generous. And so the intense danger of the

[19] Matt. 6: 2.

man contenting his better nature with this counterfeit goodness, this substitute for true charity and benevolence, this praise of men instead of the praise of God. A pretense at goodness is fearfully dangerous, for sooner or later it is likely to make the man self-satisfied and complacent even in his selfishness and hardness, convinced that he is a good and righteous person. Hence the necessity of looking oneself squarely in the face; for without this there is little chance of moral progress. This is why Jesus so bitterly denounced the hypocritical selfishness of the Pharisees, men who claimed to be the most religious individuals of the nation, while the frankly avaricious class of publicans drew no such condemnation. Selfishness frankly admitted gives more grounds for hope than selfishness that pretends that it is interested solely in religious service. Honesty of life is a basic virtue.

But when one reads the gospels one has the feeling, I think, that this insistence on honesty with Jesus is not so much on a particular virtue as it is on a certain disposition, on a kind of character rather than on a trait or department of morals. One feels that what Jesus aimed at was that luminous, open disposition that instantly attracts. There is something repelling about the person who never gives you the impression that he is being quite sincere. Those who are frank and candid draw our love, assuming, of course, that the personality thus revealing itself is one that is kind and good. When one looks at the various sayings which we have collected under this heading, the condemnation of hypocrisy, the injunction to let yea be yea and nay be nay, the warning about our being judged by our idle words, the saying, "Make the tree good and its fruit good," the conviction grows that it is this larger type of sincerity which he has in mind and not merely the virtue of honesty as it is commonly understood. And this leads on to a statement to which we will return—one amply justified, however, by what has already been said, that after all, Jesus did not so much enjoin various virtues as a certain quality of life, a life in which the several virtues merge into and unite with one another.

III

A third trait is *courage,* a courage which is the product of faith. What has been said thus far shows one thing very clearly, that the demand of Jesus' message was no easy thing. It was radically different from our halfway measures. He called men to enter the kingdom of God, to find a new life in devotion to God's purposes. But that call demands giving up all selfish interests and hopes, the things which most people hold dear. Not only so, but it involves, as no one saw more clearly than Jesus, facing the opposition of those who hold the power in this world. He called his disciples to no less a task than the elimination of evil in the world; and that means, without any shadow of question, the organized antagonism and personal hatred of those who wish to perpetuate that evil. Accordingly, the discipleship of Jesus is not for the weak and afraid. It does not simply urge heroism — it demands it.

In two ways it puts a premium on the element of courage and daring. First, in that it implies the sacrifice of all of the selfish aims of life for the sake of that which is felt to be nobler. It involves for the individual what appears to be a tremendous risk. Physical enjoyment, power used selfishly, egoism in its various manifestations—all these are immediately satisfying. Is one to renounce all these, throw away the progress one has made toward attaining them, and follow an ideal of life unselfishly lived? That involves the greatest personal risk. It means trusting in one's sense of value to the point of renouncing what most men ardently seek. Dare one do that? Has one the power of resolution, a sense of daring and courage great enough?

We are familiar with two types of temperament. One is cautious, conservative, releases no present good until a better is already in hand, is unwilling to take great chances, is afraid to turn loose the things it has known for the sake of something new. Its stirrings of soul have been trained to do nothing radical. It will not countenance a break with the old order of things either socially or personally. It is the type of mind that has become encrusted, bound within narrow confines by inhibitions and fears. It is incapable of a complete and radical decision. The other type of temperament is the sort one sees where decisions which involve risk and sacrifice are made. The decision may be to remodel a business at great risk, or to choose a career at the sacrifice of one that is financially more secure, or to subordinate personal fortunes for the sake of the public good. In all such decisions there is involved the courage to sacrifice the present for the future, security for achievement, the good already possessed for the better which may be gained. That is the spirit that is free from inner bondage and able to respond to the appeal of the highest. It is not afraid, it breaks new ground, it leads boldly. While not confined to young men, that spirit is more characteristic of youth than of age. Jesus, even when he was put to death, was a young man.

This decision to risk all for the sake of the kingdom of God, Jesus demanded unhesitatingly. He never thinks of men as halting and hesitating between two aims. He has in mind men who have courage to make a great decision. "No man putting his hand to the plow and looking back is fit for the kingdom of God," he told a vacillating follower.[20] He called the disciples to leave their occupations and homes and begin a new kind of life. "The kingdom of heaven is like unto a treasure hidden in a field; which a man found, and hid; and *in his joy* goeth and selleth all that he hath, and buyeth that field." [21] Or again, it is "like unto a merchant seeking goodly pearls, and having found one pearl of great price, he went and sold all that he had, and bought it." [22] The men in these parables had to be men not only of decision, but of a confident courage. There runs throughout the teachings of Jesus the demand for such qualities of daring as elements essential for citizenship in the kingdom. His whole conception of the life of the kingdom is based on the thought of the decisions in which men and women "for joy" give up all lesser values for the sake of the ideal good. But that requires a heroic quality of life that men often fail to realize as a Christian requirement because they have too often dulled the sharpness of that decision.[23]

In the second place, Jesus knew that the life of the kingdom would not be one of public approval. Conflict was inevitable. He knew that from bitter personal experience as well as from the simple logic of life. For the life of

---

[20] Luke 9: 62.   [21] Matt. 13: 44.   [22] Matt. 13: 45 f.

[23] It may be objected that this thought of a decision "once and for all" is in opposition to what was said in a previous chapter on progress in the life of the kingdom. The answer is that Jesus certainly thought of individuals as settling the ultimate aim or objective of life in a basic decision, but he did not think that thereby one becomes perfect. Obviously there will be habits to be brought into line, attitudes to be developed on the basis of love, graces of the spirit to be ever acquired, etc.

which he spoke was to be one of loving service and devotion, and the conflict of that sort of living with the desires of those who profit by the ignorance and want of others was obvious. He called his handful of followers to the greatest venture ever launched, the destruction of all the powers of evil. "I came to cast fire upon the earth; and what will I, if it is already kindled? . . . Think ye that I am come to give peace upon the earth? I tell you, Nay; but rather division: for there shall be henceforth five in one house divided, three against two, and two against three. They shall be divided father against son, and son against father; mother against daughter, and daughter against mother." [24] If any man would come after me, let him deny himself, and take up his cross, and follow me." [25] "But take heed to yourselves: for they shall deliver you up to councils; and in synagogues shall ye be beaten; and before governors and kings shall ye stand for my sake. . . . And ye shall be hated of all men for my name's sake." [26] He himself led the way. "A disciple is not above his master, nor a servant above his lord. If they have called the master of the house Beelzebub, how much more shall they call them of his household." [27] To one who expressed a willingness to follow him, Jesus had to reply that he must remember that the Son of Man had no place to lay his head.[28] He was called upon to endure privation, to face constant criticism and almost daily attack, to have treachery enter his intimate group of disciples, and finally to die on a hill outside the gates of Jerusalem. He well knew the result of loyalty to the kingdom.

In the face of this inevitable conflict is it any occasion

[24] Luke 12: 49-53.   [26] Mark 13: 9 f.   [28] Luke 9: 58.
[25] Mark 8: 34.   [27] Matt. 10: 24 f.

of surprise to find that Jesus placed emphasis on courage and strength of purpose? For courage is vital to the service of love that he intended. Without it, no matter how benevolent an individual may be, there will result only timidity and ineffectiveness. He had no use for the fearful and cowardly. Over and over again in the gospels we read, "Fear not," "Fear not." When he said "love," he did not mean weak sentimentality or a piety which represents an escape from the hazards and ardors of life. It was a thing that had in it the strong passion of the ancient prophets of Israel, a zeal that counted no task too difficult and no stronghold of evil too powerful to be attacked. Jesus had a contempt for weakness and fear; courage is a fundamental Christian virtue.

But it must be asked, What is the basis of this courage of which we have been speaking? Is it simply physical hardness, sheer bravado, or stoic fortitude that endures without complaint? Reckless courage that dares without ground or reason is wrong and foolish. Jesus had a very definite basis for the courage which he required. It goes back to his religious conviction, to his belief in God as active and ruling in the universe.

That Jesus did so think of God as actively working for righteousness has already been shown. How could one be afraid who realized that great fact? We are fellow-workers with God. The universe is on the side of right-eousness. "If God be for us, who can be against us?" [29] —that is the basis of Jesus' strength. To his disciples growing timid as to their powers of presenting their cause he declared, "It is not ye who speak, but the Spirit of your Father that speaketh in you." [30] When they were dis-

[29] Rom. 8: 31.   [30] Matt. 10: 20.

mayed at the ripeness of the harvest and the scarcity of workers, he reminded them of God's part in the work, "Pray ye therefore the Lord of the harvest, that he send forth laborers into his harvest." [31]   God is actively at work for righteousness; we labor not in our strength alone—that is the way Jesus regarded the problem. "So is the kingdom of God as if a man should cast a seed upon the earth; and should sleep and rise night and day, and the seed should spring up and grow, he knoweth not how. The earth beareth fruit of herself; first the blade, then the ear, then the full corn in the ear." [32]

And not only should the righteous man have courage and dismiss his fears because God is his helper and strength, but also because he may be absolutely sure of the ultimate victory. The mustard seed is tiny, but it grows into a great tree. The leaven is small in proportion, but it changes the whole lump. God not only rules, but he shall rule completely—that we have seen is the vital element in the thought of the future kingdom. "Fear not, little flock, for it is your Father's good pleasure to give you the kingdom." [33]

This is the source and ground of Jesus' confidence and courage. One sees again how his practical ethical teaching turns back to and rests upon his thought of God. We usually call this Jesus' teaching of faith in God. He constantly urged greater faith upon his disciples. "If only ye had faith like a mustard seed!" [34]   He saw that the chief bar to greatness of effort was that they did not have sufficient confidence in goodness, which is only another way of saying sufficient confidence in God. He saw they

[31] Matt. 9: 38 and Luke 10: 2.   [33] Luke 12: 32.
[32] Mark 4: 26 f.   [34] Matt. 17: 20 and Luke 17: 6.

did not really believe that goodness could be made supreme in life, that God's kingdom was actually coming. Hence they did not let go of themselves, they did not trust the issue. In the working of all his miracles of healing Jesus saw this constantly illustrated. Belief that the good could and would happen was indispensable. "Have faith in God"—that was an attitude of life which was necessary for the release of the latent powers of one's soul. On any interpretation life is a great venture, and Jesus would have men play the game with confidence and courage. Faith is not a work of supererogation, it is a basic necessity for any successful living. "Have faith in God," "O ye of little faith"—in such phrases Jesus constantly called his disciples to more courageous living.

TOPICS FOR DISCUSSION

1. The attitude which Christian humility should take toward one's own virtues, toward the faults of others, and toward the acceptance of responsibilities.

2. The causes for the boastfulness and self-assertiveness characteristic of much of American life. Is this trait confined to American character?

3. The relation of the several virtues, love, humility, sincerity, and courage—are they separate virtues or are they different phases of the same inner spirit?

4. The most characteristic Stoic virtues. Those most characteristic of Buddhism. Of Confucianism. Of Judaism. Of Christianity.

A WRITTEN ASSIGNMENT

Write three paragraphs giving your explanation and interpretation (a) of the parable Luke 18: 9-14, (b) of the parable Luke 14: 7-11, and (c) of the passage Luke 14: 26-33.

SUPPLEMENTARY READINGS

On the sins Jesus condemned:

Moffatt: "Jesus on Sins" in Case, *Studies in Early Christianity,* pp. 193-208.

Objection to Jesus' ethical teaching on the grounds that it is
    ascetic :
  Rashdall : *Conscience and Christ,* pp. 156-163, and 199-217.
Objection on the grounds of its alleged neglect of intellectual and
    æsthetic interests :
  Rashdall : *Op. cit.,* pp. 163-169.
On the "child mind" praised by Jesus :
  Bundy : *The Religion of Jesus,* pp. 218-237.

CHAPTER XIV

JESUS' TEACHING ON POSSESSIONS

The teachings of Jesus which have been passed in review in the preceding chapters constitute the core of his ethical ideal. He taught that obedience to God's will involved something more than obedience to this or that rule of conduct. It demanded a new type of inner character which would conform to the character of God. The basic and unifying element in that character should be the quality of love—love that was courageous and unafraid, though withal modest and sincere.

The meaning of this teaching will become clearer if one considers its application to certain areas of moral conflict and difficulty. The most constant of these is that of money and property. There are numerous indications in the gospels that hearers of Jesus had great difficulty, just as men do to-day, in applying this teaching of complete and unselfish love to the economic sphere.

For money is more than a number of hard, cold pieces of metal. It is the command of food and clothing and houses and autos and pictures and boats and all other things that people crave. Many of these things are necessary for living; all of them bring comfort and ease and a certain kind of satisfaction. So men constantly struggle to seize as much as possible of the stock of the world's goods. In that struggle it is the familiar story that a few are outstandingly successful, and these make the rules for the continuation of the struggle. Thus custom and law come in to aid differences in natural ability in widening the gap between rich and poor.   In the United States, for example, fifteen per cent of the people control about eighty-five per cent of the wealth, and yet, being a new country, the wealth is more evenly distributed here than in most other lands.

I

In Palestine, where Jesus lived, this contrast of wealth and poverty was obvious.   The New Testament bears testimony, the more eloquent because indirect, of the presence of the poor.   The ordinary food of Jesus' hearers was bread and fish.   Meat as food is not once mentioned in the gospels.[1]   The poor are frequently mentioned.   The number of very small coins which have been preserved from that period show the poverty of the majority of the people.   The predominant occupations were agriculture and sheep raising, and the poor soil combined with primitive processes of farming to give scanty crops.   Add to all this the fact that the country had been drained for generations by the taxations of foreign overlords.   Still, in contrast to the multitudes of poor, there were people of wealth.   Jesus watched "many rich" as they cast gifts into the treasury.   Josephus and the Mishna both speak of wealthy officials and citizens.

We must, moreover, remember that Jesus, living in this situation, was one of the laborers.   He was in all probability the eldest son of a widowed mother and there were at least six children younger than himself.   When he began his public work his followers were all men of limited means.   At different times in his brief life he must have known the pressure of want.   This was not because there

[1] See Dickey, *The Constructive Revolution of Jesus,* p. 124.

was not enough food and clothing to go around in Palestine, but because a few people had secured a disproportionate part of the supply. It would not be surprising then if we found Jesus addressing himself specifically to the economic problem, which was acute then as now, denouncing the situation in Palestine and making proposals for a new system in which all injustice would be done away.

Just such a denunciation and such proposals many people think Jesus gave. "Christ was the first great socialist"; "If anyone preached to-day as he did, he would be arrested"; "Christianity was a vast economic revolution"; "The Sermon on the Mount is really a treatise on political economy"—these are only a few quotations expressing this conviction.[2] It is pointed out that he declared it more difficult for a camel to go through the eye of a needle than for the rich man to enter the kingdom.[3] He told the rich young ruler, "If thou wouldst be perfect, go, sell all that thou hast, and give to the poor." [4] Does this not denounce wealth? He said, "Lay not up for yourselves treasures upon earth." [5] Does not that forbid private property? In the form of the beatitude which appears in Luke one reads, "Blessed are ye poor! . . . Woe unto you rich!" [6] There are several parables that point in the same direction, notably that of the rich man and Lazarus[7] and the story of the rich man who said to his soul, "Take thine ease." [8] Finally we have in Luke 14: 33 the specific and sweeping injunction: "So therefore whosoever he be

[2] For a good collection of these see Peabody's *Jesus Christ and the Social Question*, pp. 63 ff.

[3] Mark 10: 25.	[5] Matt. 6: 19.	[7] Luke 16: 19 ff.
[4] Matt. 19: 21.	[6] Luke 6: 20, 24.	[8] Luke 12: 16 f.

of you that renounceth not all that he hath, he cannot
be my disciple." Such sayings certainly seem to indicate
that Jesus opposed the acquisition of personal property
and wealth.

Before passing to the discussion of this question, it
will be instructive to notice that the exact opposite to this
condemnation of wealth has frequently been presented as
the teaching of Jesus—namely, that he offers material rewards and blessings to those who follow him. "Seek ye
first his kingdom and his righteousness; and all these
things shall be added unto you." [9] No man has left house,
or brethren, or sisters, or mother . . . or lands . . . for
my sake, but shall receive a hundredfold now in this time,
houses, and brethren, and sisters, and mothers, and lands
with persecutions; and in the world to come eternal
life." [10] These have been the texts for many an assertion
that Christianity brings material blessings to the faithful.
Nothing better illustrates than these various views the
vagueness and uncertainty of popular knowledge of the
mind of Jesus; nor could there be any better illustration
of the necessity of studying each particular saying in the
light of the whole tenor of his teaching.

What did Jesus teach about money and possessions?
He certainly did not leave the subject alone and, as the
phrase goes, "stick to religion." Did he offer a new economic system on the grounds that love is incompatible
with private ownership and hence all such personal possessions should be given away?

I think we may quickly dispose of this question. In
spite of all the quotations given above which condemn
wealth or praise poverty, we can safely say that Jesus was

[9] Matt. 6: 33.   [10] Mark 10: 29.

not opposed to private ownership, *as such,* or to the normal process of making a living. He himself earned a living in early life and probably supported by his toil his widowed mother and sisters and younger brothers. Later on, when he and his disciples traveled over Galilee and Judea, we are told that they had a money bag from which their frugal needs were met.[11] Luke tells us further that there were certain women who at one time ministered to him and his disciples of their substance,[12] which fact would show, of course, that Jesus made use of the private means of others. The homes of Peter in Capernaum and of Mary and Martha near Jerusalem he used both for his work and his rest, and there is no hint of a denunciation of such ownership of houses. But perhaps the most instructive passage is the story of Jesus and Zacchæus. The publican, in the enthusiasm of his new conviction, said, "Behold, Lord, the half of my goods I give to the poor; and if I have wrongfully exacted aught of any man, I restore him fourfold." [13] That Jesus had no objection to ownership as such is shown by his reply, "To-day is salvation come to this house," although it is to be noticed that Zacchæus by no means gave away his entire fortune. As to the injunction to the rich young man to give away his fortune, its sequel shows that we must not try to make it a universal rule. Jesus looked around and said, "How hardly shall they that have riches enter into the kingdom of God. . . . With men it is impossible, but not with God." [14]

All of which comes back to this: that love is not incompatible with personal ownership. A home in which chil-

---

[11] John 13: 29.
[12] Luke 8: 3.

[13] Luke 19: 8.
[14] Mark 10: 23, 27,

dren are to be reared and parents protected, tools which make possible serviceable labor in the work of the world, clothing against the winter's cold, and food for the day of famine—all these are in ordinary situations but the expression of a loving spirit. Jesus never denounced "taking thought for the morrow" in spite of the erroneous translation in Matthew 6: 34 (a passage which should read as the Revised Version has it, "Be not anxious for the morrow"). He recognized in many a parable the value of honest work and he commended the care of aged parents and the love of little children. He was not so blind as to condemn the necessary method of expressing such love and care.

II

What then was Jesus' teaching on the subject of riches? The number and character of his statements about riches and the rich show that he had deep convictions on the subject. What was his positive teaching in this realm that comes close home to all, rich and poor?

1. Jesus laid down the fundamental proposition that there must be no rival in the heart of the individual to the rule of God. He saw clearly how the love of money tended to become the dominant desire of life. Men get in the race, and the competition for wealth makes its pursuit the more keen. The power which it brings makes it desirable even apart from the pleasant things it will purchase. Thus possessions begin to loom larger in the thought than obedience to the will of God. Men think in mercenary terms, crave material ends, admire those who succeed in laying up riches. Thus, even unconsciously, the things of God come to take the second place. Mammon—

which is only the Aramaic word for riches—come to be
the object of worship.

But there is no membership in the kingdom of God
without singleness of heart. We have seen how absolutely
fundamental this is with Jesus. There must be no compromise as to the aim of life. "No man can serve two
masters: for either he will hate the one and love the other;
or else he will hold to the one and despise the other. Ye
cannot serve God and Mammon." [15] Why not? Because
serving God is a thing of the whole direction and dedication of the life, and the life cannot be dedicated to two
different ultimate objectives. Unless that decision as to
the aim of life be clearly faced, there will result ineffectiveness of effort, uncertainty of action, inner conflict and
confusion. That wholeness of life in loving service becomes impossible.

"Ye cannot serve God and Mammon." Ye cannot serve
God and any other competitive interest. The strongest
statement of this fundamental principle Jesus gave not in
connection with money matters; he chose instead—it must
have been consciously—the noblest human devotion, love
of family. "If any man cometh unto me, and hateth not
his own father, and mother, and wife, and children, and
brethren, and sisters, yea, and his own life also, he cannot
be my disciple." [16] The meaning of this verse is clear.
Not even the noblest devotion to this individual or this
small group can be elevated above the demands of the
kingdom. The words which follow in the text drive home
that thought: "For which of you desiring to build a
tower, doth not first sit down and count the cost? . . .
Or what king going to war doth not consider the force

[15] Matt. 6: 24. [16] Luke 14: 26.

of his enemy? . . . So therefore whosoever he be of you that renounceth not all that he hath, he cannot be my disciple." [17]   If love of parents, wife, and children must not come before devotion to the kingdom, is it any wonder that he refused to allow that primacy to the pursuit of wealth? "Seek ye first the kingdom of God"—nothing must come before that.

This is the first principle in Jesus' teaching on riches. And it was because he saw Mammon constantly usurping God's place that he declared it to be such a danger to the soul. The man seeking wealth is likely to adopt what Professor Dickey has called "a rival salvation." [18]   He comes to believe that his main satisfaction and security in life are to be obtained by wealth. He begins to trust in his money. The objects of his interest become material things. But "after all these things the Gentiles seek"— i. e., this is all paganism. The real source of trust and confidence should be God, and the main concern of life should be his will. The inadequacy and impermanence of such trust in material things become clearly revealed in the hour of death. There was a rich man once who filled his barns to overflowing and said, "Soul, take thine ease." But that night God said, "Thou foolish one, this night thy soul is required of thee." And Jesus concluded the story with the warning, "So is everyone who lays up treasure for himself, and is not rich toward God." [19]   It was because he saw riches crowding out in so many instances that "richness toward God" that he felt the love of money to be such a danger to the soul. Not necessarily so, but

[17] Luke 14: 28-33.

[18] Dickey, *The Constructive Revolution of Jesus,* p. 131. I am indebted to Professor Dickey throughout much of this discussion.

[19] Luke 12: 16-21.

actually, he saw wealth in many cases making men arrogant and proud, self-confident and worldly-minded.

2. So closely associated with the above as to make separate treatment difficult is a second principle which Jesus laid down. Seeking first the kingdom of God means, as we have seen, adopting an attitude of love toward our fellow men. It assumes that men are more valuable than money, and that the claims of human beings must never be sacrificed for anything material. The first principle stated above might be put, The rule of God above riches; the second principle, Men are more valuable than money.

Here again Jesus saw the pursuit of wealth as a special danger. The choice between personal profit and greater service to humanity is one that tests character most severely. There is an adage strangely familiar in Christian America, "Every man for himself, and the devil take the hindermost." It is the exact antithesis of Jesus' "He that is greatest among you shall be the servant of all." To extract a purely personal profit from human need, a profit that in no way returns in further service, is quite obviously unchristian. And yet the process goes on constantly. To quote Professor Dickey again, "The whole business of laying up money in the midst of human need, Jesus implies, corrupts the soul." The Christian spirit declares that human values are above all monetary returns, and it will gladly sacrifice a chance for fortune on behalf of the health, happiness, and spiritual development of men and women affected by the occupation. The law of supply and demand is no answer to the questions raised by a Christian conscience. Nor is a lawyer's opinion on the legality of a certain course of action. A corner on the wheat market, a reduction in the production of life's necessities in order to increase the price, such control of the tools of production that laborers are made to compete with each other for the chance to work—these and other practices may be legal, but they put money above the lives of men and women who suffer from them. The practical application of this principle means that the first question a Christian would ask would not be, "How much profit will this bring?" but, "How will this affect the lives of the men and women and children related to this business or profession?"

This conception of the unique value of human life is fundamental with Jesus. It goes back to his teaching that all men are objects of the divine love. "The hairs of your head are numbered, fear not therefore." "How much then is a man of more value than a sheep!" "Behold the birds of the heaven! . . . Your heavenly Father feedeth them. Are ye not of more value than they?" In all of these sayings the unique worth of human beings is clearly in mind. They are the objects of the love and care of God. Beware then of injuring them for the sake of some material consideration! "Whosoever shall cause one of these little ones that believe to stumble, it were better for him if a great millstone were hanged about his neck and he were cast into the sea." [20]

And yet for the sake of money Jesus saw men constantly crippling and starving their fellows. Not only the acquisition of it, but its centralization in a few hands, is likely to prove a temptation. We are accustomed to say that great wealth is good neither for the possessor nor for the dependent poor. Mastery over the lives and fortunes of others, which wealth involves, is a grave responsibility. The danger is that it will breed hardness of spirit and lack

[20] Matt. 18: 6.

of sympathy. On the other hand, those made dependent are likely to become bitter and resentful. The "class struggle," which seems almost inevitably to spring up, arrays both groups against each other. In the conflict the rights of men as such, the generous emotions of both parties, are likely to be wiped out, and hatred and antagonism take their place. No wonder that Jesus saw in avarice a vital danger to the soul. "Take heed that ye keep yourselves from all covetousness, for a man's life consisteth not in the abundance of things that he possesseth" [21]—that word comes in the midst of modern economic strife, calling men to peace. From Jesus' standpoint the economic struggle of the modern world is both wrong and foolish. Men are fighting for the wrong things. Possessions are not the primary aim of life. The true values are love, peace, coöperation, friendship, the joy of intelligent labor, a sense of mission. The kingdom of God is brotherhood. Property must always be subordinated to the rights of personality. The principle is so far-reaching that we have only just begun to appreciate its significance. In the mind of Jesus there are no property rights that can stand against the value of persons.

3. We might add a third principle in Jesus' teaching on wealth: that all occupations and professions should be carried on from the motive of public service, and not solely for the motive of personal profit. That is, of course, but another phase of the principle of love discussed above. But its application to the economic world has never been made. So regarded, no business would be run for its owners only, but to support the needs of the community; no farmer would plow for his small financial gain, but to feed

[21] Luke 12: 15.

a hungry world; no doctor or lawyer would practice for himself alone, but to heal and help those in distress. So regarded, every task becomes sacred. With such ideals, work is a precious thing and must not be applied to endeavors that do not minister to the physical or spiritual needs of men. Even the humblest task so regarded has its own glory. There are no "respected occupations" except those which serve the more. "He who would be the greatest must become the minister of all." [22]

These are the positive principles that Jesus would apply to economics. He had no neat scheme of economic reform. This was shown by his refusal on two occasions to take the rôle of financial legislator. They came to him on one occasion and asked him about the right of Rome to collect taxes.[23] He refused to be drawn into a definition of the limits of the Church and the State, or the rights of the State in the economic sphere. On the other occasion, a man came asking that Jesus compel his brother to divide an inheritance fairly. Here was his chance surely, if he had wished to set up the specific rules of how property should change hands and how wealth should be divided. Instead, his reply went behind the details of the case to the motive which he saw was in the man's heart and which was far worse than any injustice he had received in the division of the estate: "Man, who made me a judge or a divider over you? And he said, Take heed and keep yourselves from all covetousness." [24] He steadily refused to become a lawmaker or economic expert.

Yet these three principles cry out against any system or practice that exalts wealth above humanity and makes

[22] Mark 10: 44; Matt. 20: 27; Luke 9: 48, etc.
[23] Mark 12: 14.   [24] Luke 12: 13 ff.

the desire for selfish profit the foundation of the economic order. They are more needful to-day than they were in Palestine then, because life is so organized to-day that we do not see the results of many of our actions and cannot count on natural kindness and generosity to the degree that was possible when most transactions were face to face and carried results which were immediately visible.

III

But if these principles be given the right of way, so far as Jesus was concerned the question of wealth becomes almost an indifferent matter. He had no class prejudice. We find him dining with wealthy Pharisees as well as with the poor and the outcasts. As already remarked, at least one of the women who ministered unto him of their substance was a woman of prominence, and all of them were evidently people of competence if not actually wealthy. Jesus emphasized personality and not possessions. A certain centurion he praised as having more faith than had been found in Israel, quite irrespective of his being a person put in authority and rich enough to have "given a synagogue unto our people." [25] On the other hand, the incident of the widow who cast her mite into the treasury is instructive. The size of the donations did not excite him. It was the personal expression that went into the gift. This is the principle that runs through his teaching on wealth. Jesus thus spiritualized the whole economic problem. Money, property, and the like are but tools or implements of useful living. The vital thing is the kind of personality, the character of life which uses them, and the effect that use has on other lives. The spirit

[25] Luke 7: 5.

of man and its claims must take precedence over all material considerations.

Wealth used according to the control of these principles becomes indifferent to the owner as well. It ceases to be an occasion of personal gratification or a means of mastery over others. It becomes a trust, and the owner a steward. To him who obeys Jesus' law of love, wealth simply affords an opportunity.

To such a one trying to make the kingdom of God first in life, Jesus thought of wealth as giving two opportunities.

1. It would mean an opportunity to serve humanity. "Whosoever shall give a cup of cold water only to one of these little ones in the name of a disciple shall not lose his reward," [26] he said at one time. The Good Samaritan not only bound up the wounds of the man who was bleeding, but going on to the inn was able by his means to provide for him even after his own departure.[27] The parable of Dives clothed in purple and fine linen and feasting sumptuously finds its point in the thought of how much that rich man could have done for the beggar at his door.[28] He who has means has not only his own life to give in service, but the thought and labor of many men stored up in the form of wealth. Love will rejoice in such means of service. In Palestine, where life was simple and social relations were for the most part face to face, such service usually took the form of personal charity, and Jesus regarded all such sincere acts as a fine privilege. "Sell all that ye have and give alms; make for yourselves purses

[26] Matt. 10: 42.   [27] Luke 10: 35.   [28] Luke 16: 19 ff.

which wax not old, a treasure in the heavens that faileth not." [29]

2. But it is difficult to regard one's wealth as a means to the service and help of other people. Jesus knew this well. All his warnings against the danger of riches go back to that fact. Hence he has one other thing to say to the man who has means at his disposal. Just as the abuse of the personal and spiritual for the sake of money reveals the unrighteous heart and brings God's condemnation, so the right use of wealth brings in its train the development of character and the approval of God. This is the theme of practically all of Luke 16, which begins with the parable of the unjust steward. This man used wealth which was not his to make friends for himself against the day when his lord would take away his stewardship. "The sons of this world are for their own generation wiser than the sons of the light," is Jesus' comment on the story he had told. "And I say, Make to yourselves friends by means of the mammon of unrighteousness, that when it shall fail they may receive you into the eternal tabernacles." [30] When he says, "Make ye friends," etc., we must remember that he is continuing the general picture of the parable. The main thought is clear. Just as the sons of this world use wealth to prepare for their future days, so should the sons of the kingdom. The right use of the "mammon of unrighteousness" can bring one into "the eternal tabernacles." Wealth is simply a trust. Its stewardship is a responsibility whose proper execution wins God's own approval. In itself it may be of little moment; in its use it may win the greatest rewards God has to give. The chapter from which the above quotation

[29] Luke 12: 33.   [30] Luke 16: 8 ff.

was made goes on with this thought becoming ever clearer. "He that is faithful in a little is faithful in much; he that is unrighteous in a little is unrighteous also in much. If therefore ye have not been faithful in the unrighteous mammon, who will commit to you the true riches?" [31]

Thus Jesus' teaching on the subject of riches reveals nothing new. On examining it one finds it to be simply the application of his basic principles of the supreme value of the kingdom of God, the infinite worth of each human being, and the greatness of service, to the practical relations of life.

TOPICS FOR DISCUSSION

1. Is Christian love incompatible with the private possession of property?

2. Can the acquisition of wealth in the wrong way be justified on the grounds that it will be used for good purposes?

3. Are Jesus' teachings on possessions applicable to the choice of an occupation?

4. Is the modern economic system Christian?

A WRITTEN ASSIGNMENT

Read the passages, Luke 12: 13-21 and Matt. 6: 19-32. Then read the three accounts of Jesus' conversation with the rich ruler (Mark 10: 17-22, Matt. 19: 16-30, and Luke 18: 18-30), and write the story in your own words, explaining as far as you can the actions of the rich man, the reasons for Jesus' demand, and the meaning of his saying in Mark 10: 25. Note the supplementary reading below.

SUPPLEMENTARY READINGS

On the command, "Sell all that thou hast":
Rashdall: *Conscience and Christ*, pp. 150-156.
On Jesus' teachings on possessions:
Cadoux: *The Early Church and the World*, pp. 61-66.
Scott: *The Ethical Teaching of Jesus*, Ch. XIII.
Dickey: *The Constructive Revolution of Jesus*, Ch. V.

[31] Luke 16: 10 f.

Scott: *The Ethical Teaching of Jesus,* Ch. XIII.

Matthews: *Jesus on Social Institutions,* Ch. VI.

On the economic products, conditions of labor, trade, and finance of Palestine in Jesus' day:

Grant: *The Economic Background of the Gospels,* pp. 54-81.

On the attitude of socialist writers toward Jesus:

Peabody: *Jesus Christ and the Social Question,* Ch. I.

On the unchristian character of the modern economic order:

Tawney: *The Acquisitive Society,* Ch. 1 and 2.

Ward: *Our Economic Morality and the Ethics of Jesus.*

CHAPTER XV

JESUS' TEACHING ON FAMILY LIFE

THE family is the basis of society. More burdens are carried by it, more is expected of it, than of any other institution. It determines the lives of its members to a greater degree than any other factor or group of factors. Its obligations rest upon its members more immediately and are more pressing than any others. It generates more devotion, and on the other hand more bitterness if things go wrong. It molds the lives of its members. It is of such primary importance in the practical conduct of life that it is not surprising to find that Jesus had certain very definite convictions concerning it.

I

Here probably more than at any other point it is essential to remember the attitude of contemporary Judaism. The synagogue regarded the family with the utmost appreciation and reverence. Quotations from the Old Testament, from the Apocrypha, from the sayings of the rabbis on this point are so abundant as to make it difficult only to decide which ones to quote. The verse, "Houses and riches are an inheritance from fathers: but a prudent wife is from the Lord," [1] is typical of much of the content of Proverbs. The divine sanction for marriage went back to the days of creation when God said, "It is not good for man to be alone." [2] One rabbi went so far as to say that "God sitteth in heaven arranging marriages." "At mar-

[1] Prov. 19: 14.   [2] Gen. 2: 18.

riage all sins are forgiven," is a piquant saying of another. Jewish youths were supposed to be married by the age of twenty, and sometimes their failure so to be called forth active assistance from the congregation. One of the duties of parents was to find good husbands and wives for their children.[3]

So also in the case of children. Every reader of the Old Testament is familiar with the sadness of the childless household. The stories of Hannah, of Rebecca, and of Elisabeth, the mother of John the Baptist, come readily to mind. Over and over again we catch phrases that reflect the pride and joy of the Hebrew parents in their children, particularly if they were boys. Ben Sirach found it necessary to warn his readers against caring too much for their sons.[4] "He that maketh too much of his son shall bind up his wounds."[5] "Desire not a multitude of unprofitable children, neither delight in ungodly sons."[6] A saying from the Talmud reads, "These four reckon as dead—the blind, the leper, the poor, and the childless." On the other hand, affection for and obedience to parents in the strictest degree were enjoined upon the sons and daughters. "Honor thy father and thy mother"—that was bred in the bone by many a precept and by constant example.

The Jews were conspicuous in the ancient world for the fidelity with which marriage relations were preserved. The prophets and the law and the whole educational system

[3] Ecclesiasticus 7: 25.

[4] Ben Sirach was a devout and patriotic Jew who wrote about 175 B.C. He was a teacher of the youth and a typical "wise man." His book, *Ecclesiasticus* (or *The Wisdom of Ben Sirach*), reads much like Proverbs. It is to be found in the Apocrypha.

[5] Ecclesiasticus 30: 7.   [6] Ecclesiasticus 16: 1.

by which the law was taught to the people inculcated purity and condemned the adulterer.   That fact adds more point to the repeated use of that term to describe Israel's faithlessness to Jehovah.   We see this high moral standard reflected in the writings of St. Paul: "It is actually reported that there is fornication among you, and such as is not found even among the Gentiles." [7]   That comparison of the standard among Jews and among the Gentiles was not an expression of mere race prejudice.   It was largely because of its high moral standard in this and several other respects that Judaism was winning converts all over the Roman Empire, even before the birth of Christianity.

Thus through all Jewish life there ran this family emphasis.   It was natural in its simpler aspects to a nation that had grown out of ancient tribal elements.   The family was the unit.   The genealogy of the people was carefully kept, both because of pride in the family stock and because of the necessity of proving membership in certain families to serve in the priestly occupations.   Local affairs seem to have been pretty much run by the heads of the great houses.   Patriarchal and hereditary ideas governed in the political realm rather than anything like democratic conceptions.

But there was one dark spot in all this—the position of women.   The old conception of wives as property lingered from the earlier days of the desert.   Several illustrations will suffice.   First note the difference in what constituted technical adultery in the case of a man and of a woman.   In the case of a wife, she committed adultery if she was unfaithful, no matter who might be her partner.   But a husband was not guilty of this crime unless his act was

[7] 1 Cor. 5: 1.

committed with a woman married to another man; for then he violated the other man's rights. In the laws of divorce the same attitude comes out. A husband could divorce his wife at will. "If she find no favor in his eyes," is the language of Deuteronomy 24: 1. Hillel, the great rabbi of the first century before Christ, said, "Even if she spoiled his food," though the language here may not have been intended literally. But a wife could not divorce her husband for any reason whatever. Upon certain extreme offenses she gained the right to appeal to the local courts for release. But even then all the court could do was to compel the guilty husband to divorce the innocent wife!

Just in the period when Jesus lived many influences were coming into Palestine to change the whole set of attitudes and customs built up by the Jews toward the marriage institution. There was a sect called the Essenes who forbade marriage to its members. Greek and Roman influences were everywhere in the country tending to break down the strictness with which the Jews regarded all sex relations. One public example, and this in high life, is familiar to readers of the gospels. Herod Antipas, "that fox," [8] had married his brother Philip's wife, an offense to Jewish morals that John the Baptist did not hesitate to condemn. In Jewish circles ideas were shifting. The famous rabbinical schools of Hillel and Shammai had engaged in a warm controversy over the legitimate grounds for divorce, Hillel, however, winning out in favor of the traditional freedom for the husband. Lastly, the Roman occupation of the land and the removal of all capital executions from the hands of the Jewish authorities

[8] Luke 13: 32.

had made it impossible to carry out, even had they wished it, the Pentateuchal law of death for the crime of adultery. Thus many influences were at work to change Jewish ideas in this sphere.

II

Turning to Jesus' sayings, we find him expressing in sayings of strength and beauty the finer teachings of the synagogue as to the family. The family is the noblest institution on earth. The relations which exist between its members he makes the type and symbol of the kingdom of God. God is not like a priest, or king, or judge, or artist; he is like a father of children. That means that in Jesus' thought the family had produced the noblest figure on earth, the character most divine—parenthood. Furthermore we saw that when he spoke of the ideal relation between men and women of the kingdom he turned to the family for his word—they should be like brothers and sisters. "For whosoever shall do the will of God, the same is my brother, and sister, and mother." [9] "One is your teacher, and ye are all brethren." [10]

The claims of the family he defended against all that would usurp their place. He was not always a quiet teacher, self-contained in word and bearing. Occasionally he flamed forth in indignant rebuke. One of those occasions was when he spoke of how the religious casuistry of the hour condoned or excused those who neglected the care of their own parents. "Moses said, Honor thy father and thy mother. . . . But ye say, If a man shall say to his father or his mother, That wherewith thou mightest have been profited by me is Corban, that is to say, Given

[9] Mark 3: 35.   [10] Matt. 23: 8.

to God; ye no longer suffer him to do aught for his father or his mother; making void the word of God by your tradition." [11]   For children he had the tenderest sympathy. Not only should they be loved and helped; they should be imitated,[12] "for of such is the kingdom of God."   It were better for one "if a millstone were hanged about his neck and he were thrown into the sea rather than that he should cause one of these little ones to stumble." [13]

This interest in the children who came about him must have gone back to an earlier time.   Reference has been made to the probability that Joseph died early and the care of the family devolved on the young shoulders of Jesus.   Mary's was a household teeming with children— six, seven, maybe eight of them.[14]   When later in his teaching he speaks of the children who come asking for bread and sometimes even for a fish,[15] of children playing games in the market place and sometimes in sulky mood refusing to play,[16] of people who come to borrow after it is dark and the children have finally been all gotten to bed,[17] of brothers that are quick to suspect partiality and have to be reasoned out of their moodiness,[18] it sounds very much as if he is speaking from experience.   As Glover says, "Are we to think that the tenderness of Jesus came to him by a miracle when he was about thirty years of age?   Must we not think it was growing up in that house and in that shop?   Or did he never tell a story—he who tells them so charmingly—till he wanted parables?" [19]

[11] Mark 7: 10 f.   [12] Mark 10: 14 f.

[13] Luke 17: 2.   The term "little ones" in this verse probably included also adults of that "childlike" character that Jesus praised, as well as those actually young in years.   [14] Mark 6: 3.

[15] Matt. 7: 9, 10.   [16] Matt. 11: 16, 17.   [17] Luke 11: 7.

[18] Luke 15: 28-32.   [19] *The Jesus of History*, p. 29 f.

But this is to speculate about that home of his own in the quiet years before he went out to listen to John preaching in the wilderness. To come back to the subject of his teaching, what about marriage itself? That is usually the heart of the question. Did he appreciate that? Or did he regard marriage as a concession to human frailty and an impediment to the fullest service of God? [20]

The problem of sex and its relations has always been difficult for religion to deal with. He who exalts the spiritual is likely to deny the bodily. Spirit must rule over body, therefore the body must be conquered. Thus asceticism has ever dogged the heels of religion. And where this has been avoided an opposite extreme has sometimes appeared—license in the name of religion. The bacchanalia of ancient times, the practices at various temples, the aberrations of sects and cults in modern days, testify to the danger. Sanity is never so well tested as here. What is spirituality? Something otherworldly, opposed to the normal and the healthy? Something that would take men out of life? Or is it something that suffuses normal life processes with a meaning and a light that does not come from the clay of which we are made?

Fortunately there is an explicit statement as to what Jesus thought. It is one of those passages of critical value for getting at the mind of Jesus. They had asked him about divorce and Jesus gave in answer his whole attitude toward the relation of men and women. "From the beginning of the creation, male and female made he them. For this cause shall a man leave his father and mother and shall cleave to his wife; and the twain shall become one flesh, so that they are no more twain, but one flesh." [21]

[20] Cf. 1 Cor. 7: 7, 9, 32, 33.   [21] Mark 10: 6 f.

The thought here needs little comment. In Jesus' opinion marriage was an institution of God corresponding to the facts of creation. Men and women supplement one another. Standing alone they are incomplete. The merging of lives together was God's all-wise purpose and intent. The two shall become one flesh. Marriage is the completion of the process of creation; in entering therein we coöperate with God. It is not an accident, not a concession to human weakness, but the final divine gift of completeness of life.

Jesus was no ascetic. The kingdom of God is not a removal from life. It means carrying the mind of God into all of this normal healthy life which he has given.

"Male and female created he them; therefore shall a man leave his father and his mother and shall cleave to his wife; and the twain shall become one flesh." In higher terms than this no one can speak of marriage. Husband and wife have lost their lives to find a higher life, have died individually to find a fuller life together.

All this appreciation of marriage and the family, shown especially in the use of family terms to describe the relations of the kingdom of God, is what we would naturally expect from the principles that Jesus laid down. He declared that love was the highest attribute of man and that it should become the rule of his life. Naturally he would admire and strengthen the institution that creates love, that binds its members together in mutual devotion and service. His own language makes one quite safe in saying that Jesus' whole teaching of life and duty might be described as simply the extension of the family limits so as to include all mankind.

III

This reverence for the family was, as said above, one of the primary tenets of Judaism and was regularly taught in the synagogues. It was one of the things the rabbis emphasized. This is undoubtedly the reason that we have no more pointed and explicit sayings by Jesus on the subject of family devotion and care. It wasn't necessary in Palestine. Thus Jesus' attitude comes out indirectly, for the most part in connection with what he has to say on other subjects.

Explicitly and directly, Jesus rather seems interested in qualifying the current Jewish conception of the family. While he said that parenthood best represented the character of God and that brotherhood was the essence of the kingdom, he set himself very explicitly to teach that one's family must always be kept in a secondary position. The chief object of man's interest and the scope of his endeavor must be to do God's will. One's own family must never be exalted above that. When family ties interfere with doing the will of God, they must be sacrificed. He saw a danger to the fullest development of the moral character in an excessive devotion to one small group. The claim of the family must be subordinated to the demands of the general good.

How we would like to make it otherwise! If one could only confine one's unselfishness and altruism to members of one's own family! Every one would be willing to do that. As Jesus said with stinging force on another occasion, "If ye love them that love you, what reward have ye? Do not even the publicans the same? And if ye salute your brethren only, what do ye more than others?" [22]

[22] Matt. 5: 46, 47.

The one who seeks the kingdom of God will make family devotion but a stage or step in the service of all men. The warmer, closer affection of the smaller, more intimate group will always be kept in perfect harmony with the rights and needs of others outside. The kingdom of God must come first, and if it be made so, the claims and duties and affections of family life will fall into their proper place.

This was not an abstract academic matter with Jesus. He had to give up his own home for the sake of his mission, and—if the wording of Mark 3: 21 f. be properly translated—carried on his work against family criticism and obstruction. He saw the necessity of laying down as the first condition of discipleship that men must leave father and mother and brethren and lands and houses for his sake. There are some sayings in the gospels which seem almost harsh in their insistence that the family is subordinate to the kingdom of God. "And another also said, I will follow thee, Lord; but first suffer me to bid farewell to them that are at my house. But Jesus said to him, No man, having put his hand to the plow, and looking back, is fit for the kingdom of God. . . . And he said to another, Follow me. But he said, Lord, suffer me first to go and bury my father. But he said, Leave the dead to bury their own dead, but go thou and publish abroad the kingdom of God." [23] "If any man cometh after me, and hateth not his own father, and mother, and wife, and children, and brethren, and sisters, yea, and his own life also, he cannot be my disciple." [24] "Think not that I came to send peace upon the earth: I came not to send peace, but a sword. For I came to set a man at

[23] Luke 9: 61 f. and 59 f.   [24] Luke 14: 26.

variance against his father, and the daughter against her mother, and the daughter-in-law against her mother-in-law." [25]

The thought throughout all of these is very clear. It is summed up in Matthew 10: 37 f.: "He that loveth father or mother more than me is not worthy of me; and he that loveth son or daughter more than me is not worthy of me. And he that doth not take his cross and follow after me is not worthy of me." The loyalty to the highest must be supreme. No man or woman can enter the kingdom of God with its sweeping vision of service to all of life who makes the demands of that kingdom subservient to the desire or pleasure of some individual or group of individuals. "Even the Gentiles do the same." Devotion to this group or that group is most worthy, but it must take its place in the light of the good of the whole. The opposite is the doctrine of "My party, right or wrong," "My country, right or wrong," "My own family, right or wrong." Jesus condemned all such narrowing of the kingdom.

And in so subordinating the family he lifted it, of course, to a higher level. It becomes in his hands an agent ministering to the very highest ideal of life. The affections which it generates sweep outside its own bounds to become effective for the needs of the world. Family devotion and loyalty become filled with a new meaning, and are made the agent and vehicle of the noblest objectives. [26]

IV

We have left out thus far the question of divorce and what Jesus said about it. It is in some of these sayings

[25] Matt. 10: 34 f.

[26] Cf. Scott, The Ethical Teaching of Jesus, pp. 96, 98.

that we see most clearly the depth and power of his conception of the family.

The Jewish custom and law have already been described. They sanctioned and always had sanctioned divorce by the husband with the utmost freedom. There must only be a written certificate given to the wife which was evidence of her right to remarry. Of course the rabbis built up in time various regulations which ameliorated the cruelties of such a system, and no doubt also the great majority of Jewish marriages were broken only by the death of one of the parties. But in spite of all this, the evil was there and did not escape Jesus' keen sense for moral and spiritual values.

The passages dealing with this subject are the following: Mark 10: 2-12 and the parallel passage Matthew 19: 3-9; Matthew 5: 31, 32; Luke 16: 18; and finally 1 Corinthians 7: 10, 11.

If the student will read these carefully, he will observe that the wording of the sayings is not always the same. The fundamental thought is expressed in the several passages with differences of detail. As a result it is easy to fall into debate as to this or that feature of this teaching. For example, did Jesus forbid divorce or rather remarriage? What is the relation of the uncompromising form of the utterances in Mark and Luke to the commands in Matthew which allow one exception to the principle? To discuss these questions adequately would require more space than can be given here. But through all of these passages there runs one clear, strong, certain note. In the face of contemporary practice, Jesus declared that marriage was a union and not a contract, that it was permanent and not subject to the inclination of the moment, that it was the blending of two lives, not a temporary association.

Nowhere else does Jesus so elevate marriage and the family as here. Husband and wife belong together. Even though he allowed separation—as Paul certainly understood him to allow[27]—they still belong to each other. The bond is so sacred and intimate that it holds even though they be separated from each other. Whether we like it or not, that seems to be Jesus' teaching.

We must remember that Jesus was speaking to a people among whom divorce was easy and had been so from time immemorial. Its sanction was to be found in the Old Testament. Furthermore, he spoke to a group among whom tyrannical power was possessed by the husband. Hence the necessity for laying down absolutely and unconditionally the one principle on which the family can be built, the fundamental recognition of the permanency of marriage.

That is the important thing. Men and women must think and act and plan on the assumption that marriage is essentially a union of lives for life. It should be entered only with that thought and intention. Its problems should be met and considered with no other idea in mind. A separation of husband and wife is basically wrong. That is undoubtedly Jesus' thought.

This was because he had another solution for the discords of family life. We must not read his teaching on divorce alone as if he simply overlooked the homes where there is no harmony or peace. Jesus believed in facing wrong and eliminating it, using the only weapons effective in such warfare. We must remember that these sayings on divorce are based on the assumption that one is attempting to live the life of the kingdom. Accordingly,

[27] 1 Cor. 7: 10, 11.

if the family unhappiness be one's own fault, the obvious course will be to proceed at once to remove the evil and, like Zacchæus, make restitution many fold—the more gladly and willingly because the injury in this case has been done to one who was the object of deepest personal love. But suppose the hearer of this teaching be the injured party? Shall he or she demand certain rights or declare all personal obligation at an end? Did Jesus ever encourage such an attitude? No, he declared this to be the Christian's opportunity, that he should turn the other cheek, resist not the evil, love those who persecute and do wrong. If this be so in relations that are impersonal and distant, what is the case where the offender is the partner of one's life? Jesus once told Peter to forgive seventy times seven. He said in the Sermon on the Mount that, when impressed, we should carry the burden a second mile. How many applicants for divorces have first tried such solutions? Paul was only echoing Jesus when he wrote that thirteenth chapter of 1 Corinthians. "Love suffereth long, and is kind; love envieth not, love vaunteth not itself, is not puffed up, . . . seeketh not its own, is not provoked, . . . beareth all things, believeth all things, hopeth all things, endureth all things. Love never fails." It is against the background of this teaching of forgiveness and the changing of evil into good that Jesus' teaching about divorce must be read.

The application of this teaching to our own day is, of course, full of the most difficult questions. It may well be, indeed it seems evident in many a case, that although wrong, a separation, whether temporary or made permanent by divorce, is the lesser of two evils. People do make shipwreck of their lives and there are conditions under which it seems impossible for true home life ever to be recreated. But even here the underlying principle of Jesus' teaching remains. Such events are personal and social disasters. They should be the very last resort, and be entered only with sadness and a sense of shameful failure. That is the Christian view. Instead, we have grown into a state of mind where divorce is the normal or semi-normal experience. It is regarded with equanimity both by the parties themselves and by the general public. Without carrying Jesus' teaching to unwise extremes, is it not necessary to rediscover his ideal of marriage? With so many marriages ending in the divorce courts, and the joy and gladness of weddings turning into the bitterness and acrimony of divorce proceedings, modern society grievously needs to find again the more enduring basis of marriage that Jesus taught, that it is a sacred institution in which both participants merge themselves into a high and permanent union.

But our interest in the practical side of this question has made us overlook one of the greatest elements in these sayings on divorce. Ordinarily when we think of the rightfulness of divorce, we moderns pose the question in this form: "Has not an innocent woman the right to rid herself of a brute of a husband?" Now the interesting thing is that this alternative probably never occurred to Jesus' hearers. The only kind of divorce they knew anything about was the free divorce of wives by husbands. His words, therefore, rather meant to them such a championing of the cause of woman as they had not heard before. He challenged their whole man-made system of superiority, the unjust power of divorce which they wielded, the cruel inferiority and dependence which were forced upon women. He declared that in marriage women had the same rights as men. "Whosoever shall put away his wife, and marry another, committeth adultery against her" [28]—that was revolutionary. From the days of the Mosaic law, Jewish husbands had enjoyed that privilege. So amazing was it that in the account of this saying in Matthew we are told that the disciples replied, "If this is the case of a man with his wife, then it is not expedient to marry"! [29] To their minds, marriage on such a basis was hardly conceivable, so rigidly does the custom of centuries set the mind. Jesus thus raised woman's place in the family to a point of absolute equality with that of man. In marriage there are equal obligations before God. In this affirmation Jesus made himself one of the great champions of woman's cause.

TOPICS FOR DISCUSSION

1. Jewish family solidarity as a factor in their racial survival.

2. The place of women in ancient society. When did the change take place?

3. The limits which Jesus placed on devotion to one's own family.

4. Is divorce always wrong?

5. The original form of Jesus' saying on divorce.

6. Conditions responsible for the increasing number of divorces.

7. Why Jesus speaks so often of a father's love for his children but never mentions a mother's love.

A WRITTEN ASSIGNMENT

Write your explanation of what you think Jesus meant by the sayings recorded in Luke 8: 19-21, Luke 14: 26, and Luke 18: 15-17.

SUPPLEMENTARY READINGS

On Jewish family life:

Moore: *Judaism*, Vol. II, pp. 119-140.

Abrahams: *Studies in Pharisaism and the Gospels* (1st Series), Ch. IX.

---

[28] Mark 10: 11.   [29] Matt. 19: 10.

On Jesus' family:
  Glover: *The Jesus of History*, Ch. II.
  Warschauer: *The Historical Life of Christ*, pp. 27-31.
On Jesus' teachings about family life:
  Rashdall: *Conscience and Christ*, pp. 162, 163 and 178, 179.
  Scott: *The Ethical Teaching of Jesus*, Ch. XIV.
  Cadoux: *The Early Church and the World*, pp. 58-60.
  Matthews: *Jesus on Social Institutions*, Ch. V.
On the problem of the family in modern life:
  Ellwood: *Reconstruction of Religion*, Ch. VII.
  Ellwood: *Sociology and Modern Social Problems*, Ch. VIII.
  Adler: *Marriage and Divorce*, Ch. I.
  Groves: *American Marriage and Family Relationships*.
  Groves: *The Drifting Home*.

CHAPTER XVI

THE REWARDS OF THE KINGDOM

I

THUS far we have been speaking of the kind of life that Jesus said should be lived by those who entered the kingdom of God. Much has been said about duties and obligations, the demands he made on men, the renunciations which he declared were essential to becoming his disciple. But the primary impression that Jesus' teaching made on men was quite different—that he came preaching good news. And so true was this that the early Christians called his message by that very title, "The Good News," and this is the original meaning of the word "gospel." So whenever one uses the word "gospel" one bears testimony to the joyous character of the message that Jesus gave.

We saw in Chapters VIII and IX that this good news was summed up in the announcement that the long-awaited "kingdom of God" was at hand. And this meant in the language and thought of the day that God was ready to give his richest blessings.

Note how Jesus stressed the thought of a great reward for those who would do God's will. The kingdom is "like unto a treasure hidden in a field; which a man found and hid; and in his joy goeth and selleth all that he hath and buyeth that field." [1] It is like the "pearl of great price," worth more than all else that the merchant possesses.[2]

---

[1] Matt. 13: 44. [2] Matt. 13: 46.

Repeatedly Jesus describes the members of the kingdom as "blessed." "Blessed are they that have been persecuted for righteousness' sake: for theirs is the kingdom of heaven." [3] "Blessed are the poor in spirit: for theirs is the kingdom of heaven." [4] "Blessed are the pure in heart: for they shall see God." [5] When a woman praised him, he replied, "Nay, blessed are they who know the will of God, and do it." [6] We must not lose the force of that word "blessed." "Happy is that one," so one writer translates it. It is a word used in private letters of the day in expressions of warmest congratulation. Only as used in the gospels there is added a definite religious idea—"happy in the enjoyment of the blessings of God."

This thought of the richness of the reward is not accidentally attached to Jesus' main thought, but is one of his primary conceptions. "Love your enemies, and do them good, lend, never despairing; and your reward shall be great, and ye shall be sons of the Most High." [7] Better bodily dismemberment than miss the kingdom. "If thine eye cause thee to stumble, cast it out: it is better for thee to enter into the kingdom of God with one eye, than having two eyes to be cast into hell." [8] The reward is sure. Even deeds done in secret will not be overlooked: "Thy father which seeth in secret shall recompense thee." [9] "Whosoever shall give to drink unto one of these little ones a cup of cold water only in the name of a disciple, verily I say unto you, he shall in no wise lose his reward." [10]

[3] Matt. 5: 10.
[4] Matt. 5: 3.
[5] Matt. 5: 8.
[6] Luke 11: 28.
[7] Luke 6: 35.
[8] Mark 9: 47.
[9] Matt. 6: 4, 6.
[10] Matt. 10: 42.

II

So outstanding is this whole thought of reward in Jesus' sayings that it has frequently been charged that Christianity is a doctrine of selfishness, that it bids us do good in order to get something. It is pointed out that certain pagan moralities, particularly Stoicism, insisted on duty for its own sake without thought of reward. In comparison the ethical teaching of Jesus is thus assigned a lower place.[11]

But we have seen that Jesus was the first to criticize this unlovely type of goodness when he saw it in men around him. A good act done from a selfish motive, whether it be public charity or prayer in the market place, brought his scathing criticism. The people who perform worthy deeds "to be seen of men" "have their reward," [12] but it is not the reward of the Father in heaven. The sayings in Luke 6: 32-34 condemn specifically such selfish goodness: "If ye do good to them that do good to you, what thank have you? for even sinners do the same. And if ye lend to them of whom ye hope to receive, what thank have ye? . . . Even sinners lend to sinners in order to receive again as much." Such sayings and many others preclude the idea that Jesus allowed his disciples to "do good hoping to receive." But we do not need such specific sayings. The whole tenor of Jesus' teaching on righteousness demands a devotion of the whole man to such a degree as to make impossible anything like a selfish morality.

What, then, is the point of all these sayings of reward? We seem to have a conflict. On the one hand, Jesus tells us that the motive of all action must be love of others and

---

[11] For the treatment given this topic, cp. Scott, *The Ethical Teaching of Jesus,* p. 63 f. [12] Matt. 6: 2, 5.

not thought of self; on the other hand, he holds up to us this thought of a great reward. The answer involves two or three principles.

In the first place, Jesus speaks of a reward from God, never from men. He turns the motive away from the approval of men to the approval of God. Notice, for example, how constantly in the Sermon on the Mount he enjoined his hearers to act, not for the approval of men, but of God, "who sees in secret."

And there is a vast difference between working for God's approval and seeking a reward from men. In the former case no outward show or pretense will suffice, but only the genuine devotion of the life. As Paul said later, "If I bestow all my goods to feed the poor, . . . but have not love, it profiteth me nothing." [13] God sees into the inner heart and motive. He sees things as they really are. Hence there is eliminated all the insincerity and duplicity that attends working for human reward. For one cannot lie to God, as Peter said to Ananias and Sapphira. To seek God's approval and his recompense means in the very nature of the case to love sincerely and to act honestly.

And with this understood, working for a reward simply means trusting God that unselfish service to our fellow men will result in the highest and the best in life for ourselves. We give ourselves in sincerely unselfish service and leave the personal result to God, confident that such a devotion of our energies and our thought will not lead to genuine loss. Jesus' teaching of reward from God is ultimately an assertion that goodness is not something alien in the midst of an evil universe, standing by itself, but that goodness lies at the heart of things; and an order-

[13] 1 Cor. 13: 3.

ing of life according to its standards is highest wisdom for the individual as well as for society. It is no discredit to his teaching that it emphasizes this trust in God's care over the good.

But there is still a third factor in this teaching concerning reward. Jesus taught that we never really earn this reward from God. "All we like sheep have gone astray." Remember what was said in an earlier chapter on humility. The ideal of character is infinite, and before that standard no man can feel self-righteous or meritorious. Concerning "the eighteen upon whom the tower at Siloam fell and killed them, think ye that they were sinners above all the men that dwell in Jerusalem? I tell you, Nay: but, except ye repent, ye shall all likewise perish." [14] No man deserves God's reward, taught Jesus. We are like the workers in the vineyard who were hired at the eleventh hour. Of course they did not earn their pay. Why then did they receive it? Only because the master of that vineyard was ready to give the recompense whether earned or no. "Is it not lawful for me to do what I will with mine own?" says the master of the vineyard to his critics. "Is thine eye evil because I am good?" [15] God *gives* good things unto his children; they do not earn them—that is Jesus' thought. "Fear not, little flock; it is your Father's good pleasure to *give* you the kingdom." [16] "Verily I say unto you, Whosoever shall not *receive* the kingdom of God as a little child, shall in no wise enter therein." [17] "Even so ye also, when ye shall have done all the things that are commanded you, say, We are unprofitable servants." [18] In such sayings there comes out the thought

[14] Luke 13: 4 f. [16] Luke 12: 32. [18] Luke 17: 10.
[15] Matt. 20: 15. [17] Mark 10: 15.

that the blessings of the kingdom are really a divine gift
to men and women who fall far short of earning or deserving them.

Thus while Jesus uses the word "reward," and speaks
of working for it, what he really does is to assure men
that their trust in God and in God's way of life is not misplaced.   God is a father who is waiting to give of his
blessings in showering abundance, far in excess of what
we deserve.   From his teaching on the reward of goodness, the insincere motive is gone, the self-righteousness of
the Pharisee is gone, and humility and gratitude and joy
take their place.   When one sees the character of God that
Jesus revealed, the motive for doing good becomes grateful love rather than a desire to earn a reward.   There is
a vast difference between this and a selfish morality.

III

But what is the reward or blessing which God will give?
Did Jesus promise material blessings?   I referred above to
the fact that many people have understood him so to speak.
The passages, "Seek ye first his kingdom, and its righteousness; and all these things shall be added unto you," [19]
and the promise in Mark 10: 29 of a hundredfold of all
houses and lands given up for the cause, are quoted in
support of the contention.   Is material wealth the blessing that God waits eagerly to give?

We may dismiss this interpretation.   Wealth is not always a blessing.   Jesus himself insisted on its risk to the
soul.   "Keep yourselves from all covetousness." [20]   "Ye
cannot serve God and mammon." [21]   "Lay not up for
yourselves treasures upon earth." [22]   "It is easier for a

[19] Matt. 6: 33.
[20] Luke 12: 15.
[21] Matt. 6: 24.
[22] Matt. 6: 19.

camel to go through the eye of a needle, than for a rich man to enter the kingdom." [23] But apart from the moral risk of money, Jesus made it clear that it was not the greatest blessing. "A man's life consisteth not in the abundance of the things which he possesseth." [24] "What doth it profit a man to gain the whole world, . . ." provided he miss something else? [25] Over against the "unrighteous mammon" there is a "true riches." [26] Even our own experiences in life, limited as they are, show us that riches are not final or satisfactory in themselves. The verses which are alleged to prove that Jesus taught a materialistic reward to those who obey God's will clearly have another meaning. And if one will take the trouble to read these carefully in their own setting, there will not be much difficulty in discovering their real import. Matthew 6: 33, for example, as the preceding verses show, is certainly a promise of necessary food and clothing rather than of the accumulation of wealth.

Similar to this suggestion is the view that the reward of the kingdom is immunity from all physical ills. I remember some years ago a very sincere Sunday school teacher who maintained that a real Christian should have no fear of dangerous animals or bodily ills. He cited the verse in Luke 10: 19, "Behold, I have given you authority to tread upon serpents and scorpions, and over all the power of the enemy; and nothing shall in any wise hurt you." Paul's trials and afflictions ought to have been a sufficient refutation of the interpretation. But we need not go that far. Jesus himself, as already noted, foretold persecutions and trials, even death to some. The sons of Zebedee were to drink of the same cup of which he was to drink. The shepherd was to be smitten and the sheep scattered. Peter's viewpoint, that sufferings should not come to the Messiah, was that of men, not of God.[27]

The gospels show us that Jesus would have been the first to condemn a life of physical ease untouched by any trial and vitalized by no possible danger. That idea is below the elevation of his view of life. To him it was a thing to be bravely hazarded and freely given. "Blessed are those who are persecuted for righteousness' sake." "Blessed are ye, when men shall reproach you, and persecute you, and say all manner of evil against you falsely, for my sake. Rejoice, and be exceeding glad."[28] The service of the kingdom inevitably involves persecution.

IV

What then is the reward of obedience to the will of God, if it is not wealth and if it is not safety? What reward could be adequate for the sort of service which Jesus demanded? Obviously no small material compensation would be sufficient, no fraction of that which must be renounced. Indeed, no reward could be equal to the sacrifice demanded except one, the obtaining of a fuller and richer *life*.

It is in the Fourth Gospel that the word "life" is used most consistently of the reward which Jesus held out. "I came that they may have life, and have it abundantly."[29] "Ye would not come to me that ye may have life."[30] "He that hath the Son hath life, and he that hath not the Son hath not life."[31] In this as in other cases one sees how the author of that gospel seizes upon the essence of the

[27] Mark 8: 33.   [29] John 10: 10.   [31] John 5: 12.
[28] Matt. 5: 10-12.   [30] John 5: 40.

gospel and states it in terms that are both simple and profound.

In the Synoptic Gospels the word "life" is also used to describe the reward of the righteous, though it is not the primary expression. "Narrow is the gate, and straitened the way, that leadeth unto life, and few are they that find it." [32] "If you would enter into life, keep the commandments," said Jesus to the rich ruler.[33] "If thy hand cause thee to stumble, cut it off: . . . for it is better to enter into life maimed, than having two hands to go into Gehenna." [34] But the word "life" in these passages is only a substitute for the basic conception of the kingdom of God, a figure of speech which is common in the religious literature of the period.[35] The last quotation shows this clearly. Not only is "entering into life" the opposite of "going into Gehenna," but the next verse, which balances the one quoted, reads, "It is good for thee to enter into the kingdom of God with one eye, rather than having two eyes to be cast into Gehenna." The kingdom of God is the reward of the righteous. Other expressions are but figures to illustrate or emphasize some phase of that inclusive hope.

That this phrase described the blessed age or world to come which was to fulfill the highest Jewish hopes and aspirations has already been explained. It only remains to point out certain features of that reward as it shaped itself in the mind of Jesus.

In the first place it should be noted that that life, in contrast to the present one, will be eternal. Those who have left houses or brethren or family for the sake of the gospel

---

[32] Matt. 7: 14.   [33] Matt. 19: 17.   [34] Mark 9: 43.
[35] Dalman, *Words of Jesus*, pp. 156 ff.

shall receive much in this life, "and in the world to come eternal life." [36]   The parable of the Great Judgment closes with the words, "and the righteous shall enter into eternal life." [37]   "Make to yourselves friends by means of the mammon of unrighteousness [*i. e.,* win divine approval]; that when it shall fail, ye shall be received into the eternal habitations." [38]   In Luke's version of Jesus' answer to the question of the Sadducees about the resurrection there is the specific statement that "those that are accounted worthy to attain to that world and the resurrection from the dead . . . cannot die any more." [39]

One notes also that Jesus spoke of the fellowship with the great figures of the past that will be enjoyed in the kingdom of God. "God is not the God of the dead, but of the living," he said. Using the familiar Jewish figure of a banquet to describe the kingdom, he declared that many would "come from the east and the west, and sit with Abraham, Isaac, and Jacob in the kingdom of heaven." [40]   These were the patriarchs, the fathers of Israel, the heroes of Jewish piety and patriotism. There are other names which each of us would think of in such a connection, perhaps those of great souls who have inspired multitudes of people, others of individuals who are not known to fame but whose lives have cheered and helped those who knew them. "Life," not alone, but in association and fellowship with all who have endeavored in their age and circumstances to do the will of God, was part of the reward which Jesus envisaged.

Did Jesus attempt to say what that life shall be like? Will the conditions of that world be like ours? Are we to

[36] Mark 10: 30.   [38] Luke 16: 9.   [40] Matt. 8: 11.
[37] Matt. 25: 46.   [39] Luke 20: 36.

think literally of a city lying foursquare, with gates which are twelve pearls, and streets of pure gold? Jesus never attempted to describe the nature of that heavenly life. Why propound the familiar puzzles about the resurrection life, whose wife will the woman with seven husbands be, and all the other questions that can be asked? That life will be totally different from this earthly existence. "For when they shall rise from the dead, they neither marry nor are given in marriage; but are as the angels in heaven." [41] The pictures of the banquet are only figures. The "great gulf" and all the rest of it are only spatial terms which we are compelled to use. The only kind of life we know anything about is this bodily one; what life in the kingdom of heaven will be like we must leave in the hands of God.

It is evident that this hope of the kingdom of God in its external and future manifestation is what nowadays we describe by the word "heaven." The only difference is that in the first century this supernatural age was thought of as dawning at a particular time which would mark the end of this present world. Christian faith of to-day rather conceives of the kingdom of heaven as an eternal abode to which God takes his servants immediately at the end of their terrestrial day. The thought of the great Day of Judgment and the end of this present world order has not been given up, but only postponed, to the more distant future. The difference does not matter. Even in Jesus' day these two ways of thinking of God's reward were merging into each other. The basic conception is the same. It is the embodiment by faith of humanity's greatest hope, that of a life that is not bound

[41] Mark 12: 25.

down to decaying flesh, but is as boundless and glorious as is the life of the spirit.

How do we know there will be any such thing? That was the argument the Sadducees had been making for a long time. It is interesting to note the answer that Jesus made to them. He quoted from the Old Testament a passage about the character of God.[42] And in essence that is the only argument he makes: the Scriptures show that God is of a certain character. And after all, is that not the simplest and most abiding ground for hope, the nature and character of God as Jesus described him? There are figures and there are analogies, but the only firm assurance is belief in a God of love who "will not leave us in the dust." At any rate, that is what Jesus answered to those who doubted in his day.

V

This emphasis on the other life has produced some of the world's greatest characters. It has released man from bondage to the present. It is dangerous and otherworldly in a bad sense only when men hold it to the exclusion of interest in this present world. We have seen that Jesus was not of that temperament. He declared that the service of the kingdom also increases immeasurably the richness of the life that now is. How is this the case?

1. I begin with what Jesus said about the material things of life. He did not promise wealth and prosperity, as we have seen, but he did quite boldly declare that one of the blessings of the kingdom will be the assurance of a heavenly Father's care. And he means this in quite material things. Just as God feeds the sparrows and clothes the lilies, so will he provide for us. In one beautiful figure

[42] Mark 12: 26, 27.

after another this thought is presented in the sixth chapter of Matthew. "Behold the birds of the air." "Consider the lilies of the field." "And which of you by being anxious can add one cubit to his stature?" "If God so clothe the grass of the field, which to-day is, and to-morrow is cast into the oven, shall he not much more clothe you, O ye of little faith? Be not therefore anxious, saying, What shall we eat? or, What shall we drink? or, Wherewithal shall we be clothed? . . . For your heavenly Father knoweth that ye have need of all these things." [43] That last phrase gives the secret. These things are necessary for life and God is ready to provide for our needs. Indeed, he thinks first of these needs: "Your Father knoweth what ye have need of, before ye ask him." [44]

This teaching of God's providence has been of course one of the points over which modern men have had great difficulty. One should remember, however, several things. First, that Jesus did not promise great riches. He had in mind only what was actually needed for life. The member of the kingdom has put other things above money. Furthermore, such an individual will not be a parasite upon his fellow men. The kingdom means service, not dependence on others. Jesus certainly did not inculcate a disposition that sits idle and prays to the Lord to provide, while others are at work. Then it must be remembered that the individual who has committed himself to the ends of the kingdom always has in mind in his labor the needs of humanity. His life's work serves others. It is not unreasonable to believe that such an individual can feel

[43] Matt. 6: 25-32.   [44] Matt. 6: 8.

confident of receiving as the result of his labors enough to satisfy the necessities of life.[45]

But it is important to notice in the same passage the use to which Jesus puts this confident trust. He seems interested not so much in the food and drink and clothing in themselves as in the effect of this trust upon the human spirit. "Be not anxious, be not anxious, be not anxious" —that is the refrain. He sees in this gift of God's care the liberation of men from their burdens of anxiety and fear. Men should learn the simple lesson of the fatherhood of God. In perfect trust and confidence he taught his disciples to pray, "Give us this day our daily bread." [46] The worries and fears that undermine health and destroy peace should be eliminated by this faith in a Father who will "add these things" according to our need.

2. But this thought merges into a more general one. The life of the kingdom removes all the anxiety and fear and worry which come because of the competition and strife with other men. Can we keep up in the race with the people around us? Will this issue turn out right? Is this decision the right one? Will the important position come to us or to the other men? These and a hundred other questions like malignant spirits harass the lives of multitudes of people. To the man or woman who has

---

[45] It might be asked, Is not the assurance of the necessities of life as great for the selfish individual as for one trying to serve the kingdom? The answer is quite certainly, No. Society has no need of the former. It can dispense with the work and with the presence of one who does not serve in any way. But only by ignorance will society ever fail to give to the latter its unwavering support and protection. Our whole wage and salary system is theoretically based on this premise of proportionate reward to him who serves society most. Jesus' teaching is based on faith in God, however, not on economic theory.

[46] Matt. 6: 11

made the kingdom first in life, such attitudes and anxieties are impossible.

For if service has become the aim and not rivalry, the race to outdo and surpass others is over, once and for all. The outlook on life is changed, the ends to be sought are different. The old yearning for wealth and power and mastery are removed. One works with and for, not against, one's fellow man. Nor can such a spirit stand in fear of possible failure. In every situation and in every circumstance a loving spirit can find opportunity to serve. The aim of life has become one which neither accident nor evil can thwart. Instead of making the life dependent upon that which is external and accidental, it becomes directed from within. The ultimate issues are decided. The reins by which we have been driven are cut away. There is calmness of spirit and inner peace. The richness of such a life of coöperative activity cannot be taken away.

That Jesus had in mind this inner peace which follows the acceptance of his ideal and that he viewed it as one phase of the reward, is implied by a number of his sayings. Indeed the consciousness of the inner superiority of the life of the kingdom over other ways of living permeates the whole of his teachings. It is evident in his injunction to rejoice even amid persecutions, and to anoint one's face though fasting. It lies behind his confident declaration that those "who hear the word of God and do it" are blessed.[47] Other sayings point more specifically to this inner reward. Martha was encumbered with much serving, while Mary sat at Jesus' feet willing to let the sumptuous repast go unprepared in her desire to understand more of what the teacher had to say. "Martha, Martha,"

[47] Luke 11: 28.

said Jesus, "thou art anxious and troubled about many
things; few things are needful or even one: Mary hath
chosen the better part, which shall not be taken away from
her." [48]   The best attested saying in all the gospels is the
reiterated statement, "Whosoever shall lose his life for
my sake, shall find it." [49]   But of all the sayings about
the inner blessings of the life of the kingdom, the most
beautiful is that which begins, "Come unto me, all ye that
labor and are heavy laden," and concludes with the promise, "and ye shall find rest for your souls." [50]   What that
rest included one might debate, but it certainly involved
the substitution of calmness, and confidence, and joy for
the strife, anxiety, and inner conflict which mar the lives
of many.

3. Then, next, there is the reward of perfect social relations.   How much of the value of life comes from personal relations!   There are, of course, satisfactions which
are quite impersonal—food when hungry, a warm bed in
winter, the pursuit of knowledge for its own sake, the
enjoyment of natural beauty.   But when these things have
been quite sufficiently recognized, how barren they tend to
become without those personal values which our nature
craves.   Run over the interests and activities of the day
and consider how empty life would become if human relations were taken out, how vital they are to the completion
of the normal life of man.   Membership in the kingdom
of God means that there has taken place a right ordering
of all personal relations.   Hate, suspicion, and antagonism
are eliminated.   The circle of friendship is enlarged and

[48] Luke 10: 41.
[49] Mark 8: 35, Matt. 10: 39, 16: 25, Luke 9: 24, 17: 32, and John
12: 23.
[50] Matt. 11: 29.

deepened. The human ties that bind us to others are multiplied and made stronger. Life finds its purpose for others, the individual becomes, in the root meaning of the Latin word, altruistic. He lives for others and, as a result, bodily and mentally with others. The emphasis in life falls on personality and its values.

Hence, naturally, all values that flow into life from the right ordering of our relations to other individuals are multiplied like the seed which fell on the good ground. The elements which make one's family the most blessed thing on earth are extended indefinitely. Brotherhood assumed at the beginning as an obligation becomes by practice a treasure discovered anew each day. The generous attitude toward all is transformed into the warmth and wealth of human friendship. Love, the duty, finds its own reward.

That is what Jesus meant when he gave Peter that amazing answer. "Peter began to say, Lo, we have left all and followed thee. Jesus said, There is no man who hath left house, or brethren, or sisters, or mother, or father, or children, or lands, . . . but he shall receive an hundredfold now in this time, houses, and brethren, and sisters, and mothers, and children, and lands, with persecutions." [51] For such a man enters into the great family of humanity. Such a man, who loves his neighbor as himself, possesses many lands and many houses; lands which serve his deepest purposes of supporting the hungry of the world, houses that care for his brother's comfort and which lodge those whom he delights to serve. Such a man possesses the universe, because he has taken to his heart the men and women and children who live in it.

[51] Mark 10: 28-30.

4. Finally, Jesus spoke of a reward that transcends the relations of time and space. He spoke of fellowship with God.

Again and again in this study we have seen how everything goes back to that thought. It is the foundation of all else that he said. The first commandment of all is to love God "with all thy heart, and all thy soul, and all thy mind, and all thy strength." [52] "Blessed are the pure in heart," he said, because "they shall see God." [53] When the disciples returned from their first missionary journey, elated over their success, he pointed them to the real ground of rejoicing—not that they had power over demons, but "rejoice that your names are written in heaven." [54] In Jesus' mind this was the greatest and most inclusive good of life.

This fellowship means a likeness of character and purpose which results in a lifting of the horizons of life. It means essentially that we are to look at the world and at our own lives from the divine viewpoint, to see them as God sees them. There is a new perspective in all things. No longer are things seen from the narrow horizon of our personally centered experience; but rather, if I may borrow the phrase of a great philosopher, *sub specie æternitatis*, "in the light of all eternity." Even one standing afar off can see the meaning and purpose thus infused into life. We enter into the purposes of God. We become fellow-workers in his creative plan. A sense of mission comes upon us. We are lifted out of the trivial routine and enter into the succession of the saints and pioneers of the faith.

But this fellowship has another aspect, one which in a

[52] Mark 12: 30.   [53] Matt. 5: 8.   [54] Luke 10: 20.

sense includes the others: it means a constant sense of the nearness of God. Every page of the gospels shows how Jesus possessed that sense. It lies back of such sayings as, "Consider the lilies of the field: your Father clothes them," "Behold the birds of the heavens: your Father feedeth them." It was his strength in hours like the cleansing of the Temple and the lonely vigil in Gethsemane. The individual who possesses that consciousness of God moves in a world where he is at home because it is a world that God has made; the grass is a carpet that he has spread and the sunshine and rain are his daily ministrations. And such an individual thinks and acts no longer in his own power alone. A Father's care and a Father's strength are constantly about him. And the companion of his thought is a moral perfection that transforms his selfishness and his weakness into loving courage.

Looking back over this chapter the question recurs, Is the kingdom of God the pearl of great price? Is it worth the renunciation of all else? Is the return more than what is given up? No one can answer that for another. Each man must find the ends and values of life for himself. But we can see now what is involved in the question. The issue is simply whether the ends of life are within personality and its relations to other individuals, or in something external to it. The reward of the kingdom as Jesus taught it is the enriching, broadening, and continuation of personal experience—"life, and that more abundantly." [55]

TOPICS FOR DISCUSSION

1. Whether the thought of reward to be gained is a justifiable motive for a good action.

2. The reward gained by society if everybody would live according to the teachings of the gospel.

[55] John 10: 10.

3. The factors which make Christmas the happiest period of the year. The extent to which these factors are present in Jesus' conception of everyday life.

4. The practical meaning of fellowship with God.

5. The penalties of selfishness.

6. Is trust in God something different from trust in the nature and constitution of the universe?

A WRITTEN ASSIGNMENT

Write a sketch of the sort of heaven you would like to go to. Remember that you are going to stay there for several millenniums at least.

SUPPLEMENTARY READINGS

Jewish conceptions as to reward and punishment after death:
Moore: *Judaism*, Vol. II, pp. 377-395.
On whether Jesus taught the idea of endless punishment after death:
Rashdall: *Conscience and Christ*, pp. 294-306.
Dougall and Emmett: *The Lord of Thought*, pp. 236-249.
On the nature of the resurrection:
Streeter: *Immortality*, Ch. III.
On the life of the world to come:
Streeter: *Op. cit.*, Ch. IV.
On whether the thought of a reward vitiates the goodness of a deed:
Rashdall: *Op. cit.*, pp. 290-294.

CHAPTER XVII

JESUS' TEACHING ON PRAYER

PRAYER is the center of religion. Religion has two aspects: On the one hand it maintains certain standards of conduct, on the other it affirms certain beliefs about the ultimate nature of the universe. It is prayer which connects the two. Without it the one of these would be ethics, and the other would be theology. Prayer makes them elements in religion. In prayer the individual brings together God, life's ideal values, and himself.

It is evident from the gospels that Jesus believed in prayer, told men to pray, and prayed himself. Mark narrates how early in the morning before others are about he withdraws to the desert to pray,[1] and late in the evening after teaching the multitudes all day he goes into a mountain to pray.[2] The hours before the arrest are spent in prayer.[3] Luke is particularly interested in the prayers of Jesus, and adds to Mark's account various other references. At the time of the baptism, when the heavens opened and he saw the vision, he was praying.[4] When the multitudes crowded upon him after the healing of the leper, "he withdrew into the deserts and prayed." [5] Before choosing the Twelve, and before he asked the disciples what they thought of himself, he was in prayer.[6] The Transfiguration occurred when he was at prayer.[7] The request of the disciples, "Lord, teach us to pray," was

[1] Mark 1: 35.   [4] Luke 3: 21.   [6] Luke 6: 12, 9: 18.
[2] Mark 6: 46.   [5] Luke 5: 16.   [7] Luke 9: 28.
[3] Mark 14: 32.

266

made at the close of one of his periods of prayer.[8]   Some of these may be editorial additions in order to provide settings for sayings or incidents where the actual occasion had been forgotten, but there can be no doubt that they represent an authentic record of the practice of Jesus.

One notices immediately several facts about these acts of prayer. In the first place, a considerable number of them occur at times of decision and crisis. Important junctures and turning points in Jesus' career were approached after long periods of silent meditation and prayer. In the second place, one notes that prayer was for Jesus a refreshing and invigorating experience. From the turmoil, confusion, and fatigue of dealing with the multitudes he sought refuge in withdrawals for quiet prayer. His words to his disciples show what these retreats meant to himself. "Come ye yourselves apart into a desert place and rest awhile," he said when they returned telling of their strenuous campaign through the cities and villages of Galilee. Such experiences of rest, reflection, and prayer Jesus himself had found necessary in order to carry on the spiritually and emotionally exhausting undertaking in which he was engaged. Such a practice of prayer throws valuable light on Jesus' own religion. In spite of his clarity of mind and intuitive understanding of religious and moral matters, in spite too of his independence and the authority with which he taught, it is evident that Jesus had no sense of religious self-sufficiency and personal adequacy. His intuitive moral judgments and his consciousness of authority to proclaim God's will were rather the results of these hours in which he sought to ascertain the purposes of God and to be led by him.

[8] Luke 11: 1.

If one should ask what Jesus taught about prayer, it must be answered that he gave very little definite teaching. There were certain things he said about it, but he gave no set rules or systematic directions for prayer. To him it was an intensely personal thing, and never to be reduced to form or ritual. Professor Bundy, speaking of Jesus' retreats for the purpose of prayer, remarks that there was no regularity about these retreats. "They were in no sense a part of a prayer system. For Jesus prayer was not a traditional religious exercise to be engaged in and observed at certain set hours, but the spontaneous impromptu practice of an intense personal piety." [9] Indeed we learn more about prayer as Jesus practiced it from his own prayers recorded in the gospels than from any instructions he gave about praying. By putting together precept and practice one can learn something of his conception of prayer and the objects for which he thought men should pray.

1. First and foremost should be placed the fact that Jesus repeatedly and in the strongest possible language urged his hearers to pray. "Ask, and it shall be given you; seek, and ye shall find; knock, and it shall be opened unto you: for every one that asketh receiveth; and he that seeketh findeth; and to him that knocketh it shall be opened. Or what man is there of you, who, if his son ask for a loaf, will he give him a stone; or if he ask for a fish, will he give him a serpent? If ye then, being evil, know how to give good gifts unto your children, how much more shall your Father who is in heaven give good things to them that ask him?" [10] On other occasions he was even more emphatic. "If ye have faith as a grain of mustard

---

[9] *The Religion of Jesus,* p. 191.   [10] Matt. 7: 7-11.

seed," he said in extreme illustration, "ye shall say unto this mountain, Remove hence to yonder place; and it shall remove; and nothing shall be impossible unto you." [11] By such words he tried to impress upon his hearers that God gives heed to prayer. For he knew that the reason men do not pray is that they do not believe that anything will be accomplished by it. God does hear and answer the prayer of faith. To Jesus prayer was not a process of autosuggestion or a devotional ritual with subjective values, but an actual source of power for accomplishment.

2. Prayer as Jesus regarded it is a purely private and personal affair. "When ye pray, ye shall not be as the hypocrites: for they love to stand and pray in the synagogues and in the corners of the street, that they may be seen of men. Verily I say unto you, They have received their reward. But thou, when thou prayest, enter into thine inner chamber, and having shut thy door, pray to thy Father who is in secret, and thy Father who seeth in secret shall recompense thee." [12] That is the only real sort of prayer. The public utterance is too likely to be ostentatious, formal, and of no personal value. Jesus was familiar with such public prayers, and he saw in them the absence of that intense sincerity, that striving to know the divine will which should mark true prayer. His own acts of praying are all done in places of quiet and escape from public gaze, not literally in a closet, but alone, where the most secret things of the heart could be expressed to God and criticized in the light of his universal purposes. Public prayer is no doubt valuable to a degree, but only to the degree that individuals echo and repeat for them-

[11] Matt. 17: 20, Luke 17: 6, and Mark 11: 24.
[12] Matt. 6: 5, 6.

selves the thought of the leader. Even where that is done, public praying falls short of what Jesus meant by the word. Prayer in its deepest sense will be personal and earnest beyond what most of us think. In it the individual relates his deepest problems and desires to the will of God. Such praying, Jesus taught, God hears and answers.

3. Prayer will be brief, to the point, and the soul of simplicity and sincerity. "In praying use not vain repetitions, as the Gentiles do: for they think that they shall be heard for their much speaking. Be not therefore like unto them: for your heavenly Father knoweth what things ye have need of before you ask him." [13] Verbose and rhetorical prayers, prayer-chains, prayer-beads—all such Jesus regarded as typical of paganism. The true prayer is a cry from the heart, a word, a single petition. Jesus' own prayers are all short. Except for the Lord's Prayer, only one of them is longer than a single sentence. Professor Bundy has pointed out how lacking in detail they all are. "In none of his prayers does Jesus catalogue his needs; he does not rehearse the situation in which he finds himself; he does not elaborate upon all that is involved for himself." [14] That is because his faith in God was real and personal. "Your Father knoweth what ye have need of." It is also noteworthy that the prayers of Jesus contain no laudatory introductions or flattering addresses. Most of them begin with the simple expression, "Father." Prayer is not telling something to God. Neither is it wheedling something out of God. It must be neither formal, nor elaborate, nor rhetorical. It is a deeply sincere

[13] Matt. 6: 7 f.   [14] *The Religion of Jesus*, p. 201.

endeavor to know and to correlate oneself with the purposes of God as they work themselves out in the world.

4. Prayer should be insistent, continuous, unceasing in its endeavor to attain an answer to one's need.

In illustration of this phase of his thought Jesus gave two parables which have caused considerable difficulty. One is the parable of the man who went at midnight to the house of a friend asking for the loan of some bread to feed an unexpected guest.[15] The man inside replies that the door is shut and that he is in bed with his children —I have often felt sorry for that man—and that he does not wish to be troubled. Nevertheless, says Jesus, "though he will not rise and give him because he is his friend, yet because of his importunity he will arise and give him as many loaves as he needs." The other parable is one of a wicked judge to whom a widow came crying for justice and who refused to give it. Finally, when she was insistent, the judge said to himself, "Though I fear not God nor regard man, yet because this widow troubleth me, I will avenge her, lest she wear me out by her continual crying." [16] Now neither the man who would not get out of bed to help his friend nor the wicked judge are very edifying characters, and people have wondered that Jesus should tell these stories to illustrate the value of insistent prayer to God. This is because they forget that the parables illustrate a single theme; they are not allegories in which each detail of the story has a corresponding point in the moral. The theme of these two parables is quite clear. Luke, indeed, points out the moral in the introduction which he gives to the second one. That parable was spoken "to the end that they ought always to pray and

---

[15] Luke 11: 5.   [16] Luke 18: 3-5.

never to faint." Prayer must not be perfunctory, the affair of a moment. The individual brings his problem before God and does not cease until he has an answer. Prayer must be an insistent endeavor to obtain light and help. Even when making requests of earthly friends or people who are not friends, this sort of insistence, said Jesus, gets results. How much more is God ready to answer those who cry urgently and insistently to him! These parables, which incidentally show clearly that sense of humor of which we get glimpses elsewhere, do not teach that verbal repetition, begging, or cajoling should mark true prayer, but that prayer should be constant and continued, with confidence that to such prayers God gives answer.

There is a quotation from Adoniram Judson, the great missionary to Burma, which may perhaps illustrate this point. Fosdick in his book, *The Meaning of Prayer,* tells how at the close of his life Judson made the statement, "I never prayed earnestly and sincerely for anything, but it came; at some time—no matter at how distant a day—somehow, in some shape—probably the last I should have devised—it came." "But Judson," continues Fosdick, "had prayed for entrance into India and had been compelled to go to Burma; he had prayed for his wife's life, and had buried both her and his two children; he had prayed for release from the King of Ava's prison and had lain there months, chained and miserable. Scores of Judson's petitions had gone without an affirmative answer. But *Judson* always had been answered. He had been upheld, guided, reënforced; unforeseen doors had opened through the very trials he sought to avoid; and the deep desires of his life were being accomplished not in his way but beyond his way." [17]   Similarly it should be recalled that Jesus himself was not always answered in the way in which he would have preferred.   Luke says that he prayed before the Twelve were chosen, but Judas nevertheless turned out to be a traitor.   He prayed in the Garden of Gethsemane that the cup might pass, but the petition was not granted.   There must have been many other prayers of his which were not literally granted as first formulated. But Jesus himself was answered, even in the case of that last prayer in Gethsemane.   Rising from his knees, we are told that he roused his sleeping disciples with the injunction that they too should turn to prayer in the face of the impending temptation. [18]

These various aspects of the prayers of Jesus and of his words about prayer lead to the question of the proper objects of prayer.   For what did Jesus pray and for what did he urge his disciples to pray?   It will be observed that these cover a considerable range of human experience. The following may be regarded as types of many similar prayers:

(1) There is the prayer of thanksgiving.   The only actual quotation of one of Jesus' prayers of this sort are the words, "I thank thee, Father, Lord of heaven and earth, that thou didst hide these things from the wise and understanding and didst reveal them unto babes; yea, Father, for so it was well-pleasing in thy sight." [19]   The whole spirit of grateful thanks, however, pervades all of Jesus' thought.   It is to be seen in his words about how God clothes the lilies, feeds the sparrows, and cares for men.   Gratefulness or gladness is a necessary part of the

[17] *Op. cit.*, p. 130 f.
[18] Mark 14: 38, "Watch and pray, that ye enter not into temptation."   [19] Matt. 11: 25.

true religious spirit, and its most natural expression is in spontaneous words or expressions of prayer.

(2) There is the prayer for the necessities of life. "Give us day by day our daily bread." [20] That Jesus believed in God's care for the material needs of the individual has been shown in the last chapter. So believing, he declared that men should pray with reference to them. The statement, "Your Father knoweth that ye have need of these things," is not to be taken to preclude prayer for such daily necessities. To eliminate prayer for these things would be to eliminate the belief that God provides for man's daily needs and to destroy the gratitude which men correspondingly owe him. Jesus does not go into details; he does not elaborate the various daily wants, but he does include in his model prayer petition for the basic needs of life.

(3) There is the prayer for forgiveness. Obviously, this is an element in all true praying. To stand before God in sincere and honest manner is to be painfully aware of one's failures and sins. To be unconscious of them would be to show the unattractive self-complacency of the Pharisee in Jesus' memorable parable of the two men praying in the temple. The attitude of true prayer is one of humility. It asks for forgiveness. It never catalogues its virtues.

In the Lord's Prayer request for divine forgiveness is coupled with another statement, "Forgive us our sins as we have forgiven those who have sinned against us," and this clause is reiterated in the First Gospel after the close of the prayer. The thought here is very simple. It is not a tit-for-tat morality. Jesus' whole teaching is directly

[20]Luke 11: 3; cp. Matt. 6: 11.

contrary to such a conception. Recall his striking saying in connection with the parable of the servants who, after they have labored in the fields all day, are then commanded to prepare and serve supper to their master, "Even so ye, when ye have done all the things that are commanded, say, We are unprofitable servants; we have done that which it was our duty to do." [21]   To *claim* God's forgiveness on the basis of one's own goodness in forgiving others would be to repeat the self-righteousness of the Pharisee in the parable. The meaning of the additional clause in the Lord's Prayer seems more consistently and more naturally to be explained in another way. It is now well known that the teaching of the divine forgiveness was one of the most constant ideas of Judaism of the first century. Jewish teachers indeed felt called upon to warn the people that they should not presume upon God's willingness to forgive.[22] Jesus repeated over and over again that God forgives sinners. But such forgiveness presumes a sincere repentance. No one has a right to claim it who does not adopt toward his fellows the same attitude which he prays God to show toward himself. In other words, the sincere prayer for forgiveness brings one into a circle of ideas in which continued animosity against a fellow man is impossible. To come into the presence of God in a sincere manner inevitably involves consciousness of one's own sins and regret for them. But of these sins the greatest and most obvious, from Jesus' standpoint, would be ill-will toward a brother. Thus, says Jesus, no man can genuinely pray, "Forgive me my sins," without adding, "as I do also forgive those who have sinned against me."

[21] Luke 17: 10.   [22] See Moore, *Judaism,* Vol. 1, pp. 508 ff.

(4) There is the prayer for moral deliverance: "Bring us not into temptation, but deliver us from evil." [23] The word "temptation" here means severe trials, trials of the flesh or of any special circumstances which are liable to lead to sin. This is obviously one of the most natural, most elemental, and most unquestioned objects for which the religious man prays. Prayer as a source of strength means first of all moral strength to meet the difficult issues and severe trials of life.

Two questions have often been raised about this petition. In the first place, it is argued that temptation is a good thing since by it character is built. The objection is casuistical. No man would willingly pray that he should be tempted. To do so would indicate a species of spiritual pride as well as an unhealthy interest in and willingness to test out one's moral condition. When the word "temptation" is taken in its wider sense of trials, this becomes even clearer. To pray for trials and temptations (or for that matter, trials or temptations) would be a species of asceticism. It brings to mind some of the ascetic practices of the monks of the fourth and fifth centuries. The normal, healthy prayer of a sincere and humble person will be that one be delivered from all trials and temptations.[24]

The second question which has often been raised is

---

[23] Matt. 6: 13; cp. Luke 11: 4 without the second clause.

[24] James 1: 2, "Count it all joy, my brethren, when ye fall into manifold temptations [trials], knowing that the proving of your faith worketh patience," etc., has often been cited in contrast to this petition in the Lord's Prayer. It need only be pointed out that James is writing to Christians who had been undergoing trials. He is writing after the fact and congratulating them on the chance that the trials give of proving their faith. Verse 12, "Blessed is the man that *endureth* temptation," reveals the point of his words. This is a very different thing from praying for temptations to come.

whether God brings men into temptation. James 1: 13, "Let no man say when he is tempted, I am tempted of God: . . . for God himself tempteth no man," seems a direct contradiction of the petition in the Lord's Prayer, and indeed seems the sounder religious idea. This is a real point. It is the issue around which the story of Job is built. Job's friends declare to him that his trials and sufferings are sent by God and are due to his sins, while Job maintains his innocence. The worst phase of Job's experience was the constant reiteration by his companions that his sufferings were God's direct act. Surely Jesus did not turn back to this ancient and morally trying doctrine that God himself brings temptations and calamities upon men merely in order to try them. Of this thought there is no other indication in Jesus' teaching. To Peter sleeping in the Garden of Gethsemane Jesus says, "Watch and pray, lest ye *come* into temptation"—there is no suggestion that God is directly tempting him. So also in the great trial of Jesus' life. His prayer, "If it be possible, let this cup pass from me," shows that he was not thinking of God merely as trying or tempting him, but rather of this experience as an inevitable part in God's plan to bring in his kingdom, a cup which he was willing to drink for the sake of that great end. So in the prayer the text, "Bring us not into temptation," is no doubt the Greek equivalent of the Aramaic original, "Cause us not," or "Permit us not to enter into temptation." One of the most unfortunate conclusions which could be drawn from this petition would be the idea that in times of moral conflict and struggle, when one's very soul seems almost at stake, it is God who has brought the experience merely as a temptation.

(5) There is the prayer for others, the prayer of inter-

cession. Two such prayers of Jesus are referred to in the gospels. One was for Simon, the leader of the disciples. It is quoted in Luke's account of the Last Supper: "Simon, Simon, behold, Satan asked to have you, that he might sift you as wheat: but I made supplication for thee, that thy faith fail not; and do thou, when once thou hast turned again, establish thy brethren." [25] Jesus knew well the weakness of Peter's character and had prayed that the coming events might not destroy him. Peter fell, but he turned again and became one of the founders and leaders of the Church. The second intercessory prayer of Jesus is also found in Luke, but a great many of the oldest manuscripts do not have it in their texts, and it may be that it was not an original part of the gospel. Be that as it may, the utterance has enshrined itself in Christian memory never to be lost. It is Jesus' word from the cross, "Father, forgive them; for they know not what they do." [26] In addition to these two prayers of intercession there are suggestions of many others; the prayer before the choice of the Twelve, for example. We may be sure that in Jesus' prayers the names of other people, his disciples, acquaintances he had met, his own family no doubt, were often to be heard.

(6) There is the prayer for help and guidance in hours of perplexity and despair. This, too, is an obvious and fundamental aspect of prayer.

The experiences in which men need the help and guidance which come in prayer are too numerous to classify, but two dominant types may be distinguished. One type is that of the confusion of loyalties and ideals, when the beautiful, true, and good are twisted with evil in combina-

[25] Luke 22: 31 f.   [26] Luke 23: 34.

tion so strange and perplexing as to seem almost the work
of devils.   The choice of action in such cases is fraught
with uncertainty and danger.   In such cases the great
souls have always found their way by means of prayer.
The second type is that of the meaningless tragedy, the
blasting of one's hopes and the death of one's efforts.
Both of these types converge in the prayer of Jesus in the
Garden: "Abba, Father, all things are possible unto thee:
remove this cup from me: howbeit not what I will, but
what thou wilt." [27]   In this prayer we see reflected all the
uncertainty and doubt which were inevitable in connection
with his choice of the path of death, as well as his deep
distress as he faced the apparent end of all his efforts in
failure.   His prayer was one which sought to find the
meaning of the experience, which would make it endura-
ble.   That he found it is evident from his exhortations to
his disciples to watch and pray, as well as from his calmness and poise during the dramatic scenes which followed,
the arrest, the trials, and the actual execution.

(7) All these objects of prayer come to a focus in one
great theme, prayer for the coming of God's kingdom.
The good man is inseparable from his endeavor to realize
the rule of God.   His prayers for himself, for others, for
light in hours of difficult decision, are parts of his endeavor to live the life of the kingdom, to extend its rule,
and to bring about its final consummation.   Two prayers
of Jesus embody this inclusive desire.   One is general:
"After this manner pray ye; Our Father who art in heav-
en, . . . thy kingdom come.   Thy will be done, as in
heaven so on earth." [28]   The other is more specific: "When
he saw the multitudes, he was moved with compassion.

---

[27] Mark 14: 36.   [28] Matt. 6: 9 f., cp. Luke 11: 2.

. . . Then said he to his disciples, The harvest is plenteous, but the laborers are few. Pray ye therefore the Lord of the harvest, that he send forth laborers into his harvest." [29] For the coming of the kingdom he prayed just as he lived and labored for it, and this great objective in prayer as well as in effort he endeavored to inspire in his disciples.

The high level on which this prayer life of Jesus moved is evident. None of his prayers contained selfish or insincere elements. The subjects of his praying were both subjective and objective. Jesus prayed for others, he prayed for the coming of more workers into the harvest, for bread, the removal of the last cup from him. His prayers cover the gamut of the highest religious aspirations. They are the best proof of the purity and nobility of his own religious life.

It is obvious that Jesus' words on prayer were not uttered as part of a theoretic exposition of the subject. His approach to prayer was direct, sincere, and practical. The theoretic difficulties which modern scientific thinking propounds were not present to his mind. He prayed at first no doubt because prayer was part of his religious inheritance, but then because in prayer he found strength and guidance and a means by which he believed and taught that God's power for good could be brought into the world.

This is not the place for a detailed discussion of the problems of prayer in its relation to a world of cause and effect, but certain aspects of the subject are evident. Taking prayer in the sense in which Jesus practiced it, the withdrawal from the tumult, the sense of the presence of

[29] Matt. 9: 36-38; cp. Luke 10: 2.

God, the endeavor to understand God's will, the devotion of oneself to the universal reign of goodness and truth, the presentation of one's desires and difficulties to God, all this with no set formula, no repetitious rhetoric, but with the utmost sincerity and realism—taking prayer in this sense, certain things are obvious. It is evident that prayer is essential for religion. It is a natural corollary of belief in God, and varies in its intensity with the definiteness with which one believes in God. It is also clear that such prayer is necessary in the modern world. In an age of intellectual flux and moral change, when older standards are being modified and the true values of life are ofttimes obscured and confused, one needs more than ever to strive through prayer to find the eternal values which God is creating in the world. As to the limits of prayer's effectiveness one might debate; its necessity, no religious person would question.

TOPICS FOR DISCUSSION

1. The difficulties of prayer.
2. The wrong kinds of prayer.
3. The effects of prayer on the one praying.
4. Should one pray at stated times and places?
5. Is communion with God in prayer merely emotional, or does it require thought and effort?
6. The Lord's Prayer; its divisions, its main ideas, its two different forms.

WRITTEN ASSIGNMENTS

Write a comment on the Lord's Prayer, comparing the two forms in which it has been preserved, and explaining the meaning of each petition. (Matt. 6: 9-13 and Luke 11: 2-4.)

SUPPLEMENTARY READINGS

On Jesus' teaching on prayer:
Bundy: *The Religion of Jesus*, pp. 170-209.

Bundy: *Our Recovery of Jesus*, Ch. VI.
Robinson: *The Sayings of Jesus*, Ch. X.
Glover: *The Jesus of History*, pp. 110-118.

On the Lord's Prayer:
Plummer: *An Exegetical Commentary to the Gospel of Matthew*, pp. 95-105.
Bundy: *Our Recovery of Jesus*, pp. 307-310.
Rall: *The Teachings of Jesus*, pp. 89, 90.
Smith: *In the Days of His Flesh*, Ch. XIX.
Abingdon Bible Commentary, pp. 965, 966.

On the nature of prayer and its problems:
Fosdick: *The Meaning of Prayer*.
Streeter: *Concerning Prayer*.
Brown: *The Life of Prayer in a World of Science*.

CHAPTER XVIII

JESUS AND THE JEWISH SCRIPTURES

How did Jesus relate these teachings of his as to the kind of righteousness which God desires to the official religion of the day, the religion of the law? Did he declare that his teachings constituted a new religion which his hearers should embrace? Did he declare the body of ceremonial laws—the laws of circumcision, of abstention from certain foods, of the cleansing of vessels and the like —to be valid no longer? What was his attitude toward the Scriptures in which these laws appear?

It will be seen immediately that these questions are of importance from several angles. On the one hand there is involved in it the whole problem of the relation of the early church to the synagogue. Was it from the first a new religion or was it only forced to become one by excommunication and persecution? One recalls the struggle which took place among the first Christians over the question of obedience to the Mosaic regulations. Paul declared that circumcision was of no importance for Christians, but not all the members of the church agreed with him.[1] Indeed on this issue the church of New Testament times was very nearly split in two. In the second place, there is involved in this topic the basic problem of Jesus' conception of the religion of his fathers. Did he feel that it had become an outworn garment now to be discarded for one that was new? His parables of the patch of new cloth upon the old garment and of the new wine which

[1] Acts 15: 1 f.

must be put in new bottles come to mind. Did Jesus regard himself as founding a new religion? In the third place, one must remember that these questions are of practical importance. Many people to-day are uncertain concerning the Old Testament. Was it God's message to men? Have we outgrown it? Amid the arguments pro and con, the bitter feeling and the actual strife, it is well worth inquiring as to Jesus' attitude toward and use of those Scriptures of his people.

I

We must begin by recalling the conception of righteousness which was taught in the synagogues. Righteousness before God consisted in one thing, said the scribes or rabbis—obeying the law of God. And this law had been revealed centuries before to Moses. Whatever was contained in that revealed law was divinely commanded. Man's duty was to obey its precepts—not to reason why. Obedience would bring God's favor, neglect or violation his sure judgment.

This law of Moses contained many different regulations. Some of its regulations prohibited murder, adultery, theft, false witness, the making of graven images of gods, etc. Others gave rules as to abstaining from certain foods. Still others ordained a particular sacrificial cultus which should be carried out by individual and nation. Others demanded separation from the heathen nations around about, lest Israel be led by them into idolatry and sin. All of these various regulations, being part of that divinely revealed law, were binding upon those who would live as God commanded. One could not pick and choose. All the precepts were commands of God. A passage in the Talmud states the belief: "Even if one says, 'The Law is from God with the exception of this or that verse which Moses, not God, spoke from his own mouth,' then applies to him the judgment, The Word of the Lord he has despised." Being divine in its origin, man's duty was to keep its commandments, not to obey some rule of his own contriving.

This conception of righteousness is thoroughly logical. Convinced of the inspiration of the law of Moses the scribes developed the implications of the doctrine with scholastic thoroughness. If the law was given by God to Moses, it contained what was necessary for man's salvation. No one could point out any errors in it or take away anything from it or add anything to it. The prophets who had written after Moses only elaborated and applied to different situations what Moses had decreed. They had nothing essentially new to reveal as to God's will. Any teacher who spoke against the law of Moses was a deceiver of the people and guilty of blasphemy.

With such a conception of revelation it was necessary of course to see to it that God's revealed law was correctly understood and taught. Hence the scribes had built up a professional scholarly guild in which each individual who aspired to become a religious teacher learned from his predecessors and masters the accepted interpretation of the law. This body of official interpretations and applications of the law constituted that oral law or "tradition of the elders" which is spoken of in the New Testament.[2] This body of official decisions had grown up gradually as the result of the study and discussion of generations of scholars. It insured uniformity of teaching and, as far as it was obeyed, uniformity of action on the part of the people.

[2] Mark 7: 3.

Being the official interpretation of the written law, the oral law was regarded as of divine authority also, much as the decisions of various judges concerning the statutory law to-day constitute a body of "case law" which possesses authority in the courts.

This conception of the revealed law of Moses was the basic underlying premise of Judaism. One can see immediately certain consequences which inevitably followed from it. It placed the religious guidance and instruction of the nation in the hands of those who had been professionally trained for the work, and condemned all teaching which did not conform to the accepted pattern. It attributed the greatest possible authority to the law of Moses and branded as heresy all conceptions which did not agree with that law as interpreted by the scribes. On the other hand its positive value was that it emphasized obedience to a code—namely, a goodness of action—and carefully instructed the people in that law. Thus it built up in time the most ethical society which the ancient world produced.

The conception of righteousness current in Jesus' day thus was one of obedience to specific laws of conduct, some of these ethical, others ceremonial or ritual. Both of these sides of the Mosaic legislation had been developed and expanded under the leadership of the scribes. As one attempts to recover from the mists of the past the exact situation with which Jesus had to deal, one finds both of these phases. On the one hand, one meets with the most elaborate sets of requirements concerning the accurate performance of the ceremonial duties of the law, rules concerning vessels that had become ceremonially unclean, concerning the exact payment of the tithes and other taxes due to the temple, concerning the various acts which were legal and illegal on the Sabbath, etc. But one also finds

expressed by the scribes and taught in the synagogue ideals
of conduct of surpassing nobility. Two sayings of the
great Rabbi Hillel, who lived just previous to Jesus, will
illustrate this ethical development. "Be of the disciples
of Aaron," he taught, "one that loves peace, that loves
mankind, and brings them nigh to the Law." [3] To a
Gentile who came asking that he be told the whole law
while standing on one foot Hillel answered, "What you
would not have done to thyself, do not to another; that is
the whole law, the rest is commentary. Go and learn it." [4]
Such sayings, with many others which could be quoted,
show that the Judaism of Jesus' day had reached an exalted
ethical pitch, but this was bound up with and partly obscured by the ceremonial and racial elements which had
come down from its ancient past.

II

Jesus was not educated in the schools. He was not a
professional scribe. He was an artisan, a worker with
his hands. The message which he felt impelled to deliver
to his people came to him from the depths of his own conscience, not from study in the learned guild of scholars.
In the preceding chapters it has been pointed out that its
central element was the simple but revolutionary conception that what God wants of men is a complete and
joyous devotion of the self to the service of others. How
did he relate this to the religion of the law, to the Scriptures of his people? Did he discard the books of Moses,
the writings of the prophets, the psalms, all the great
literature which we call the Old Testament? If he recognized these writings as divinely inspired, how did he

[3] Aboth 1 : 12.   [4] Shabbath 31 a.

justify his teaching which neglected much that they enjoined?

Nobody ever came to Jesus and asked him whether the Scriptures were inspired. That question would not have occurred to a loyal Jew. The belief in the fact was the foundation of the whole Jewish scheme of things. We do happen to have preserved, however, a specific statement of Jesus given in connection with another matter which shows conclusively his view of the Scriptures. The passage is the one in which he speaks of the Messiah as David's son. He introduces the quotation of the opening words of Psalm 110 with the phrase, "David said in the Holy Spirit, Sit thou on my right hand," etc.[5] This phrase was the regular formula used by pious Jews to refer to inspiration by the Divine Spirit. Such expressions as, "Moses said in the Holy Spirit," "Daniel saw in the Holy Spirit," etc., are found constantly in Jewish writings which reflect the thought of the day. The expression passed over into Christian usage and is to be found in such passages as Hebrews 3: 7 and 10: 15.

This expression has more in it than appears at first glance. The Jews divided their Scriptures into three sections: the law, which was the most sacred of all; the prophets, which came next in the order of authority; and a third section called "the Writings." This last was the least venerable and least authoritative of the three. Among these "Writings" was the Book of Psalms. The fact therefore that Jesus refers to the Psalms as having been written "in the Holy Spirit," shows his attitude toward the other books of the Old Testament as well.

To depend too much on an introductory phrase, how-

[5] Mark 12: 36.

ever, is precarious. In this case it is unnecessary. An examination of the gospel material shows that Jesus' reverence for the Scriptures was natural and instinctive. He lived in their language and thought. Constantly he was content simply to give a quotation from the law or the prophets when questions of deep importance were addressed to him. "What is the chief commandment?" and he answers from Deuteronomy and Leviticus.[6] "Will there be a resurrection of the dead?" and he develops his answer from the words of Exodus, "I am the God of Abraham, Isaac, and Jacob." [7] "Is divorce right?" and he quotes from the story of creation, "Male and female created he them." [8] He was so saturated with the very words of its pages that it is sometimes difficult to tell whether he is citing a passage or merely putting his own thoughts in phrases that the prophets had used. Compare for example Matthew 23:23 with Zechariah 7:9. Again and again he uses the words of some prophecy or psalm in sentences of his own. Note how he closes his lament over Jerusalem with words borrowed from Psalm 118, "For I say unto you, Ye shall not see me henceforth, till ye shall say, Blessed is he that cometh in the name of the Lord." [9]

Furthermore he quite clearly regarded the Scriptures as containing the moral requirements of the coming kingdom. A rich man came to him and asked, "What shall I do to inherit eternal life?" Jesus was content to reply, "Thou knowest the commandments: Do not commit adultery, do not kill, do not steal, do not bear false witness, defraud not, honor thy father and thy mother." [10] On

[6] Mark 12:29.   [8] Mark 10:6.   [10] Mark 10:19.
[7] Mark 12:26.   [9] Matt. 23:39.

a second occasion a lawyer asked, "Master, what shall I do to inherit eternal life?" Jesus answered, "How readest thou in the law?" and when the man quoted passages from Deuteronomy and Leviticus enjoining love to God and to one's neighbor, he said to him, "Thou hast answered right. This do and thou shalt live." [11] Obedience to these words of the law, he taught, would bring eternal life.

But even deeper are we carried by the evidence as to Jesus' own personal dependence on the Old Testament for help and guidance. When the temptation came in three alluring forms we find him each time turning for his reply to words from his Bible. Luke's dramatic story of the initial appearance in Nazareth is just as significant: "He opened the book, and found the place where it was written,

> The Spirit of the Lord is upon me,
>
> Because he anointed me to preach good tidings to the
>   poor:
>
> He hath sent me to proclaim release to the captives,
>
> And recovering of sight to the blind,
>
> To set at liberty them that are bruised,
>
> To proclaim the acceptable year of the Lord.

And he closed the book . . . and began to say unto them, To-day hath this scripture been fulfilled in your ears." [12] Thus he was content to say of himself and his work, "It is like Isaiah's description." When criticized for permitting his disciples to pluck grain on the Sabbath he cited as a precedent the story of David and the shewbread told in 1 Samuel.[13] When he drove out the money

---

[11] Luke 10: 25 ff.; cp. Mark 12: 28 ff.   [13] Mark 2: 26.

[12] Luke 4: 17 ff.

changers and the traders from the temple he quoted the words of the prophets, "My house shall be called a house of prayer."[14]   When his opponents faced him with words of Moses which contradicted his own teaching concerning divorce, he went to the pages of Genesis for authoritative support for his view.[15]   To the Scriptures, too, he turned for light on the perplexing problem of his own fate.   In the sacred writings he found assurance that the path of suffering and death which he was forced to tread was in accordance with God's will.[16]   And in the last moments of his life we find upon his lips the opening words of the twenty-second Psalm.[17]

And then his teaching.   The description of God as "Our Father" he had found in the Scriptures.[18]   Jesus describes him as the God of Abraham, Isaac, and Jacob.[19] The kingdom of God which he announced is to be understood only by going back to the writings of the prophets. The great principle of love which he declared to be God's primary commandment had been affirmed in the words of the law.[20]   The title "Son of Man" which he seems to have applied to himself came from the book of Daniel.[21] His rejection of the regal and military conception of the Messiah he based on Psalm 110, which, he declared, proved that the Messiah would not be like David.[22]   All of this supplies the content and the meaning when we find Jesus describing the Scriptures as "the word of God" and "the commandment of God."[23]

[14] Mark 11: 17.   [16] Mark 9: 12 and 14: 21.
[15] Mark 10: 6.   [17] Mark 15: 34.
[18] See Isa. 63: 16 and 64: 8; Jer. 3: 4, Exod. 4: 22, Deut. 32: 6, etc.
[19] Mark 12: 26.   [20] Deut. 6: 4 f. and Lev. 19: 18.
[21] Dan. 7: 13.   [22] Mark 12: 36 f.   [23] Mark 7: 8, 9, and 13.

III

On the teachings of these books Jesus had meditated profoundly. He had heard them from his earliest childhood, he had listened to them read in the synagogue services, he had witnessed in the great temple court at Jerusalem the sacrificial ritual which they commanded. They furnished the spiritual food on which he had been nourished.

As he meditated on these teachings he had become convinced that not all of their precepts were of equal importance and value. Certain ones were of vastly greater importance in the sight of God than others. Indeed there were two commands which he felt to sum up and focus the meaning of the whole divine revelation. These were the commands which were to be found in Deuteronomy and in Leviticus that men should love God with all their strength and their neighbors as themselves. His spiritual intuition convinced him that this love was "the one thing needful," the goodness which the Father in heaven desired of his children. This unselfish love would even characterize the kingdom of God to come, for it was of absolute value and worth and nothing superior to it could be conceived.

In comparison with this teaching of love and service Jesus regarded the other commands of the Scriptures as subordinate and secondary. We shall see that he had no attack to make upon the ritual. He spoke of the temple as hallowing the gold used in its service, and of the altar as making holy the gift offered upon it.[24] He enjoined one who had quarreled with his brother first to become reconciled with him, then to return to the temple and offer

[24] Matt. 23: 17, 19.

his sacrifice.[25]   To his own disciples he gave the example of paying the regular tax for the support of the temple.[26] Against the exercises of the Day of Atonement, the various feasts of the Jewish calendar, the laws of circumcision, the regulations of the ritual and cultus, he made no attack.   But he perceived that his countrymen in great numbers, and even the religious leaders themselves, had missed the supremely important thing amid the multiplicity of rules and laws.   To love God and one's fellow man completely was the universal and imperative duty of life.   Nothing could take the place of or be allowed to hinder that.   How pitiful were the attempts to please God by tithing mint and anise and cummin while neglecting the weighty matters of the law!

This conception of the essential nature of the goodness which God desires became the central part of his teaching of the people.   Those who were blessed were the peacemakers, the pure in heart, those persecuted for righteousness' sake.   Man's duty was to forgive even an enemy, for God gives his gifts of rain and sunshine to good and evil alike.   One should do unto others as one would have them do unto oneself—that was the sum of the law and the prophets.   One should feed the hungry, give drink to the thirsty, entertain the stranger, clothe the naked, and visit those in prison in order to receive the approval of the Great Judge.   Not only did he teach this standard of righteousness, but he demonstrated it in his own life.

This teaching and this demonstration brought him into conflict with the scribes.   For occasions arose when acts of service and love inevitably involved neglecting or violating some of the commands of the ceremonial law.

[25] Matt. 5: 24.   [26] Matt. 17: 27.

They had no objection to Jesus' teachings on love and service, indeed they said things very similar themselves. But they did object when he allowed this very general ideal to interfere with obedience to some of the specific commands of the Mosaic law. How this conflict came about will become clear if we consider several of the actual situations which arose.

1. Within the bounds of Judaism there were a number of people who were notorious for their neglect of the law. There were of course such public sinners as the harlots and the bandits. Then there were the publicans who disregarded the law and cheated the people by their excessive charges at the tollhouses. Besides these there were others who were known to be careless about the payment of the tithes commanded by the law or who neglected the laws of ceremonial purity. All such violators of the law were put in a class together and scrupulously avoided by the Pharisees. They were called "the people of the land." Law-observing Jews were forbidden to eat with them, to trade with them, to marry any member of the class, and in other ways to ostracize them. The motive behind this separatism was the practical judgment that if one associated with such people, one would be drawn inevitably into violations of the law.

But it was Jesus' great objective to bring all such people into the kingdom of God. Instead of ostracizing them or treating them as outcasts, he ate with them, stayed in their homes, and became known as "the friend of publicans and sinners." By so doing it was inevitable that he himself violated some of the Mosaic regulations. Even if prohibited foods were not served on such tables, the dishes used were ceremonially unclean, the furniture was not pure, in all probability the food itself had not been prepared with attention to the Mosaic dietary laws nor tithed in accordance with the law. Here arose a conflict of Scriptural duties. Should one refrain from intercourse with such people in order to avoid these violations of the law? Or should one ignore these ceremonial requirements in order to befriend and win these ostracized individuals and groups?

In this issue Jesus did not hesitate. He knew that these laws stood in the Scriptures. But to obey them at the expense of the opportunity to serve and save the outcasts was to him a perversion of the Scriptures and a misunderstanding of the true will of God. Not only his mission but his ideal of life was to "seek and to save the lost." [27] "Those who are well," he answered his critics, "do not need the physician, but those who are sick. I came not to call the righteous, but sinners." [28] "There shall be joy in heaven over one sinner that repenteth," he declared on another occasion, "more than over ninety and nine righteous persons who need no repentance." [29] He told the parable of the shepherd who left his sheep in the fold to go out in the mountains and find the one that was lost, concluding the story with the statement, "Even so it is not the will of your Father which is in heaven that one of these little ones should perish." [30] This was the sort of activity which he declared to be God's chief command, not the observance of rules and seasons.

Jesus thus disregarded the ritual laws involved and became known as the "friend of publicans and sinners." [31] Such limitless service of others he declared to be the basic teaching of the law. It was enunciated in the command

[27] Luke 19: 10. [28] Mark 2: 17. [29] Luke 15: 7.
[30] Matt. 18: 14. [31] Matt. 11: 19 and Luke 7: 34.

to love one's neighbor as one's self. It was illustrated in the story of David, who gave the sacred loaves of the shewbread to satisfy the needs of his famished men. It was proclaimed by the prophets in words like those of Hosea, "I desire mercy, and not sacrifice; and the knowledge of God more than burnt offerings." [32] If men would only read the Scriptures with understanding, they would see its teaching as to the will of God.

Therefore Jesus mingled freely with the "people of the land." He violated the laws as to vessels. He ate no doubt untithed food and food which had not been prepared in the proper way. He did not require his disciples to practice the custom of ceremonial hand-washing. He had no criticism of these laws (except in the case of the last named, which was not part of the Mosaic code), but he refused to accept the fact of obedience or disobedience of them determining man's righteousness in God's sight. Dishes could not make a man clean or unclean before God.[33] Nor could hands washed a certain way, nor the eating of certain foods.[34] It was obedience to "the weightier matters of the law" which counted. He refused to let these ceremonial precepts, even though they stood in the Scriptures, hinder or prevent his mission to those children of Abraham whom he felt most needed his message.

2. An even clearer illustration of the way in which Jesus subordinated certain precepts of the law to others of deeper import and value is afforded by his attitude toward the Sabbath.

In the books of Genesis, Exodus, and Leviticus appear

[32] Hos. 6: 6.

[33] Luke 11: 39 f.; Matt. 23: 25 f.

[34] Mark 7: 2 f. and verse 15.

certain categorical commands: "The seventh day shall be to you a holy day; . . . whosoever doeth any work therein shall be put to death." [35]   "On the seventh day is a sabbath of solemn rest; . . . ye shall do no manner of work." [36]   "Ye shall kindle no fire throughout your habitations on the sabbath day." [37]   Such laws make no distinction between work for one motive and work for another.   Healing is as much forbidden as harvesting—as the Pharisees repeatedly insisted.   Plucking grain on the Sabbath day and husking it in one's hands violated the principle of the Sabbath just as much as reaping on a larger scale.   If the law be God's revelation, then such acts as healing the sick and plucking grain, though good in themselves, must be postponed until the following day. To do otherwise was to desecrate the Sabbath and hold up before the people an example of disregard for God's law.

Now Jesus read with reverence the same passages, but he did not read them mechanically.   He read with a deep sense of their moral purpose and of the value of the Sabbath institution.   He remembered that in two lists of the Ten Commandments the purpose of the Sabbath is explained to be the humanitarian desire "that thy manservant and thy maidservant may rest as well as thou, and thou shalt remember that thou wast a servant in the land of Egypt." [38]   And he allowed no statement of Sabbath duties, whether in the law or out of it, to contradict this fundamental purpose of making the Sabbath serve human need.   The law declared, "Whosoever doeth any work therein shall be put to death," but he went back of such legal expression and challenged his opponents with the question, "Is it lawful on the sabbath day to do good or to do harm, to save life or to kill?" [39]   He permitted his disciples to satisfy their hunger by plucking on the Sabbath the grains of wheat, an act regarded as labor, citing the Scriptural precedent of David and the shewbread. He healed upon the Sabbath various individuals, pointing out that the law permitted lifting animals from a pit into which they had fallen on the Sabbath. "How much more then is a man of more value than a sheep?" [40]   Service to men and the saving of life Jesus thus regarded as expressive of the spirit and teaching of the law, even though such acts might violate the specific law of Sabbath rest.

3. A third illustration of Jesus' subordination of certain portions of the Scriptures to other portions is afforded by his teaching on divorce. The facts in this case have been considered and need not detain us at this point. The Pharisees asked Jesus concerning divorce. "Moses said for the husband to give her a bill of divorce and put her away," they pointed out.[41] And in Deuteronomy 24: 1-7 stands the law to which they referred. Nevertheless Jesus held to his position. He had seen the cruelty and pain involved in such a system, and he was convinced that it did not represent God's purpose for marriage. "For the hardness of your hearts Moses wrote you this commandment," he replied. The real purpose of God was to be found expressed not in that verse but in the story of creation, where in the very beginning it is stated, "Male and female created he them." Moses' per-

---

[39] Mark 4 f.   [40] Matt. 12: 11 f.   [41] Mark 10 2 ff.

mission of divorce had to be understood as a concession from this divine purpose.

4. The Old Testament also had much to say about a Messiah of military character and a kingdom of political grandeur. But though Jesus regarded the Scriptures as inspired, he remained unaffected by these passages. In the kingdom of which he spoke one finds no hint of such conceptions as Ezekiel's valley full of the dry bones of Israel's enemies, nor of Jerusalem becoming "a cup of reeling unto all the peoples round about her," [42] nor of a Messiah who should "break (the nations) with a rod of iron and dash them in pieces like a potter's vessel." [43] But there are other passages of the Old Testament on which Jesus did found his mission: the passage from Isaiah which he read in the synagogue of Nazareth; the phrase "Son of Man," which became his title; the cry of Zechariah, "Rejoice, O Jerusalem: behold, thy king cometh unto thee meek, and riding upon an ass." [44]   Probably even more present to his mind than these were the great passages of Isaiah 49, 52, and 53 which sing of a suffering Servant of Jehovah, who was despised and rejected of men, a man of sorrows and acquainted with grief, wounded for our transgressions and bruised for our iniquities. In these descriptions he found his own lot most truly pictured and the end of his own career foreshadowed. All the sayings of a king glorious before his enemies and surrounded by his court he put aside, and went to his death saying to his own intimate disciples, no doubt with these passages from Isaiah in his mind, "The Son of man goeth even as it is written of him." [45]

---

[42] Zech. 12: 2.

[43] Psa. 2: 9.

[44] Zech. 9: 9. See Matt. 21: 5.

[45] Mark 14: 21.

Thus we see that Jesus not only accepted the statement but lived in the assurance that the Old Testament was an inspired revelation of God to men. But he did not regard that revelation as requiring mechanical obedience to the letter nor as all of the same value. Certain portions had to be supplemented by others, some were given in an earlier day and were adapted to the hardness of men's hearts. One needed to get back of the letter to the spirit of the whole. He regarded his own message as but the unfolding and development of ideas which the Old Testament had expressed. "I came not to destroy the law, but to fulfill it." In its pages he found messages of God and of life which were of eternal validity. "Thou shalt love the Lord thy God with all thy heart"; "Like as a father pitieth his children, so the Lord pitieth them that fear him"; "The Lord is my shepherd; I shall not want"; "Put away the evil of your doings from before mine eyes"; "Seek judgment, relieve the oppressed, judge the fatherless, plead for the widow." With these and numberless other precepts before his mind, no wonder Jesus was willing to say to the young man, "Thou knowest the commandments; do these and thou shalt live." But always it was obedience to the spirit which comes to fullest expression in passages like those just given.

Jesus had no intention of founding a new religion, but rather of inducing men to live in accordance with God's will as it had been revealed in the law and the prophets. But those ancient writings had to be understood aright. He did not regard them as a series of precepts and teachings all on the same plane of value. They could not be read and obeyed mechanically. One must see certain truths which they taught so clearly and strongly that they would become tools by which the remainder could be examined, rejected, or interpreted anew. It was Jesus' work to disentangle, restate, and develop this eternal element which he found in the law and the prophets. And in so doing and in exemplifying this perfect obedience in his own life, he added to that revelation its consummation and fulfillment.

TOPICS FOR DISCUSSION

1. The several divisions of the Jewish Scriptures, their relative antiquity and importance.

2. Jewish attitude toward the law of Moses. Compare this with the attitude of some Christian circles toward the Bible.

3. The logic of the scribal criticism of Jesus' neglect of certain laws.

4. Jesus' distinction between what was primary and secondary in God's sight. Is such a distinction as easy to grasp as hard and fast rules of behavior?

5. The connection between Jesus' attitude toward the Scriptures (*i. e.,* the Mosaic law) and his death.

6. Early Christian misunderstandings of Jesus' attitude toward the law. The reflection of this in the passage Matt. 5: 17-20.

WRITTEN ASSIGNMENTS

Read Mark 10: 17-20, Luke 10: 25-28, Matt. 5: 17-20, Mark 2: 23–3: 6, Mark 7: 1-15, Mark 10: 2-12, and write on the topic, "The two sides to Jesus' view of the Scriptures."

SUPPLEMENTARY READINGS

On Jewish conception of the inspiration of their Scriptures:
    Moore: *Judaism,* Vol. I, pp. 235-251.
    Branscomb: *Jesus and the Law of Moses,* pp. 5-33.
On the oral law of the scribes:
    Herford: *The Pharisees,* Ch. III.
    Moore: *Op. cit.,* Vol. I, pp. 251-263.
    Branscomb: *Op. cit.,* pp. 33-49.
On Jewish "joy in the law":
    Schechter: *Some Aspects of Rabbinic Judaism,* Ch. XI.
On Jesus' attitude toward the Mosaic law:
    Branscomb: *Op. cit.,* Ch. VII.
    Bosworth: *The Life and Teachings of Jesus,* Ch. X-XII.

Dickey: *The Constructive Revolution of Jesus*, Ch. II.
Scott: *The Ethical Teaching of Jesus*, Ch. IV.
Rashdall: *Conscience and Christ*, pp. 95-108.
Klausner: *Jesus of Nazareth*, pp. 363-376.
On the saying in Mark 7: 15:
Branscomb: *Op. cit.*, pp. 175-182.
Montefiore: *The Synoptic Gospels*, Vol. I, pp. 152-161.
On the saying in Matt. 5: 17:
Branscomb: *Op. cit.*, pp. 226-229.
Montefiore: *Op. cit.*, Vol II, pp. 46-55.

CHAPTER XIX

JESUS AND THE TEMPLE

It has already been remarked that in Judaism of the first century, as in other ancient religions, no very distinct line was drawn between ceremonial and ethical duties. Both were parts of the revealed will of God. The books of Moses pass from laws regulating the sacrifices and the annual festivals to those dealing with the relations of men to their neighbors without any consciousness of any difference between them. In the Judaism of Jesus' day the ceremonial and the moral, the ritual and the ethical, were all parts of the one great many-sided code of social and individual dealings which had the sanction both of the Scriptures and of the great leaders and teachers of the past. True, there are some sayings of the rabbis which recognize that the ritual duties in themselves were on a different level from the ethical duties. Johanan ben Zakki, the rabbi who reorganized Judaism after the destruction of Jerusalem in 70 A.D., for example, speaking of the regulation that one who touches a dead body becomes unclean and must purify himself with water, declared, "A corpse does not actually defile nor water make clean, but it is a command of the King of Kings." [1] But the fact that the King of Kings had definitely and specifically commanded these various ceremonial precepts made them exactly as obligatory as the other duties enjoined in the law.

Of course much of this Jewish ritual was a matter of

[1] *Tanhuma* (ed. Buber), Hukkat No. 26.

social habit as well as of religion. For example, the prohibition of certain foods involved no burden on the people. Such forbidden foods would not be served on respectable tables, nor would they be sold in the markets except in communities where Gentiles also lived. Similarly the observance of the Sabbath and the regular festivals of the religious calendar would be the custom of the community, just as Thanksgiving, Easter, and Christmas are observed to-day by people who have no church allegiance. Much that has been written about the "burden of the law" upon Jews of the time of Jesus is beside the point. The law in most respects was a noble standard of religion and morals, a very humanitarian code of law, a standard of personal decency, and, being these things, it was also an intellectual delight to those who studied it.

In the case of the laws concerning ceremonial uncleanness it must be remembered that many of these would not be a matter of vital concern to people who did not live in Jerusalem and frequent the temple. Ceremonial uncleanness had only this bad effect, that it barred the person from entering the temple while in such a state. Consequently Galileans and others who only went to the temple on rare occasions did not bother much about such regulations. It is obvious also that much of the ceremonial law found in the Pentateuch deals with the manner in which the sacrifices shall be performed and other matters of temple routine, and these would be the concern of the priests only.

The difficulties in connection with the ritual and ceremonial laws therefore were not as great as many of the older theological books might lead one to believe. They seem to have centered chiefly around three points. In the first place there was the question of taxes which went to the support of the temple, the priests, and the levites. The fact that these taxes were sanctioned by religion does not seem to have made them any easier to pay. There were a number of different taxes, but the basic one was the tithes of the agricultural produce of the land. The peasantry, and indeed the people as a whole, seem to have been very lax in this matter and to have been upbraided constantly by the leaders for defrauding God in the person of his ministry in this fashion. It was one of the characteristics of the pious group, the Pharisees, that they paid their tithes scrupulously, tithing even the mint, anise, and cummin which grew in their gardens.

A second set of difficulties centered around the laws of ceremonial uncleanness. These laws originally had in mind people who lived near the temple and frequented it, so that the regulation that one could not come "before the Lord" (*i. e.*, into the temple) in an unclean state, was tantamount to requiring that the people should largely keep themselves ceremonially clean. But as pointed out, these laws could be and were virtually ignored by great numbers of Jews who resided away from Jerusalem. This caused considerable distress to the more pious Pharisees, who contended that these laws about ritual cleanness should be observed even though one was not expecting to enter the temple. They banded together, as we have seen, and separated themselves from all who were not so careful.

A third area of difficulty was created by the inevitable fact that occasions arose when different laws conflicted with each other. For example, the law that a child should be circumcised on the eighth day frequently conflicted with the law of Sabbath rest; the duties enjoined upon the priests in the temple also conflicted with the laws of

the Sabbath; the law of exact fulfillment of vows conflicted sometimes with duties which had been disavowed
by a rash oath. In all such cases the scribes worked out
a system of precedents which they justified by casuistical
arguments. But more important than these conflicts was
the fact that the ritual and ceremonial duties sometimes
conflicted with the ethical obligations which the law enjoined. We shall see that Jesus was particularly sensitive
to this sort of conflict, and that his position with regard
to them involved him in very serious difficulties.

So much by way of introduction.

II

The gospel accounts, though written some years after
the events they record and after the Church had separated
from Judaism and had almost entirely ceased to observe
the Mosaic law, make it clear that Jesus made no attack
on the ritual and ceremonial practices of Judaism. Indeed it is evident that so far as external practices were
concerned he lived the life of a loyal and devoted Jew.

In the first place, the very garments that he wore were
in accordance with the provisions of the law. Mark
speaks of how the people sought to touch the "border" of
his garment.[2] The word here translated "border" really
means the fringe or tassel which Jews wore on the corners of their robes in accordance with the command in
Numbers 15: 37, 38: "Jehovah spake unto Moses, saying, Speak unto the children of Israel, and bid them that
they make them tassels in the corners of their garments
throughout their generations." This tassel or fringe virtually constituted a uniform by which a Jew could be

[2] Mark 6: 56.

recognized and distinguished from a Gentile, so much so
that it was forbidden to sell a garment to a Gentile unless
the tassels were first removed.[3]   Obviously such matters
of dress must have been dictates of custom and social
habit rather than of theology, but they were customs only
of good Jews.   Jesus in one of his rebukes of the scribes
and Pharisees ridiculed them for making their tassels or
borders wide[4] and we can be sure that he was not ostentatious in this matter any more than in any other phase
of his personal piety.   The fact remains, however, that he
conformed in this particular to the mode enjoined in the
law book.

Jesus' attitude toward fasting confirms this general
conclusion.   The law did not require personal or private
fasts, its only requirement in this direction being the fast
on the Great Day of Atonement.   But from time immemorial fasting had been a means by which men "afflicted
themselves" while supplicating God or while preparing
for some great undertaking or decisions.[5]   Jesus imposed
no fasts upon his disciples; indeed he was criticized because he did not do so.[6]   His reputation was definitely
non-ascetic.[7]   But he did not object to fasting.   On the
contrary Jesus himself fasted, we are told, for forty days
and nights just before beginning his ministry.[8]   He also
gave instructions to his disciples as to the proper way to
fast.[9]   Thus it is clear that he believed in the value of

[3] *Jewish Encyclopedia,* Vol. V, p. 522.   [4] Matt. 23: 5.

[5] As when David fasted in supplication to God for the life of his
child (2 Sam. 12: 16); or when the Christian leaders in Antioch
fasted before sending Paul and Barnabas on their mission (Acts 13:
2).   [6] Mark 2: 18 ff.   [7] Matt. 11: 19.

[8] Matt. 4: 2.   The number forty is probably conventional.

[9] Matt. 6: 16 f.

external practices as an aid to religious thought and devotion.

Similarly in the case of the regular religious festivals of the Jewish calendar. The gospels mention a number of these in which he took part. In the Gospel of John we read of a journey to Jerusalem in the earlier part of his ministry in order to celebrate the Passover.[10] An unnamed feast mentioned in 5: 1 of the same gospel has been conjectured to be the Feast of Purim, a rather boisterous feast which celebrated the deliverance of the Jews from Haman as narrated in the book of Esther. In 7: 2 we find Jesus again at Jerusalem joining in the celebration of the Feast of Tabernacles, and in 10: 22 he is present at the Feast of Dedication. Finally, all four gospels speak of the Passover meal which his disciples were preparing when he was hurried off to trial and execution.[11] The references to these feasts are largely incidental and indicate how thoroughly Jesus participated in the religious cultus of his compatriots.

The two chief institutions of Judaism, however, were the synagogue and the temple. It has already been pointed out that Jesus was a constant attendant at the synagogue.[12] Did he have the same appreciation of the purely formal services at the temple? Did he have any sympathy with a worship of God which consisted in the sacrifice of doves and oxen and sheep?

Whatever we might have expected to be Jesus' attitude

[10] John 2: 13.

[11] The Synoptic Gospels describe the Last Supper as the Passover meal (Mark 14: 12 ff.). According to John 13: 1 and 18: 28, however, the Passover meal was not eaten until the evening of the day of the crucifixion. John's account for certain reasons appears preferable.

[12] See above, p. 99 f.

toward the temple, the fact is that he had great reverence
for it.   There are several pieces of evidence which show
this.   In the first place we have just noted that Jesus
made a number of pilgrimages to the temple even before
his last journey to Jerusalem.   Not to count the journey
when he was only twelve years old and was found by his
parents in the temple, there are four such journeys to
Jerusalem mentioned in John.[13]   The narratives show
that it was in the temple that he spent his time while in
the Holy City.

But more important than the fact of his repeated presence there are certain of his sayings concerning the temple.   "Woe unto you, ye blind guides, that say, Whosoever shall swear by the temple, it is nothing; but whosoever shall swear by the gold of the temple, he is bound.
Ye fools and blind: for which is greater, the gold or the
temple that hath sanctified the gold?   And, Whosoever
shall swear by the altar, it is nothing; but whosoever shall
swear by the gift upon the altar, he is bound.   Ye blind:
for which is greater, the gift, or the altar that sanctifieth
the gift?" [14]   Even more indicative of his attitude is the
saying which follows these words: "He that sweareth
by the temple, sweareth by it, and by *Him that dwelleth
in it*." [15]   From these words it is clear that Jesus thought
of the temple as God's house in a very definite and special
sense.

In the light of this fact it is not surprising that he
made no attack upon the temple ceremonies or sacrifices,
but on the contrary rather regarded them as of religious
value.   The gift (sacrificial offering) laid upon the altar

[13] John 2: 13, 5: 1, 7: 14, 10: 22.   [15] Matt. 23: 21.
[14] Matt. 23: 16 ff.

becomes sacred, he said in the words quoted above. More familiar is the saying in the Sermon on the Mount: "If thou art offering thy gift at the altar, and there rememberest that thy brother hath aught against thee, leave there thy gift before the altar, and go thy way, first be reconciled to thy brother, and then come and offer thy gift." [16] Thus he had no word of criticism or condemnation for the sacrificial offerings themselves. Rather, by his word, he encouraged them. It is not surprising to note that he paid the half-shekel tax which all loyal Jews paid for the support of the temple.[17]

This reverence for the temple comes to strong expression in the dramatic incident with which he opened his final ministry in Jerusalem.[18] Coming into the great outer court of the temple on the first day after his triumphal entry, he found in its midst vendors, hucksters, money changers, oxen, sheep, doves, noise, and confusion. Worse than these was the spirit of bargaining and profit-seeking which reigned instead of that reverence and awe which he felt should dominate all who entered that sacred place. So deeply did he value the temple and what it stood for, that he flung down his challenge to the priestly authorities who controlled the temple and who reaped their share of the profit from these exploitations of the piety of the people. Seizing a piece of rope and quoting the words of the prophets, "My house shall be a house of prayer, but you have made it a den of thieves," he drove them out of the temple inclosure. No doubt the Galilean pilgrims, indignant at the profiteering prices which they found themselves obliged to pay, joined in the undertaking, while the guards who always stood at the gates were

[16] Matt. 5: 23 f.   [17] Matt. 17: 24 ff.   [18] Mark 11: 15.

either unwilling or afraid to interfere.   To Jesus the
temple was the shrine of his people, ordained by the law,
and hallowed by a thousand scenes of partiotism and devotion.   On that spot the nation's sacrifices had been offered since the days of King Solomon.   In its courts
saints like Simeon and Anna had worshiped, waiting for
the kingdom of God.   There devout mothers had presented their children to the Lord and penitent individuals
like the publican in the parable had turned to God.   It had
been the nation's place of worship for many generations,
and so far as it lay within his power, Jesus would keep it
such in all its purity.

Over against this varied evidence stands the statement
in Mark that Jesus declared that the temple was going to
be destroyed.   "And as he went forth out of the temple
one of his disciples saith unto him, Teacher, behold what
manner of stones and what manner of buildings!   And
Jesus saith unto him, Seest then these great buildings?
There shall not be left here one stone upon another which
shall not be thrown down." [19]   This statement is not only
repeated in Matthew and Luke, but the charge that Jesus
declared that the temple would be destroyed appears in a
garbled form in the accounts of his trial.[20]   Furthermore,
a year or so later Stephen is charged before the council
with having taught that "this Jesus of Nazareth shall destroy this holy place." [21]   Evidently Jesus did say something about a coming destruction of the temple.

Why did he say this?   In the light of the above evidence of his constant presence in the temple and his appreciation of its services, such a prophecy cannot have
been because of any belief that the temple was an impedi-

[19] Mark 13: 1 f.   [20] Mark 14: 58.   [21] Acts 6: 14.

ment to the progress of true religion. No such thought can be found in the records of his work. He never denounced the sacrifices or spoke against the temple.[22]

The explanation is very likely to be found in a different direction. Toward the close of his life it is evident that Jesus spoke repeatedly of the refusal of the nation's leaders and, indeed, of "this generation" to heed his teachings. Matthew 23 is a vehement condemnation of the scribes and Pharisees. "Behold, your house is left unto you desolate," he is quoted as saying to unheeding Jerusalem.[23] The parable of the vineyard in Matthew closes with the words, "Therefore I say unto you, The kingdom of God shall be taken away from you, and shall be given to a nation bringing forth the fruits thereof."[24] This whole area of Jesus' teaching has undoubtedly been colored by the experiences of the early church and it is difficult to recover exactly what was Jesus' position in this respect. But this much seems certain: Whatever statement he may have made about the destruction of the temple is to be taken as a prophecy of a punishment to fall upon the unrepentant nation, rather than as an indication of a view of the temple as an impediment to the progress of the kingdom.

[22] Matt. 12:7, which quotes the saying from Hosea, "I desire mercy, and not sacrifice," has been regarded as proof of such an attitude on Jesus' part. The one passage, however, can scarcely support so radical a conclusion. In the first place it appears only as an addition by the first evangelist to the narrative which he takes from Mark. In the second place, even if an authentic saying, the Semitic idiom would not necessarily mean other than, "I desire mercy more than sacrifice," just as "Lay not up treasures on earth, but lay up for yourselves treasures in heaven" is not a condemnation of earthly treasures as such, but an emphatic assertion of that which is of superior worth.

[23] Matt. 23:38, Luke 13:35.   [24] Matt. 21:43.

III

Thus it is quite evident that Jesus did not object to the ceremony and form of his ancestral religion. He would not have shared the feeling of some modern sects who ban all musical instruments from their churches and who refuse to have any sort of ordered service. Jesus on the contrary found value in the cultus ordained by the law. It spoke to him of things unseen, of the spiritual heroes of former days and of spiritual values which could be expressed only by means of symbol. It is true that the world is too much with us, and the life of the spirit must be nourished by experiences which portray symbolically and make vivid that which is beautiful and true and good.

But constantly where emphasis has been placed upon form and ceremony these things have come to be regarded as important in themselves. Not the effect upon the worshiper, the thing which is symbolized, but the symbol itself is regarded as of vital importance. Thus the history of the church tells many a story of people who have regarded the *way* of ordaining the ministry or of baptizing converts or of administering the Lord's Supper as in themselves matters of tremendous moment which justified not only separation from other Christian organizations but even antagonism toward them. Over and over again forms of service have displaced justice, mercy, and faith as the weightier matters of the law of God.

Now Jesus' appreciation of the temple and of the elaborate ritual that went with it was coupled with a clear sense of the secondary importance of all such matters of ceremony and form. The evidence for this is more or less familiar and some of it has already been cited:

1. In the first place he made it quite clear that sacrifice

was not so important as reconciliation with an estranged brother, indeed that it was of no value if the spirit of the one offering the gift was filled with enmity.[25] The vigor and strength of the saying quoted above on this point is not appreciated unless one recalls the circumstances of the time. Sacrifices at the great altar at Jerusalem were necessarily rare experiences for those who lived outside Jerusalem. Many people might never have the privilege of making such an offering, and for the great majority it would occur only a few times during their lives. In any case such an experience would be one of the supreme religious moments of a lifetime. Now Jesus says that if at such a moment one recalled that one had done an injury to some neighbor or acquaintance and had not made proper restitution, one should leave the gift at the great altar, and first effect a reconciliation with the angry brother, and then return and offer in joy and gratitude the gift. Not even those rare moments of sacrifice at the nation's shrine were as important or significant as reconciliation with a person one had injured.

2. A second clue to Jesus' evaluation of the temple and its ritual is afforded by his remark about an offering which he saw a widow place in the treasury of the temple. As he sat in the court watching, several rich men came up and cast very considerable sums into the trumpet-shaped receptacles into which gifts for the temple were placed. "And there came a poor widow, and she cast in two small coins worth about a penny. And he called his disciples, and said to them, Verily I say unto you, this poor widow cast in more than all they that are casting into the treasury: for they all did cast in of their abundance, but she of

her want did cast in all that she had, even all her living." [26]   That saying shows the way in which Jesus translated all the external side of religion into terms of inner motive and evaluated it from that standpoint.   The priests who were present guarding the chests and the bystanders who were in the court no doubt regarded the widow's gift as not worth notice.   What would that contribution amount to in paying for the temple services or in caring for the poor?   Such people, like conventional ecclesiastics of our own day, interested in constructing great edifices and keeping the machinery of a religious organization going, looked rather to the total.   Jesus, on the contrary, saw the heroism of the widow's tiny gift. Though unnoticed by men, he declared that it was a great gift in God's sight, greater than any of the others which had been made.   These other gifts would provide many more sacrifices, would buy expensive equipment for the temple or take care of many priests, but in God's sight the sincere service of the heart was worth more than all these external symbols of religious worship.

3. A more specific saying was one which Jesus uttered in connection with a criticism of his disciples for violating the law of Sabbath rest.   They had rubbed the wheat grains between their hands in order thereby to husk it and satisfy their hunger.   The Pharisees objected on the grounds that this was plainly to violate the law of the Sabbath.   Jesus answered by referring to a famous Scriptural instance of the violation of the ceremonial law.   On the table at the sanctuary there stood certain loaves of bread called the shewbread, and it was unlawful for anyone to eat this bread except the priests.   One day David

[26] Mark 12: 41 ff.

and his men came to the sanctuary at Nob in a famished
condition, and being unable to obtain common bread they
ate the holy loaves which stood upon the altar.[27]   According to the notions of the time—and of ours in parallel cases—that was high sacrilege.   But Jesus read the
story and saw in it a basic principle of religion.   The
holiness of the shewbread was of no importance in comparison with the hunger of men.   The priest at Nob was
right in giving the shewbread to David and his men.   No
ceremonial law, no holiness of *things,* should be allowed
to interfere with service to men and women.   That Jesus
grasped the principle quite clearly seems evident from the
fact that the criticism of his disciples was not for eating
holy bread, but for violating a quite different law of the
cultus.

4. A fourth phase of the evidence as to Jesus' attitude
toward the ceremonial can be stated quite briefly, for the
data was explained in the last chapter.   One of the fundamental issues with which he was faced was that of the
separation of the pious Pharisees from the "people of the
land" who constantly broke regulations of the law.   To
fraternize with such people was dangerous from the le-
galistic standpoint, particularly to eat with them.   Their
food was not prepared in the proper way, their dishes
were not kept ceremonially clean, their food was not correctly tithed, the furniture in their houses was religiously
defiling from contact with forbidden things, and even
their garments were not ritually clean.   But these laws
of the cultus, he was convinced, should not be allowed to
stand in the way of service to these sons and daughters
of Abraham who needed his message and his help.   Ac-

[27] See 1 Sam. 21: 3 ff.

cordingly Jesus ran all the risks of these violations of the law and was known as "the friend of publicans and sinners." "Woe unto you, scribes and Pharisees, hypocrites," he once declared to his critics, "for you tithe mint, anise, and cummin, and have left undone the weightier things of the law, justice and mercy and faith. . . . Woe unto you, . . . for you cleanse the outside of the cup and the platter, but within they are full from extortion and excess." [28] All such meticulous observance of ceremonial and ritual laws to the neglect of human kindness and love he labeled hypocrisy. Foods in themselves could not make a man unclean in the sight of God, but the state of his heart. "There is nothing from without the man that going into him can defile him; but the things which proceed out of the man are those that defile the man." [29] This great saying, uttered in all probability in reply to some specific criticism, became in time the slogan by which the church was to emancipate itself from the Mosaic legislation.

Thus we see again how the pure spiritual genius of Jesus transformed and revalued everything with which it came in contact. The evidence is convincing that he accepted the ceremonial aspects of Judaism and made no attack upon them. There is nothing in the teachings of Jesus which reads like the famous utterance of Amos, "I hate, I despise your feasts, I will take no delight in your solemn assemblies." [30] We find him rather participating in the festivals, attending upon the temple, speaking of the altar which hallows the gift upon it, and of the temple which makes holy the gold upon its pillars. But this magnificent ceremonial, the origin of which was com-

[28] Matt. 23: 23, 25.   [29] Mark 7: 15.   [30] Amos 5: 21.

monly supposed to go back to Moses, should be neglected in order to be reconciled to a brother. It was all to be valued in terms of its meaning for inner personal piety. It should never be allowed to become a stumblingblock which should impede the fullest service to men in need. In the greatness of his spirit the ritual was appreciated, but subordinated to the ethical. Love toward God and worship of him was to be expressed primarily by service to mankind, not by elaborate chants by employed choirs nor by expensive sacrifices on the great altar.

Jesus did not abrogate the elaborate cultus of Judaism, but in the light of his teaching the church soon dropped it from its thinking. It was valuable for those who took part in it sincerely and with a desire to please God, but it was not a necessary duty, and other forms answering the need of those who had been reared differently came in time to take its place. Paul later put all this into a theology. Jesus gave no theological system. His was the creative moral force which broke through the older inhibitions and dogmas and which provided the materials, so to speak, out of which the new systems of religious thought could be constructed. The church owes its theologies to others; to Jesus it owes its knowledge of how complete the spirit of love can be and how great is the beauty and the power of love.

TOPICS FOR DISCUSSION

1. The difference between the services in the temple and those in the synagogues.

2. The origin of some of the laws of the Jewish cultus.

3. The plan of Herod's temple.

4. The various uses to which the temple and its courts were put.

5. Religious conservatism in the realm of ritual.

WRITTEN ASSIGNMENTS

Write a discussion of the place of form and ritual in contemporary religion, and of its true function and value.

SUPPLEMENTARY READINGS

On the temple of Herod:

    Edersheim: *The Life and Times of Jesus,* Vol. I, pp. 242-246.

    Hastings: *The Dictionary of the Bible,* Article "Temple," Section IV, p. 711 ff.

    Smith: *Jerusalem,* Vol. II, Ch. XVIII.

On the services in the temple:

    Schürer: *The History of the Jewish People in the Time of Jesus Christ,* Div. II, Vol. I, pp. 273-298.

On the two fundamental observances of Judaism—circumcision and the Sabbath:

    Moore: *Judaism,* Vol. II, Ch. II.

On Jesus' attitude toward the temple:

    Dickey: *The Constructive Revolution of Jesus,* Ch. III.

On the cleansing of the temple:

    Bosworth: *The Life and Teaching of Jesus,* pp. 308-313.

CHAPTER XX

JESUS AND THE GENTILES

VERY soon after its establishment Christianity spread
from Palestine to Syria, Asia Minor, Greece, Egypt, and
Rome and drew into its membership representatives of
the varied races of the Roman Empire. Almost from its
beginning it was an international religion. Judaism, on
the other hand, has always been the religion of a particular race of people, and if at different periods its missionary spirit has been strong, it demanded of those it converted that they become Jews in their manner of life.
Because of this marked contrast it has often been assumed that Jesus was directly responsible for this separation of the religion of his fathers from its ethnic connections.

Now this is one of the points on which the gospel
records are fraught with considerable uncertainty. Not
only is the material bearing on the question meager, but
it is contradictory. On this point, as on the question of
Jesus' attitude toward the Mosaic law, it seems evident
that the early difficulties and experiences of the Church
have left their effect on the tradition of Jesus' sayings.
One can observe in the records the development of an
anti-Jewish polemic, and also one can see certain anticipa-
tory references to Gentile acceptance of the gospel. Indeed so difficult is the problem that it might fairly be
argued that in a study of this sort where much must be
omitted anyhow such a theme should give way to other
topics. The answer to this is simply the interest and im-

portance of the theme. Did Jesus break with his people, deny the special claims of Israel, and address himself directly to the varied peoples of his day? If so, the fact should be recognized. On the other hand, if Jesus only had in mind in his work the Jewish people and thought of himself and his mission in terms of them only, how can it be claimed that he was the founder of this most international of all the religions? Should not the credit for this fall to Paul? In a word, what was the relation between Jesus, his thought and work, and the great movement that so soon after his death swept across the distinctions of race and color and ethnic inheritance? That topic seems too important to be omitted.

II

The gospels contain an abundance of evidence that Jesus lived in his complex and racially mixed environment the life of a loyal and devoted Jew. Much of this has already been cited and need not be repeated. Furthermore it should be clear from all that has gone before that Jesus' thought and teaching was not borrowed from Gentile or pagan circles, but came out of the heart of the religion of Judaism. But there remain to be noted certain more specific facts concerning his relation to Jew and Gentile respectively.

1. It is an obvious fact that Jesus conducted no mission to the Gentiles or on Gentile soil. His work was confined to his Jewish compatriots. True, there were individual Gentiles who were attracted by his teachings, but these were exceptions or accidents, not the result of a campaign among or expressly for Gentiles. It is also true that on one occasion he left the soil of Judea and Galilee and journeyed in the regions of Tyre and Sidon, the great

pagan cities of the Phœnician coastal plain,[1] but we read of no preaching or teaching while on this journey. On the contrary, Mark says expressly that while on this journey he did not wish his presence to be known.[2] No incident is recorded from this tour except one case of healing that forced itself on him.

2. It is also a fact that in several sayings in the gospels Jesus speaks of the Gentiles in a distinctly disparaging way. "In praying use not vain repetitions, as the Gentiles do: for they think that they shall be heard for their much speaking."[3] "Ye know that they who are accounted to rule over the Gentiles lord it over them, and their great ones exercise authority over them. But it is not so among you."[4] In these sayings the right or true spirit or practice is inculcated by contrast with the pagan ideas of the Gentiles. A little different is the saying, "If he [an offended brother] hear not the church, let him be unto thee as the Gentile and the publican."[5] Here there is implied an approval of Jewish separation from all Gentiles, though the mention of the publicans, of whom Jesus was notoriously the friend and consort, casts some doubt on the accuracy of the wording of the passage. A fourth saying, however, is much more serious than these. This is the reply which Jesus made in answer to the request of the Syrophœnician woman, "Let the children first be filled: for it is not right to take the children's bread and cast it to the dogs."[6] The harshness of that saying is not mitigated by pointing out, as sometimes is done, that the word used for dogs is a diminutive and

---

[1] Mark 7: 24, 31.   [3] Matt. 6: 7.   [5] Matt. 18: 17.
[2] Mark 7: 24.   [4] Mark 10: 42.   [6] Mark 7: 27.

means "little dogs"! How this saying should be understood had best be postponed for later discussion.

3. Even more specific than the above were the instructions which we find Jesus quoted as giving to his disciples when he sent them out to preach. The mission charge to the Twelve in Matthew 10 begins with the words, "Go not into the way of the Gentiles, and enter not into any city of the Samaritans: but go rather to the lost sheep of the house of Israel." [7] This is followed later in the same discourse by the statement, "When they persecute you in one city, flee into the next: for verily I say unto you, Ye shall not have gone through the cities of Israel, till the Son of man be come." [8] I must admit a lingering suspicion concerning the authenticity of these verses. They seem to savor of the conflict in the early church as to whether Christian missionaries should go off to Cyprus, Samaria, and elsewhere rather than to preach the good news to Jews. But it must be admitted that the sayings are quite in line with Jesus' choice of his own field of work. They are also in line with another part of the reply made to the Syrophœnician woman, "I was not sent but unto the lost sheep of the house of Israel." [9]

These several sayings, particularly when taken with the general facts mentioned in the first paragraph of this section, make it quite certain that the burden of Jesus' thought and activity was directed toward his own people. Why was this the case? Was Jesus a narrow nationalist, believing that no good could come out of any land or people except his own? Had he no interest in other peoples, or, worse than that, no respect for them? These questions must be given a fair answer.

[7] Matt. 10: 5.   [8] Matt. 10: 23.   [9] Matt. 15: 24.

III

Much the most satisfactory answer seems to me to be along the lines of certain indisputable facts of a general nature which bear upon the problem, rather than by the citation of this or that passage, some of which are of questionable authenticity. There are four of these general facts which are related to the question under discussion:

1. Jesus shows a complete lack of any anti-Roman prejudice or feeling.

Rome was the arch-enemy of all Jewish nationalists. Roman power dashed to the ground the last hope of Jewish independence. The Roman general Pompey had penetrated into the Holy of Holies which it was lawful only for the high priest himself to enter. The Romans had carried off thousands of captives to Rome. Their minions had killed the last of the Maccabean princes. Roman legionaries were quartered in Jerusalem in the citadel overlooking the temple. Roman hirelings collected taxes from the people. The Roman generals and governors had more than once turned their troops loose upon the defenseless populace. No wonder hatred and the desire for revenge smoldered in the hearts of the people. Among the racial prejudices of the Jews hatred of the Roman was at this period the most dominant.

Now it is an important clue to Jesus' attitude toward foreigners to note that he seems to have transcended in his own feelings this national animosity. Simkhovitch in his book, *Toward an Understanding of Jesus,* has shown how this issue was one which Jesus, dealing in popular fashion with the multitudes, could not escape. Yet we have no word of denunciation for the Roman power or rule. Perhaps that is not so significant; the

Pharisees also adopted the policy of submission to Rome, leaving her punishment in God's hands. More important is it that in Jesus' picture of the future kingdom of God, when righteousness shall be established over all the earth and all evil shall be destroyed, there is no echo of that rampant nationalism which comes to expression in apocalyptic books of the period. Jesus' thought took other lines. On one occasion this issue of the attitude to be adopted toward Rome was forced upon him. He was asked the outright question, Should taxes be paid to Rome or not? Calling for a coin, we are told that he asked, "Whose is this image and superscription?" When they replied that it was Cæsar's, he uttered his famous saying, "Render unto Cæsar the things that are Cæsar's, and unto God the things of God." While the main point of this oft-quoted dictum might be debated, the reference to the actual sovereignty of Cæsar and the statement that the tax should be paid, shows that Jesus' normal clearsighted judgment was not warped and twisted in this area by an anti-Roman complex.

To these indications of Jesus' attitude toward Romans should be added that furnished by Jesus' preachings of non-retaliation, forgiveness of enemies, and love even toward those who persecute one. The sayings expressing these ideas have already been examined and they need not be repeated. If the reader will only call to mind the vigor and the inclusive character of these sayings, he will be convinced that they were unlimited, applicable to all personal enemies, whether they be Jew or Gentile, indeed, even though they be Samaritan or Roman. That this is the case is borne out by one of the illustrations by which Jesus impressed this teaching—namely, that if one be impressed to go a mile, instead of retaliating in whatever way possible one should go two miles. The illustration refers to the system of *corvée,* by which representatives of the government had the power to levy service on individuals. Not all exercising this right would be Romans or other foreigners—at least not in Galilee where Herod Antipas still ruled—but Roman soldiers and officials would certainly be included in the minds of those who heard this saying.

2. In the second place, Jesus shows no anti-Samaritan prejudice.

That the Samaritans were despised and hated by the Jews of Jesus' day is clear from the gospels as well as from the other literature reflecting the life of that period. Half-Jews—from the standpoint of the Jerusalemites—they were regarded with the contempt and the bitter feeling characteristic of family feuds and intimate racial cleavages. When Jesus' opponents wished to apply to him the supreme insult, they said, "Thou art a Samaritan, and hast a demon." [10]

Now in spite of the mission charge to the disciples, "Enter not into the way of the Samaritans," it may be safely said that Jesus did not share this feeling of contempt and hatred. The hero of one of his greatest parables was the Samaritan who ministered to the wounded man after a Jewish priest and Levite had passed by on the other side.[11] Similarly in the story of the ten lepers the one who returned to give thanks was a Samaritan.[12] There is a third passage that is instructive. It narrates how on one occasion Jesus and his disciples had to suffer the indignity of being refused lodgings in a Samaritan village. So moved with indignation were the disciples

---

[10] John 8: 48.   [11] Luke 10: 33.   [12] Luke 17: 16.

that they urged Jesus to call down fire from heaven and consume the whole village. Jesus, however, was far from sharing such a feeling. Evidently his attitude was in marked contrast to theirs. "He turned and rebuked them," says the narrative, "and they went unto another village." [13] In the Fourth Gospel this suggestion of friendly relations with the Samaritans is carried further. We read of a conversation with a Samaritan woman at a well near Sychar, and of the interest which was aroused in Jesus in the village. The story concludes with the suggestive statement, that Jesus "abode there two days, and many believed on him." [14] Thus in the case of the Samaritans, as in that of the Romans, Jesus seems to have shown no racial prejudices, but rather to have accepted them, as he did Jews, on the basis of the character and worth which they revealed.

3. The next fact to be noted in this attempt to grasp the outlook of Jesus is one which has been abundantly established in the preceding pages. He did not join in the current separation from "the people of the land" because of their neglect of ceremonial and ritual laws. On the contrary, he declared with reference to them that a goodness of humanitarian and ethical behavior, even though coupled with a neglect of certain laws of the cultus, was acceptable in God's sight.

The point of this is obvious. It shows that Jesus' attitude was of the prophetic rather than the priestly type. It is difficult to believe that one who sought out "the lost sheep" as he did, who declared that there was more joy in heaven over one sinner that repents than over ninety and nine just persons who need no repentance, who de-

---

[13] Luke 9: 55.   [14] John 4: 40 ff.

clared that the publicans and harlots who had repented would go into the kingdom of God before the self-righteous and ceremonially clean Pharisees—it is difficult to believe that such a one would not have been generously and kindly disposed toward the Gentiles who, in Paul's phrase, showed "the works of the law written on their hearts." [15] His whole moral and religious outlook recognized no barriers to the divine forgiveness, and no basis for the divine approval except that of one's state of heart. And that he was thus ready to recognize without restraint Gentiles who showed the character of the kingdom as well as Jews is strikingly borne out by his praise of the Roman centurion, "Verily I have not found so great faith, no, not in Israel." [16]

4. Similarly suggestive of Jesus' temperament and outlook is the general fact of his unsparing condemnation of those who, though descendants of Abraham and observant of the externals of the law, did not show that righteousness of inner purpose which he declared to be God's desire. Neither scribes, Pharisees, nor temple priests were free from his condemnations. No more than John the Baptist, did he regard physical descent from Abraham as in itself a ground for confidence as to the future. His prophecy of the destruction of the temple shows that he, like the ancient prophets, saw no immunity from the judgment of God to be afforded by the sacred history or special opportunities of his people.

5. Lastly, there are several sayings in the gospels in which Jesus seems to make definite reference to the conversion of the Gentiles to share in the joys and privileges of the future kingdom. As remarked above a number of

[15] Rom. 2: 15.   [16] Matt. 8: 10.

these are, in their present form, of doubtful authenticity, and reflect the later experiences of the church. Matthew 21: 43, for example, is an addition which the First Gospel makes to the account taken from Mark. Mark 13: 10 also is open to serious question, since it gives an explanation of why the return of the Lord must be delayed. But there is one great saying which is fully as deserving of mention as some of those of the opposite tenor which have been cited. It is a declaration of judgment upon the unrepentant Jews: "I say unto you, that many shall come from the east and the west, and shall sit down with Abraham, and Isaac, and Jacob, in the kingdom of heaven; but the sons of the kingdom shall be cast forth into the outer darkness." [17] In this saying, the severe tone of which is supported by other utterances, Jesus places himself squarely in line with the prophets of the past who proclaimed the rejection of unrepentant Israel and the gathering of other people into the kingdom of God.[18]

These several facts, taken together, prove that Jesus belonged to the liberal side of Judaism. If so, it is strange that there are so few undoubtedly genuine sayings concerning the conversion of the Gentiles. Two considerations, however, throw light upon the fact:

(a) In the first place, it must not be forgotten that Jesus' career was extremely brief. At most it lasted only about three years. How he would have developed and expanded his message and his activity had he been allowed

[17] Matt. 8: 11 ff.; Luke 13: 29. The wording is slightly different in Luke, but the point of the saying is the same. The setting of the First Gospel is obviously due to the editor, since it appears differently placed in Luke.

[18] See Isa. 19: 23-25, 56: 6-8, the Book of Jonah, the Testament of Levi 4: 4, of Benjamin 9: 2, and of Asher 7: 3.

to continue his work we have no way of knowing.   During this brief period he was engaged in one supreme undertaking.   Time never permitted the application of his principles to themes related to that central purpose.

(b) In the second place, it must be remembered that the Judaism of Jesus' day was itself strongly missionary. Josephus, the Book of Acts, the classical writers, and, indeed, all the extant literature of the period show how widespread and successful was the endeavor of the Jews to win Gentiles to membership in the synagogue.   "Woe unto you, scribes and Pharisees, hypocrites," reads one of the sayings of Jesus, "ye compass sea and earth to make one proselyte." [19]   The real issue of Jesus' day was not whether Gentiles should be converted, but rather, to what sort of religion they should be converted.   In other words, there was no necessity for Jesus to declare that righteous Gentiles would be accepted into the kingdom of God.   That was commonly accepted.

Now it was here that Jesus made his contribution, one which made the work of the apostles and the spread of the gospel over the Roman world a natural consequence. He redefined the essence of Judaism.   His conception of the obedience which God wanted was different from that of the scribes.   The imperative, unlimited obligation of man before God was to practice justice and mercy and truth, to love God and serve one's neighbor with all one's strength, and to become great in ministering to others. We have seen that he did not attack the ritual and cultus, but he subordinated them even to the point of ignoring some of their provisions.   This was to lay the foundation of a new definition of the religion of Israel, as Paul and

[19] Matt. 23: 15.

other Christian teachers were quick to see. Such teaching emancipated the ethical and religious in the teachings of the prophets and lawgivers from the peculiar ethnic and racial practices which marked off the Jews and their proselytes from all other peoples. In the vigor and strength of his conviction of the primacy of the ethical in God's sight Jesus laid the basis for the international and universal character which Christianity so soon achieved.

But Jesus himself did not develop all the consequences of his views. He was limited by time, he was limited by the single-mindedness with which he gave himself to his task of bringing Israel into the kingdom, and he was limited by his apocalyptic outlook. The material presented in the first half of this chapter shows clearly that the object of his ministry was the lost members of his own people. Israel was the people whom God had chosen. To and through Israel the law books had been given to the world. In and for this nation the great prophets of the past, Isaiah, and Jeremiah, and Ezekiel, and Zechariah, and others too numerous to mention, had labored and suffered. Ezra and Nehemiah had given up comfort and success in Babylon to build up Jerusalem's walls and to reorganize the state on the basis of obedience to the law. For its sake the martyrs of the Maccabean period had given their lives. Out of all this history had come the synagogue and the law, and the temple and its ministry, the Scriptures and the traditions. In Jesus' sight his nation and his nation's religion was a precious thing. But yet he saw his countrymen and their leaders blindly failing to see the essence of all that goodness and beauty and love which had been revealed in the past. Instead of an overwhelming passion of good will toward others, he saw them concerned about dishes and hand-washings and tithes, not to speak of those who, oblivious of the coming kingdom, gave themselves to gross sins and pleasures. But God's judgment was surely coming, and from his kingdom all who were impure and avaricious and selfish and cruel would be excluded. Thus Jesus took upon himself the task of awakening Israel to its opportunity and its danger and of showing to his countrymen the true way in which God would have them walk.

His objective thus concerned itself with his own countrymen. Through them the Gentiles would be saved— that was the promise of the Scripture and the logic of all the facts at his disposal as well. In his work of saving his own people he came into contact with individual Gentiles, Roman soldiers, Samaritan villages, a Syrophœnician woman, a group of Greeks who came asking to see him, and these he accepted on the basis of the character which they displayed. He had no prejudice against Gentiles as such. But he made no missionary expeditions into neighboring Gentile lands. He may even have directed his disciples not to dissipate their energies by attempting to preach also to Gentiles and Samaritans while on the mission on which he was sending them. But the motive was not one of racial prejudice, but rather a conviction that the significant problem of the hour and the task to which he was called was to purify and restate the religion of Israel and to save the people of Israel.

But Jesus' teachings of God's forgiveness and glad acceptance of all men who repent and of God's requirement of loving service unto others even to the extent of neglecting ritual requirements, soon broke over racial and national lines. The disciples were surprised to find an even greater response from Gentiles than from Jews, particularly from those Gentiles who had been drawn to the synagogue by its non-idolatrous monotheism and high ethical demands, but who were repelled by the requirements of the cultus. They carried the gospel from Judea and Galilee to Samaria, Cyprus, Antioch, Athens, Alexandria, and even to Rome, the capital of the Empire, and in so doing they were convinced that they were acting under the influence of his spirit and only developing the implications of his teachings. They were aware that he had confined his own work to the chosen people, but they understood this to be only part of a plan that the gospel should be offered to the Jews "first." [20]   In his own lifetime he had not given specific instructions for the evangelization of the distant corners of the world, but the disciples, meditating on his words and under the influence of his spirit, were sure that the risen Christ had given them the command, "Go ye therefore, and make disciples of all the nations, . . . teaching them to observe all things whatsoever I commanded you: and lo, I am with you always, even unto the end of the world." [21]

Appendix on the Story of Jesus and the Syrophœnician Woman (Mark 7: 24 ff. and Matt. 15: 21 ff.)

This story has to be read completely for its harshness to be fully appreciated. Jesus is traveling with his disciples in alien territory. He does not want his presence to be known. The woman comes beseeching him not for herself but for her daughter, who, according to the simple diagnosis of the day, was "afflicted with a demon." The disciples apparently urged Jesus to heal her daughter so as to get rid of her. (Note the similar use of the Greek word translated "Send away" or "Let go" in Luke 14:

[20] See Mark 7: 27.   [21] Matt. 28: 19.

4.) Jesus' reply, according to Mark, reads, "Let the children first be filled: for it is not meet to take the children's bread and cast it to the dogs." No amount of critical exegesis can get rid of the comparison. Nor can the story be dismissed as unauthentic: the tendency at the time the gospels were written was rather to eliminate such pro-Jewish features.

Various expedients have been suggested to get rid of the difficulty: Jesus was trying the woman's faith, or he was presenting for his disciples' benefit the prejudiced Jewish point of view in order to show its ugliness, or he was debating in his own mind what he should do. None of these are satisfactory. Nevertheless, the incompatibility of this scene with all else that we know about Jesus makes it difficult to accept the story as it appears on the surface. Warschauer has a fine passage on this point: "One would not have imagined but that He who had been so strongly moved by the entreaties of Jairus, who had so tenderly ministered to the little maid at Capernaum, who was so sensitive to the charm and the helplessness of childhood, would have immediately responded to this distressed mother's appeal; instead we read that 'He answered her not a word,' and that, when at last he spoke, it was words which no ingenuity of interpretation can make otherwise than appalling in their want of common humanity, their narrow nationalist bigotry, their gratuitously insulting character. . . . Instinctively we decline to believe that Jesus would have flung a term of abuse at a woman agonizing for her child. . . . What 'legitimate' claimant to the Lord's healing gifts was being deprived of anything by his compliance with this poor Gentile's petition? Neither can we suppose that the same mind which expressed itself so beautifully in the parable of the good

Samaritan . . . would have refused for a single moment to succor a sick child because she was not an Israelite." (*The Historical Life of Christ*, p. 189.)

Warschauer's solution is "to content ourselves as best we may with the surmise that the harsh words attributed to Jesus were spoken by one or other of the disciples." This is quite arbitrary and unjustifiable. The best explanation of the episode seems to be one supplied by the circumstances of the moment. Jesus had just been forced out of Galilee by the opposition of the scribes and by Herod's attempt to kill him. Traveling on foreign soil, he does not wish to be known. To grant the woman's request would seem to be but the beginning of a wonder-working career among the Gentiles, perhaps even the acceptance of a Gentile field of labors. The saying in the text expresses both his depth of feeling at having been driven out of Israel and his decision not to be forced into giving up his work for his own people.

Such an interpretation does not eliminate the harsh comparison between Jews and Gentiles, but it makes Jesus' statement one directed to himself and his disciples and dealing with one of the larger issues of his life, rather than a direct and gratuitous insult to the woman. The statement was impersonal, but the woman overheard it and quickly turned it to her own use.

TOPICS FOR DISCUSSION

1. The causes of racial antagonism.

2. The unchristian aspects of racial antagonism.

3. The ethical values of pride and loyalty to one's own racial or national group.

4. The special race problems of America.

5. Jesus' conviction of Jewish moral and religious superiority—was it justified?

A WRITTEN ASSIGNMENT

Discuss the theme, The Patriotism of Jesus.

SUPPLEMENTARY READINGS

On the causes of racial antagonisms:
  Oldham: *Christianity and the Race Problem*, Ch. III.
On racial equality and inequality:
  Oldham: *Op. cit.*, Ch. V and VI.
On the relation of Christianity to the problems of race:
  Oldham: *Op. cit.*, Ch. II.
On Jesus' statement to the Syrophœnician Woman:
  Holtzman: *Life of Jesus*, pp. 311-313.
  Rashdall: *Conscience and Christ*, pp. 175-177.
  Warschauer: *The Historical Life of Christ*, pp. 188-190.

CHAPTER XXI

JESUS' WORDS ABOUT HIMSELF

I

MANY people have been accustomed to think of Jesus as suddenly appearing in Galilee after his years of preparation, announcing to the people that he was the expected Messiah, performing various miracles to prove the statement, and calling upon men to accept his claims and follow his commands. This is indeed the impression which a reading of the Fourth Gospel leaves. It seems to us the natural thing for him to have done. But it was not Jesus' method. He did go through the towns and villages with a great announcement, and he did stir the whole district with his wonderful deeds of healing. But the proclamation that he made was not about himself, nor were the miracles merely "signs" to convince an unbelieving people.

He began his work, according to Mark, in the following way: "After John was delivered up, Jesus came into Galilee, preaching the gospel of God, and saying, The time is fulfilled, and the kingdom of God is at hand: repent, and believe in the good news." [1] Matthew says that the subject of this preaching was, "Repent: for the kingdom of heaven is at hand." [2] Obviously there was much more than just these words, but they contain the subject of his preaching. It was about God and his rule. Jesus placed before his hearers the challenge of the kingdom of God and would not let them divert him to other topics. By the seaside, on a mountain slope, in a house, sitting in a

[1] Mark 1: 14, 15.   [2] Matt. 4: 17.

boat, at the synagogue service, he kept speaking of God and his complete rule. He talked about the value of being in that divine "kingdom," the kind of life that it demanded, the danger of neglecting the invitation. And like his predecessor, John, he called on those who heard him to repent that they might not be left outside. Interruptions of all sorts occurred, from possessed people, from the religious leaders, from the civil authorities. Still he kept to his theme, speaking of the coming kingdom and urging men to repent.

If one will turn to the sayings which the gospels have preserved from this Galilean ministry, one may see for oneself that this was the content of his message. Take the Sermon on the Mount as the clearest example. Here is a discourse, three chapters long in the first gospel, which Matthew presents as an illustration of Jesus' teaching. It is all about the life of the kingdom. The people who are truly blessed, the right way to pray and fast and give alms, the loving care of God, the true righteousness compared with contemporary misconceptions, the folly of neglecting God's message—these are the subjects he talks about. As one reads these sayings one after another —pearls on a string, they have been called—one can see how Jesus was holding up to his hearers the picture of a new life, showing now one side of it, now another, enticing, persuading, warning. But there is nothing about himself, his title, his authority, except at the close where he emphatically rejects one who might hail him personally as Lord, but "does not the will of my Father in heaven." [3]

Mark does not have much teaching material, especially in the first half of the gospel. Aside from special sayings on particular occasions, there are in the first half of his

[3] Matt. 7: 21

gospel only three sections of discourse, all short: the series of parables on the kingdom,[4] the charge to the disciples departing for their first missionary effort,[5] and the sayings about what makes one clean or unclean.[6] In all of these there is that same absence of sayings about himself and his own place in the divine plan. He constantly talked about God and his perfect rule, and he quietly lived according to it.

There were individuals who caught glimpses of a deeper significance in his person than he expressly asserted. There was a sick man once who cried out suddenly in the synagogue, "Thou Jesus of Nazareth! I know thee who thou art, the Holy One of God."[7] But Jesus rebuked him and said, "Hold thy peace." At the close of that Sabbath day in Capernaum when he healed many sick at the door of Peter's house, there were evidently a number of such cases. "He cast out many devils," says the evangelist, "and he suffered not the devils to speak, because they knew him."[8] Later we read that certain other unclean spirits cried out at him, "Thou art the Son of God," and that "he charged them much that they should not make him known."[9] When at Cæsarea Philippi the disciples themselves finally made their great confession, we are told again that Jesus "charged them that they should tell no man of him."[10] Instead of making an open claim to his unique authority and position he seems on the contrary to have restrained those who wished to make such claims on his behalf. Thus it came about that at the close of his life, when his opponents sought witnesses on whose testimony they could accuse him to Pilate, they found

---

[4] Mark 4.   [7] Mark 1: 24.   [9] Mark 3: 12.
[5] Mark 6: 7-11.   [8] Mark 1: 34.   [10] Mark 8: 30.
[6] Mark 7.

none and were forced to secure from Jesus himself an admission that he was the Christ.[11]

The multitude took him for a prophet, one of the great ones of Israel. After witnessing the raising of the son of the widow of Nain, "they glorified God, saying, A great prophet is risen among us." [12] The disciples told Jesus that men thought of him as "John the Baptist, Elijah, or one of the prophets." [13] Even at the close of his work when he made his triumphal entry into Jerusalem and when all the city was stirred, wondering who he might be, we are told that "the multitudes said, This is the prophet, Jesus, from Nazareth of Galilee." [14] So again the scribes and Pharisees, though they wished to destroy him, "feared the multitudes, because they took him for a prophet."[15] We even find that he acquiesced in the title, using it of himself. "A prophet is not without honor save in his own country," [16] he declared of himself. And he said to the friendly Pharisees who informed him of Herod's intention to kill him, "I must go on my way to-day and to-morrow and the day following: for it cannot be that a prophet perish out of Jerusalem." [17] Thus according to the Synoptic Gospels Jesus said nothing himself as to his Messiahship, restrained others who wished to make it public, and accepted without question or qualification the title of one of Israel's prophets.

II

So impressive is the evidence supporting this statement that many scholars have felt that it warrants a much more sweeping conclusion. It is recalled that the gospels came

---

[11] See Mark 14: 55-62. [14] Matt. 21: 11.   [16] Mark 6: 4.
[12] Luke 7: 16.   [15] Matt. 21: 46.   [17] Luke 13: 33.
[13] Mark 8: 28.

out of and reflect the faith of the early Christian Church, and that the center of that faith was the conviction that Jesus was the expected Messiah. When, therefore, the records show that Jesus himself did not go about claiming the Messiahship, restrained individuals who would make such a claim for him, and only on the occasion of his trial—an occasion when the disciples were not present —ever stated in public that he was the Messiah, the conclusion is drawn that Jesus never claimed to be the Messiah at all, but that this faith of the early Church was read back into the story of his life. According to this reading of the facts, Jesus was a prophet of the coming kingdom and thought of himself only as such, a successor of John the Baptist whose burden he took up after the latter was cast into prison. It is admitted that Jesus spoke repeatedly of "the Son of Man" who should establish the kingdom at his coming,[18] but they explain these statements as referring to a glorious figure yet to come whom Jewish apocalyptic writings expected to appear upon the clouds of heaven. The conception of a "Messianic secret" to be kept by the disciples is the natural conclusion, it is argued, from the fact that these first Christians firmly believed in the Messiahship of Jesus and yet were aware that it was common knowledge that during his lifetime Jesus had not appeared before the public in that rôle. He must have compelled his disciples to have kept the matter a secret.[19]

This view is a consistent and intelligible view of the facts. It explains in a simple way many phases of the

[18] As in Mark 8: 38, "Whosoever shall be ashamed of me and of my words in this adulterous and sinful generation, the Son of man also shall be ashamed of him when he cometh in the glory of his Father with the holy angels."

[19] For the literature expressing this point of view see the end of the chapter.

gospel narrative, in particular, why Jesus did not openly state his Messiahship. It also makes Jesus himself an easier figure to understand, since according to it he only thought of himself as a prophet of God's coming judgment. It clashes sharply with our inherited ideas about Jesus, but does not contradict the central faith of Christianity. For Christian faith almost from its beginning has proclaimed Jesus to be a far greater figure than simply one who fulfilled the Jewish Messianic expectations of his day. Paul's language, for example, describing Jesus as "the image of the invisible God, the first born of all creation" and declaring that "he is before all things and in him all things consist," [20] sweeps far beyond the conventional Jewish concept of the Messiah. The same can be said about the Prologue to the Fourth Gospel.[21] Christian faith in Jesus could admit the conclusion that Jewish Messianic ideas were not adequate to describe the person of Jesus and even that he did not apply these ideas to himself, without losing its essential character.

But while this is true, the view under consideration seems ruled out on the basis of the evidence. There are two phases of the gospel narratives which seem to require the acceptance of the view that Jesus did regard himself as the expected Messiah.

1. The first of these is the account of the Passion. This is the one part of the story of Jesus' life which is told in something approaching a detailed and consecutive account. This part of the narrative moves against the background of known historical facts, and the gospel statements here concerning the limited powers of the Sanhedrin, the movements of the Roman governor, the complications of the Passover festival, the name of the

[20] Col. 1: 15 f.   [21] John 1: 1-18.

high priest, the influence of the ex-high priest Annas,
the method of execution, are strictly confirmed by the
knowledge which modern research has amassed from other
sources. Now according to the unanimous testimony of
these accounts Jesus was accused before Pilate of being
an insurrectionist against Rome, and over his cross was
nailed a placard which bore the charge "The King of the
Jews." [22] These statements cannot be eliminated from
the history, and if historical they must reflect Jesus' own
admission. For to accuse a simple Galilean peasant who
had never raised his arm in civil disturbance, who had
specifically enjoined the payment of taxes to Cæsar, and
who had confined himself to religious and ethical teaching,
of leading an insurrection against Rome and claiming to
be king of the Jews would have been the height of ab-
surdity had he not given certain grounds for the accusa-
tion. It is the clear evidence of all the sources that the
basis of the charge against Jesus was a Messianic claim
which he himself admitted.

2. The second difficulty in accepting the view outlined
above is that a "Messianic consciousness" seems implied
by a large part of the narrative even where no specific
claim to that effect is made. Granted that the evangelists
have read that element into the story at places where
originally it was not present, yet nevertheless there are
too many incidents and sayings where this sense of Messianic authority and mission seems to supply the clue to
the understanding of the passage for it to be dismissed.
The story of the triumphal entry into Jerusalem is an
excellent illustration. Here in Mark's account, which is
earliest, no specific claim is made by Jesus nor do the

---

[22] See Mark 15: 2, 9, and 26 and the parallel accounts in Matt. and
Luke.

cries of the populace go beyond, "Blessed is he that cometh in the name of the Lord," and, "Blessed is the kingdom of our father David." [23] Yet if Jesus regarded himself only as one of the many prophets, why this peculiar mode of entry so highly suggestive of the Messianic prophecy of Zechariah 9:9? A recent writer on the life of Christ, one who is himself a liberal Jew, has put this point perhaps as clearly as it can be stated. Speaking of the gospel presentations of Jesus as the revealed Messiah, Professor Cohon says: "Shall we dismiss these Messianic elements in the portraiture of Jesus as the pure invention of his disciples and as the mere expression of the faith of the early Church without the least warrant on his own part? Such a claim is not far removed from the negation of the historicity of the gospels altogether. In view of the persistence of the testimony it is difficult to escape the conclusion that, sometime in his ministry, Jesus grew conscious not only of a unique personal relationship to God, but that in addition he came to think of himself as the long-expected Messiah. From this consciousness of himself sprang his entire mode of conduct, his sense of special authority in healing and teaching, his peculiar attitude toward sinners, and his apocalyptic teachings. The Prophetic lesson, which, in accordance with Jewish practice, he read on the Sabbath in the synagogue at Nazareth, from the sixty-first chapter of Isaiah, he thought fulfilled in himself. It is the ideal which he sought to translate into his life. He felt that the Spirit of God was upon him, that he was consecrated to preach good tidings unto the poor, to proclaim freedom unto the fettered, sight for the blind, liberty to the oppressed, to proclaim the Lord's year of favor. The Messianic

[23] Mark 11:9 f.

era, to which the people eagerly looked forward, was at hand and he was 'its principal agent and predestined head.' In keeping with the general atmosphere of secrecy which enveloped Messianism he avoided speaking of it in public, but intimated it to his trusted disciples in private. Without such a suggestion coming directly from him, it is hardly possible to explain the faith of his disciples after the tragic shock of the crucifixion. While this unique consciousness presents a psychological puzzle to moderns, it explains best the history of Christianity from Apostolic times to the present." [24] This statement expresses the case clearly. The Messianic element is woven too thoroughly into the warp and woof of the gospel history for it to have been simply a later conjecture on the part of the disciples.

III

Why then did he not say so plainly to the multitudes and to his opponents? The record is clear that he did not do so. One explanation which has been offered is that the Messianic conviction grew slowly in his thinking and that the dramatic and symbolic story of the temptation represents the inner struggle of Jesus during the Galilean period during which he was engaged outwardly in conflicts with the scribes and Pharisees over the meaning of the law. The view need not be debated here. If correct, it obviously explains only a portion of his silence. We are driven deeper into Jesus' motives and methods for a more complete explanation.

One such motive is easy to see. To have announced that the Messiah, expected for centuries, had at last ap-

[24] Cohon, "The Place of Jesus in the Religious Life of His Day" in *The Journal of Biblical Literature,* Vol. 48 (1929), pp. 86 f.

peared would have produced excitement, confusion, and misunderstanding wherever he went. Some would have understood that he was proclaiming a war of political liberation. Certainly the Roman authorities would have interpreted the announcement in this way and acted accordingly. Others would have expected a constant stream of miracles and marvels to flow from his hands. Others would have been incredulous and would have taken his time with arguments and questions as to his right to the claim. And this tumult and excitement would have made impossible his primary object, to bring Israel to rethink God and his relation to their lives.

There is a story in Mark—it is the sequel to the healing of the people at Peter's door—which gives a clear indication of the attitude of Jesus. Early that morning, before anyone else was about, Jesus slipped out of the town into a desert place. "And Simon and those with him followed after him; and they found him, and say unto him, All are seeking thee. And he saith unto them, Let us go elsewhere into the next towns, that I may preach there also; for to this end came I forth." [25] From the excitement and notoriety he fled away. In the face of such a situation he could not bring about that repentance of the heart which he sought. This would be accomplished by instruction, exhortation, and example, not by gathering together great crowds of curious to see some marvelous work. It is easy to see that this is also the explanation of his injunctions to those whom he healed to keep silent about it.[26]

But there was a deeper reason than this desire to avoid excitement and confusion which lay back of Jesus' refusal to speak of his own position and authority. He

[25] Mark 1: 36 f.   [26] Matt. 8: 4, 9: 30, and 12: 16.

preferred that men might see his work and learn from it how to regard him. It was easy to claim to be the Anointed One. Many impostors had already done that, men like the wandering Egyptian mentioned in Acts 21: 38 who, according to Josephus, led thirty thousand people out to the Mount of Olives to witness the fall of Jerusalem. Such men came through the country gathering the credulous and gullible to their banner. Jesus cared for no such following. He did not ask that men should confess any faith in him apart from a knowledge of what he taught and the ideals for which he stood. Any true confession of him apart from such knowledge and understanding was impossible. He asked for disciples who would believe in him and his mission on the basis of a realization of his meaning for Israel rather than on any personal claim that he might make.

Note the way in which Jesus called men to discipleship. He did not begin by demanding that they should believe something about him, but that they should believe in him and in the message that he spoke. "Come after me," he said to Simon and Andrew, "and I will make you to become fishers of men." [27] That was a call for coöperation with him in the task. He passed by the tollhouse where sat Matthew, the publican, taking in the customs, and said to him only, "Follow me." [28] And Matthew rose and followed him because his heart responded to the opportunity of allegiance to such a cause and leader. To the rich young man who came running to him he commanded that he sell all that he had, give it to the poor, and come and join him in his work.[29] He called another, who asked if he might first return and bury his father.

[27] Mark 1: 17.   [28] Matt. 9: 9.   [29] Mark 10: 17 f.

"Leave the dead to bury their own dead, but go thou and publish abroad the kingdom of God," was the reply he gave.[30] In all these cases we observe that Jesus makes the work of the kingdom the basis for fellowship with and recognition of himself.

Then consider the way in which he dealt with the Twelve. He called them, Mark says, "that they might be with him." [31] They were men of spiritual appreciation and promise. They were eager for the coming of the kingdom and went out on Jesus' command to proclaim it through the cities of Israel. And yet it is quite evident, from the account of the great confession at Cæsarea Philippi, that during all this early period they had not yet come to the realization that he, their leader, was the Messiah. Nor had he ever told them. He called them to fellowship with and coöperation with him in his task and he left their designation of him to flow out of that experience.

But there is an even clearer illustration still. The growing reputation of Jesus reached John as he lay in prison. He sent two of his disciples with directions to ask the specific question, "Art thou he that cometh, or look we for another?" [32] The reply which Jesus makes to so direct a question from the man by whom he had been baptized is very significant. "Go your way and tell John the things which ye do hear and see: the blind receive their sight, and the lame walk, the lepers are cleansed, and the deaf hear, and the dead are raised up, and the poor have good tidings preached to them. And blessed is he, whosoever shall find no occasion of stumbling in me." What does he mean? Simply that John must make the work

[30] Luke 9: 60.   [32] Matt. 11: 3 f. and Luke 7: 19 f.
[31] Mark 3: 14.

which Jesus was accomplishing the basis of any decision concerning him. He makes no demand, he utters no claim, he tells of no inner experience; but blessed is the man with the eyes to see. Jesus never forced his Messiahship upon anyone, but let it grow out of knowledge of himself and his work.

IV

But Jesus was and is inseparably bound up with those principles and ideals which he taught and by which he lived. He did not speak of something abstract, a theory or a philosophy, but of a practical way of living. And he personified that way of life, was both its evangel and its example. Hence the attitude that men took toward the kingdom was most clearly and most quickly revealed by the attitude which they displayed toward him. He summed up and expressed that new life of which he spoke, in his teaching of men, in the good that he went about doing, in his spirit of love, in his opposition to certain institutions and practices. And men showed even in spite of themselves their attitude toward that kind of life by the response which they made to Jesus. As John's Gospel put it, "This is judgment, that the light is come into the world, and men loved the darkness rather than the light." [33]

This fact Jesus fully recognized and made explicit in his teaching. It is involved of course in his imperative command that men should leave their fishing nets, their tollgates, even the obsequies of deceased parents, and should accept his leadership and example. "Blessed is he who shall find no occasion of stumbling in me," he said to the messengers of John the Baptist. "Whosoever shall

[33] John. 3: 19.

lose his life *for my sake* and the gospel's shall find it."[34]
"Verily there is no man who hath left house, or brethren,
or sisters, or mother, or father, or children, or lands,
for my sake and the gospel's . . ." but will receive a
hundredfold reward. "Blessed are ye when men shall
reproach you, and persecute you, and say all manner of
evil against you falsely, *for my sake*. Rejoice, and be
exceeding glad." [35] These examples taken at random
from his sayings show that Jesus did not hesitate for one
moment to demand loyalty to himself. He was fully
conscious of his mission as founder and representative of
God's kingdom, and he called unto himself the allegiance
and devotion of those who would enter therein.

Some of the disciples understood this to involve personal
ministry and service to him as an individual. It was
natural that they should want to give it, and Jesus appreciated of course the motive that prompted such acts. Witness his consideration of and thanks to the woman who
came into the house and bathed his feet with the precious
ointment. But this was not the kind of service that he
demanded of men. "The Son of man came not to be
ministered unto, but to minister." [36] There is a most
interesting story which Luke preserves of a journey
through Samaria. Evening coming on, "he sent messengers before his face; and they went, and entered into
a village of the Samaritans, to make ready for him. And
they would not receive him, because his face was as though
he were going to Jerusalem. And when his disciples James
and John saw this, they said, Lord, wilt thou that we bid
fire to come down from heaven, and consume them?" [37]

[34] Mark 8: 35; Matt. 10: 39; Matt. 16: 25, and Luke 9:24 (with
minor variations in the wording of the second phrase).

[35] Matt. 5: 11, 12.   [36] Mark 10: 45.   Luke 9: 52.

But the inhospitality of these Samaritans had no reference to the work that Jesus was accomplishing or the spirit he represented. To them he was merely a Jew traveling through their country, very likely against his own desire. They had never heard of him before and never expected to see him again. In such cases Jesus demanded no more consideration for himself than for other individuals. "He turned," goes on the narrative with vivid brevity, "and rebuked them. And they went unto another village." The loyalty that he demanded was to himself as the representative of the kingdom and was to be expressed in service to that great ideal. He asked neither that men should apply to him some set title or description, nor that they render physical service to his person. He required only that they should meet the moral challenge of his life and work.

This is the thought that lies behind Jesus' reply to John on another occasion when that disciple demonstrated his partisan spirit. The story this time is told by Mark. "John said unto him, Master, we saw one casting out devils in thy name: and we forbade him, because he followed not us. But Jesus said, Forbid him not: for there is no man which shall do a mighty work in my name, and be able quickly to speak evil of me." [38] It was enough for Jesus that the man was doing the work of the kingdom.

But perhaps the most striking of all the sayings or incidents which express this attitude is the oft-quoted (though not always happily quoted) verse about the sin against the Holy Spirit. This occurs in Jesus' reply to the charge of the Pharisees that by the power of Beelzebub, the prince of devils, he performed his marvelous works,

[38] Mark 9: 38, 39.

and in particular his cure of a possessed person. A more malignant charge cannot be imagined. In his reply Jesus distinguished between insults that were purely personal and those which attacked through him the goodness and love that he represented. To take such obvious blessings as had been witnessed in this case and describe them as works of the devil evidenced an intentional malice that God would not forgive. "Whosoever shall speak a word against the Son of man, it shall be forgiven him; but whosoever shall speak a word against the Holy Spirit, it shall not be forgiven him." [39] Thus he made sharp distinction between himself as an individual and as the agent or representative of the spiritual forces of God.

V

If it be asked, What was the thing of such permanent significance that he regarded himself as doing and was the basis of his belief in himself as the Messiah? it will be answered, The establishment of God's kingdom on earth. In many ways he saw this being accomplished. In the wonderful works which he was able to do he saw the signs of the coming kingdom: "If I by the Spirit of God cast out demons, then is the kingdom of God come unto you." [40] He saw its beginnings also in the group of men and women whom he called into glad obedience to the true will of God, and he declared on hearing of the extension of his own efforts through the work of his disciples, "I saw Satan fallen like lightning from heaven." [41] He was conscious of preparing the way for the kingdom as he expounded the essence of God's will as it was taught in the Scriptures, and as he portrayed to men the true character of God. He seems also to have

[39] Matt. 12: 32.   [40] Matt. 12: 28.   [41] Luke 10: 18.

thought of hastening the advent of the kingdom by the power of prayer, teaching his disciples to pray, "Thy kingdom come," and reiterating in many a saying the lesson that the prayer of faith will be answered.[42]   Thus as the herald and interpreter of God's coming rule and the leader and creator of a group of men and women who accept that divine rule upon themselves, he was conscious of a Messianic mission.

To some, however, it might appear that instead of establishing the kingdom he ended his life in humiliation and defeat.   Judas thought this as he saw drawing ever nearer the high cross and the mocking soldiers.   The eleven others saw in the impending event only a ghastly execution and the deathblow to all their hopes.   Jesus too had seen this end to be inevitable.   One can have little doubt that the prayer uttered in Gethsemane had been voiced many times before, "Father, . . . remove this cup from me; however, not what I will, but what thou wilt." [43] He had fought out the issue through weeks and perhaps months of prayer and inner struggle.   The path was one to be followed to the end, for it was the Father's will, and he saw in it not the defeat of all for which he stood and hoped but the means by which the kingdom would be brought nearer.   It was his greatest victory, that conviction that his death, being God's will for him, would be the effective means by which the kingdom would be brought to realization.   It is quite probable, as many scholars have thought, that he was helped to this conclusion by the words of Scripture, in particular by those marvelous pictures in II Isaiah of the ideal Servant of Jehovath, "despised and rejected of men," esteemed to be "stricken,

[42] As in Matt. 7: 7 f.   [43] Mark 14: 36.

smitten of God, and afflicted," but who in reality was the Servant of God and the means of man's redemption. Whether or not that be true, it is certain that he saw in his approaching death a final service he could render toward the establishment of the kingdom.

He made that clear to his disciples on the very night in which he was betrayed by a symbolic act which they could never forget. "As they were eating, he took bread, and when he had blessed, he brake it, and gave it to them, and said, Take ye: this is my body. And he took a cup, and when he had given thanks, he gave it to them and they all drank of it. And he said unto them, This is my blood of the covenant, which is poured out for many. Verily I say unto you, I will no more drink of the fruit of the vine, till that day when I drink it new in the king-dom of God." [44]   In that simple ceremony three thoughts stand out vividly against the dark and sinister background of the event of that night.   On the one hand it was a symbolic act of fellowship and communion by which the unity of the group now about to be broken was pledged anew.   They all ate of the same loaf, they all drank of the common cup.   Not even death would break the bond of fellowship.   In the second place, Jesus declared that this death, the shadow of which already lay across their com-mon life, was not simply a meaningless tragedy, but was a willing offering of himself for their sakes, a sacrifice like that of the Passover lamb, in which they all had their part.   In the third place this death was to be effective in God's establishment of his kingdom, the means of bringing in the glad new day which had been so long awaited, and which he symbolized in the familiar figure of a joyous banquet.   However others regarded his death, it is clear

[44] Mark. 14: 22-25.

that in Jesus' mind it was his final act of dedication to the cause of God's universal rule. Though he could not fathom the mystery of its necessity—note his prayer in the Garden of Gethsemane—he was willing to drink the cup which the Father gave to him. This was his triumphant faith. And every cross which Christian devotion has lifted since that fateful night, whether on lofty cathedral or on rude walls amid savage tribes, bears testimony to the fact that in this faith he was not mistaken. On the hill called Golgotha, outside the city walls, he carried his mission to its conclusion and its culmination.

In all this he was conscious of establishing the kingdom. And as those peasants and fisherfolk followed with him and heard him speak they, too, became conscious of it. Thus of their own accord they acclaimed him Messiah, "The Anointed One," who would bring God's rule to be. Loyalty to that rule was identical with loyalty and devotion to him. For he was not only the founder of the kingdom but its embodiment as well. That which his teaching described and illustrated in the abstract, his life presented in person. He and the cause are inseparable. No man can be devoted to the brotherhood of man and hate Jesus. No one can admire loving service, and despise the young man from Nazareth who saw so clearly its beauty and value and gave himself so completely to the ideal. One cannot accept his teachings and reject him. One does not do so, except perhaps by ignorance of his real character and thought.

TOPICS FOR DISCUSSION

1. The arguments for and against the view that Jesus did not think of himself as the Jewish Messiah.

2. The significance of the disciples' acclaim of Jesus as the Messiah.

3. The difference between the Messiahship of Jesus and the divinity of Jesus.

4. The way in which the narratives and discourses of the Fourth Gospel should be read.

5. The meaning of the Last Supper. The meaning of the Lord's Supper to one partaking of it to-day.

6. What one must believe about Jesus in order to be a Christian.

SUPPLEMENTARY READINGS

On whether and when Jesus came to regard himself as the Messiah:

Case: *Jesus—A New Biography*, Ch. VII.

Bousset: *Jesus*, Ch. IX.

Scott: *The Kingdom and the Messiah*, Ch. VI.

Warschauer: *The Historical Life of Christ*, Ch. VI.

Barton: *Jesus of Nazareth*, Ch. XVI.

On what Judas betrayed:

Warschauer: *Op. cit.*, pp. 294-298.

Schweitzer: *The Quest of the Historical Jesus*, pp. 394, 395.

On Jesus' thought of the heavenly future of the Messiah:

Wendt: *The Teaching of Jesus*, Vol. II, pp. 265-286.

On the meaning of the Last Supper:

Scott: *The Outline of Christianity*, Vol. I, pp. 92-98.

Rall: *The Life of Jesus*, Ch. XX.

Barton: *Op. cit.*, Ch. LVII.

Warschauer: *Op. cit.*, pp. 279-308.

CHAPTER XXII

THE ORIGINALITY AND AUTHORITY OF JESUS' TEACHINGS

In the previous pages an attempt has been made to present an outline of Jesus' teachings. This survey has been incomplete and inadequate, but at least a general impression will have been gathered as to the contents of his message. It remains now to ask, To what extent were these ideas original with Jesus and what is their value and authority to-day?

As regards the first of these questions, that of the originality of Jesus' teachings, it has been repeatedly pointed out that many of his convictions and beliefs were drawn from the great religious teachers of Israel's past. His conception of God was essentially that presented by the prophets, the psalmists, and the compilers of the law books. His conception of man's duty might be summed up in the commandment from Leviticus, "Thou shalt love thy neighbor as thyself." His firm belief in the resurrection and a future life is expressed earlier in the Book of Daniel and elsewhere. His teaching that God shall establish his rule over all the earth, banishing all evil and wickedness and rewarding and blessing the righteous, is simply a development and application to new conditions of the words of the great prophets of the preceding centuries.

During recent years this relationship of Jesus' teachings to the religion of the synagogues has been more and more clearly established. Jewish scholars have been studying the gospels and have declared that Jesus' sayings contain little that cannot be paralleled from those of the scribes and rabbis. Christian scholars likewise have been studying the Talmud and they have found much which resembles and illustrates the gospel accounts. As a result of such studies the connection between Jesus' teachings and that of the scribes has been clearly established. Dr. Klausner, a leading Jewish scholar of the Nationalist or Zionist School, declares for example, "Without any exception he [Jesus] is wholly explainable by the scriptural and Pharisaic Judaism of his time." [1]

If such a statement as this can be made—even granting that it may contain an exaggeration—what can be said with reference to the originality of Jesus' thought? Did he only echo the best which previous writers or teachers had expressed? Was his work merely to gather up the best thought current in the synagogues? Wherein lay his greatness? Or is the belief in Jesus as the world's greatest leader and teacher one of those mistakes of history which modern criticism is clever enough to correct?

This last can be readily dismissed. Jesus was a teacher of great independence and originality. That is evident from the fact that Pharisaism rejected his teachings, as well as from the fact that Judaism has developed along lines quite separate from his thought without any break with its previous history. Jesus had something new and different to say that was not being said by the scribes— that much is clear. But before we proceed to single out the specific phases of his contribution one preliminary remark is necessary.

That is to remind the reader that originality in the sphere of morals and religion is a very different thing from what it is in the world of science, where so many

[1] *Jesus of Nazareth*, p. 363.

discoveries have been made in recent years. In the latter field it consists in finding out something absolutely new, something that no one knew anything about before, like a new metal or a new ray. That is because scientific research deals with the material world, with that which is other than ourselves. But moral and religious questions are questions about ourselves, our hopes, fears, failures, desires, aspirations. In other words, religion deals with the inner life and sets forth a conception of the way it should be lived to attain its fullest realization. The materials with which religion deals cannot be something new and strange and novel. For men have from the beginning of things known and talked about love, hate, fear, peace, trust, and those other attitudes and experiences out of which the fabric of our lives is woven.

Professor E. F. Scott in his illuminating essay "The Originality of Jesus" has expressed this fact in so clear and striking a fashion that one cannot do better than quote his words. "From the beginning men had been concerned with the great moral questions. The true answers had been forced on them by all the experiences of life and by the very conditions of man's being. Their judgments had indeed been warped by custom and tradition and strange beliefs, but there has been no religion outside of mere savagery in which the principles of right living were not in some degree recognized. In Judaism they had been discerned with marvelous insight by a long succession of great thinkers, and a noble and comprehensive moral code had been built up, on the basis of the ten commandments. Jesus therefore had all his materials ready to his hand. It is the very proof of his originality that he was content to work with them as they were. The temptation of inferior moralists, as of second-rate poets and artists, is to despise what lies before them and strain after novelty and paradox. These cheap substitutes for originality are painfully familiar to us in our own day. Jesus did not resort to them. He perceived that everything was given in those truths which men knew already. Over all his teaching might be written the great text, "Say not, Who will ascend into heaven? Who will go down into the deeps? For the word is very near thee, in thy heart and in thy mouth." [2]

This fact must always be remembered. Jesus' teaching would have been something very strange and queer had he talked about ideals and attitudes that no moral teacher of the past had ever thought about. He took over from the great succession of Jewish teachers many of the permanently valid answers to the problems of life. Wherein, then, lay his greatness and his originality as a teacher?

1. In the first place, it is to be seen in what he rejected or ignored in the religious tradition of his people. A great deal has been written on the extent of the resemblances between Jesus and the scribes of his day, and one is inclined to forget how much there is in the Old Testament or in the collections of rabbinical teaching which Jesus would never have repeated or indorsed. The imprecatory psalms are never heard upon his lips. The emphasis in the law codes and in the Talmud upon the exact performance of the ceremonial regulations he does not repeat. Pharisaic injunctions to separate oneself from sinners he ignores. The pictures of the Messiah sitting upon the throne of David he rejected. The Pentateuchal law of divorce he declared to be simply a concession to

the hardness of men's hearts. The nationalistic aspirations expressed on many a page of Scripture he transformed. In the great Jewish religious tradition there were many different voices to be heard; Jesus was deaf to all that did not find an echo in his own soul. And this independence of the heavy hand of the past was no small part of the contribution which he made.

2. In the second place, Jesus intensified the ideal of love and service which Judaism taught so clearly. That this was the case has been suggested in the preceding pages. One need not argue whether this or that verse in the Sermon on the Mount is stronger than some similar saying in the rabbinic literature. Jesus' attitude toward the ceremonial commands is proof of the point. In his mind the duty of loving service to those in need was so imperative that one should even neglect specific requirements of the Mosaic law in order to render it. With the rabbis this duty of humanitarian service was inculcated with great force and winsomeness, but along with it they demanded strict attention to certain ritual duties commanded by the Scriptures, and in some cases their training and logic compelled them to demand attention to these duties at the expense of service to men in need. The proper observance of the Sabbath and the separation from the "people of the land" are cases in point. One might say quite correctly that Jesus' teaching on these points differed from that of the scribes in that the latter were governed by love and logic, while with Jesus the dictates of love were all triumphant. History has shown that love was the surer guide.

It was in the depth and power of this conviction of loving service as the center of man's duty to God that Jesus' contribution to the world's thought primarily consists. It is not in the number of different ideas that one may advance that greatness consists. Small thoughts on many themes are rather indications of an inability on the part of the thinker to unify and correlate his own ideas. Jesus' teaching consisted of a few principles which are both profoundly true and profoundly simple. These he declared should be the bases of life.

3. This leads to another phase of Jesus' originality. Though inheriting many of the concepts which he employs, he welded them into a unity which made them parts of an ethical and religious conception which was something new.

This is one of the great underlying facts which emerge from any study of the teachings of Jesus. While it is true that he did not present his thought systematically, nevertheless there is an underlying unity which binds his sayings on various topics into a whole. This unity is due to the fact that in all his teaching Jesus had in mind a certain type of character which he declared to be the character of those who are sons of God and shall be admitted to his kingdom. The central element in this character is a changed will that has made the service of other men its primary object, but to this central element the other virtues of the life of the kingdom are related in close and organic fashion. This type of character in its infinite perfection he declares to be that of the heavenly Father. The relationship of the good man to God is accordingly one of grateful trust combined with humility and reverence, so that man's goodness shows none of the defects of self-satisfaction and pride. The first commandment of all is to love God with all one's strength, but love to God is shown primarily by devotion to his beneficent purposes and coöperation with his will. Demonstrations of this inner unity of Jesus' teachings are always likely to leave a misimpression by obscuring the freshness and the immediate pertinence of his sayings, many of which were replies to casual questions; but if the reader will read thoughtfully some such collection as Matthew 5-7 or Luke 17-18, I think he will glimpse the fact that these sayings are more than "pearls on a string," fine sayings on various phases of the good life. They spring from a conception of character which imparts to the sayings themselves both unity and originality.

Here perhaps I may be permitted another quotation. Mr. Claude G. Montefiore, a liberal Jew of great delicacy and sympathy in his treatment of the gospel narratives, one who has contributed much not only to Christian understanding of the gospels but also to good feeling between Jews and Christians, has this comment to make as to the originality of Jesus: "There are combinations in the picture of Jesus which, as a picture, at any rate, seem to me unique, and which I am inclined to think are not merely picture but portrait. I mean such combinations as his humility and his sense of authority; his sternness and his gentleness; his great pity and his great purity; his tinge of asceticism and his lack of asceticism; his constant living with God and his compassionate forthcomingness toward many sinners; his hatred of sin and his active friendliness and sympathy with the outcast and the 'lost.' I mention these combinations quite curtly, partly because they are so familiar, partly because of limits of space; obviously they could easily be drawn out at length. Now I would not deduce from these combinations that Jesus was therefore more humble, or loved God more ardently, or felt God more near to him, than any Rabbi. That is where I part company with the Christian believer; but I do deduce from them that Jesus was original—original in his character as also in his way of life: a new phenomenon among the Jews, which has scarcely been repeated." [3]   To this quotation no comment need be added.   The combination of qualities and their unity in the single type of character which Jesus delineated was, as Mr. Montefiore states, "a new phenomenon."

4. A fourth contribution of Jesus is to be seen in his emphasis upon the individual, his rights and values, as opposed to the claims of the social body.

Judaism had come out of a past in which the rights and claims of the tribe or nation over the individual were almost complete.   It had gone through a long development and many of these ideas had been eliminated.   But in many ways this social solidarity was preserved.   Due to it, no doubt, the Jew has been able to survive during the past twenty centuries in spite of ostracism and persecution.   Now one aspect of the Judaism of Jesus' day which reflected this older way of thinking was its belief in the authority of tradition.   God's will had been revealed once and for all; it was revealed in the past; furthermore the true interpretation of its meaning was to be found in the sayings of the great teachers of the past.   As for the present, there were of course many questions still to be answered, but the final authority on all such matters of morals and religion was the guild of scholars who were learned in all this lore of the past, the official body of the scribes.   These scribes decided matters by a majority vote; what was thus voted was law and duty.   No individual was recognized as having the right to interpret or expound the law who had not studied under the official scholars.

[3] "The Originality of Jesus," in *The Hibbert Journal*, Vol. XXVIII, No. 1 (Oct., 1929), p. 101.

Judaism thus believed that the final authority in matters of conscience as well as law was past tradition as interpreted or expounded by the scribal body; or to put it the other way around, the moral authority was the majority vote of a body of scholars who were trained in interpretations and rulings of earlier scholars. It is obvious that there was no room here for individual convictions which deviated from the established rule.

This was one of the basic issues in Jesus' conflict with the scribes. They denied his right to expound God's law —this not merely because of personal prejudice, but as part of their theory of social guidance and control. If untrained, unlicensed teachers were to be permitted to say what they thought God's will was, there would be no unity of understanding and practice on the part of the people, and confusion and disobedience would result. This is an intelligent position. Its merits should be recognized as well as its defects. They are rather obvious in this day of democratic control.

Jesus, on the other hand, repudiated in practice this system of social control. Guided by his own conscience, he declared to his hearers the will of God. Furthermore he did not hesitate to act contrary to the rulings of the scribes. He repudiated the authority of the scribal tradition. A few years later we read that when the Sanhedrin "beheld the boldness of Peter and John, and had perceived that they were unlearned and ignorant men, they marveled; and they took knowledge of them, that they had been with Jesus." [4] For these disciples were but carrying on Jesus' denial of the moral authority of the rulings of the scribal body. As one of the prophets he maintained the authority of the individual conscience.

[4] Acts 4: 13.

In another way Jesus contributed to the realization of the value of the individual. I refer to his teaching of the supreme value of each person in God's sight. God knows the number of hairs on each individual's head, and controls the growth of each one's body. "Ye are of more value than many sparrows," he said enforcing the lesson of God's personal care and love. It is not God's will that one of the little ones perish. God is like the shepherd who leaves the flock to seek the one sheep. Furthermore Jesus embodied this ideal in his own endeavor to save the outcasts and the sinners, and in this it is recognized that he introduced a new spirit into Judaism.[5] I would rather point out the larger truth, that his whole outlook was one which has tremendously fostered what one may call the spirit of individualism, the recognition of the rights and values of the common man over against the more primitive view of the claims of the tribe or nation. Jesus did not apply his principles to practical political questions, but how much the whole movement toward democracy in state and elsewhere owes to the teachings of Jesus can scarcely be determined.

In still a third way one sees this individualism of Jesus coming to expression. Over against the legislation of the scribes as to good deeds, he kept insisting on the good motive. Here again the question of the proper observance of the Sabbath serves as an illustration. The scribal rulings declared what deeds were forbidden; Jesus kept insisting on any deeds which expressed certain motives or attitudes, irrespective of whether these deeds fell within

[5] See for example, Montefiore, *The Synoptic Gospels,* Vol. I, p. 55: "Jesus did not avoid sinners, but sought them out. This was a new and sublime contribution to the development of religion and morality."

the prohibited categories or not. The scribes, it must be understood, did not object to good motives. On the contrary, they demanded that they must accompany the external obedience to the law for such obedience to have value. But they were compelled to object to Jesus' view of goodness on the grounds that it was neither according to the law nor socially enforceable. No court could pass on men's motives, and to substitute motives for performance was really to overthrow the conception of a code of behavior commanded by the law and enforced upon the people by scribal judgment. In other words, it was to make religion a distinctly personal matter. It left the judgment as to the rightness or wrongness of a deed between man's conscience and God. The implication of this teaching of Jesus on the inwardness of morality was destined to break up the ancient system of religion by which it was the affair of the state or social group. It was to make religion personal and individual. Dr. Klausner sees this quite clearly and affirms that the reason why loyal Jews could never accept Jesus is that his teaching implied "the negation of national life and of the national state." [6]

Jesus himself did not develop all the implications of this individualism, but this sense of the value and moral authority of the individual is implied in his whole outlook and teaching.

5. Lastly should be added a point which is really the underlying truth of all the above. The originality and greatness of Jesus' teaching is to be found in the fact that he embodied his ethical ideal, that he lived it.

It must never be forgotten that Jesus was not a philosopher, enunciating truths about the good life. He

[6] *Jesus of Nazareth,* p. 374.

was instead one whose whole soul was filled with good will toward others. He gave himself to the cause of love out of love for those whom he saw ignorant of its present values and its future rewards. This involved a course of action which brought upon himself the contempt of worldlings, the sneers of the intellectually trained, the opposition of religious and secular authorities, the misunderstanding of his own family, and finally betrayal by a friend and a cruel and shameful death. In spite of this he did not waver. More important still, in spite of all this he declared that the life of love and service was worth all the sacrifice. "Blessed are those who are persecuted for righteousness sake;" "He who loses his life shall find it." His teachings as to God's will and man's true life were simply the embodiment in words of his own moral convictions and experiences rather than solely or even primarily conclusions arrived at by intellectual processes.

Herein was Jesus' contribution—himself. By virtue of the fact that he embodied his ideal, what he said was living and vital and impelling. For religion is a personal thing. It can never become an abstract principle. It is a way of life. But this is something that cannot be read in a book or understood by disputation and discussion. Jesus chose his disciples that they might be with him, and that has been the Christian secret ever since. Drop out the person of Jesus from the gospel, and it becomes an ethical system, convincing perhaps in its wisdom and insight, but not impelling. Jesus talked about a new character, life lived in ordinary surroundings from a new center. In himself we see what it involves in our kind of world. It will always be true that the words of Jesus are most valuable as showing the kind of heart and soul from which they sprang.   Like the early disciples our primary task is to strive to apprehend through word and deed the life and character which was Jesus' greatest gift to the world.

II

But what about the value and authority of this teaching for our own day? Granted that Jesus' message was very original and very inspiring for the first century, has not the world's thought moved beyond it?   Should not the teachings of Jesus be regarded in much the same light as the dialogues of Plato, which men still treasure as priceless records of the best thought of another day but do not consider as solving the philosophic problems of the present?

In answering these questions it is essential to make certain distinctions.   In the first place, it must be freely admitted that the beliefs which Jesus held about science, geography, history, medicine, and the like are no longer accepted as true by educated men.   In these respects he shared the ideas of other men of that day.   He spoke, for example, of how God makes the sun to rise on the just and the unjust, without any thought or knowledge of the astronomy of Copernicus, much less that of modern scientists.   He accepted apparently the belief of his contemporaries that illnesses and abnormalities of behavior were due to evil spirits or demons which had entered the individual, though physicians nowadays recognize in the details of some of the stories symptoms of diseases that are now well known.   He used the conventional language of his day as to the location of various mental and emotional functions in certain organs of the body; the heart, for example, was the center of thought; pity and compassion were referred to the abdomen. Just as he accepted the demonology of that day, so also he spoke of angelic hosts who were at hand to do God's bidding. He had inherited from his social environment a belief in a new age which would bring to an end this present age and all that belonged to it. As regards history one can see that he thought in terms of the Old Testament story, of Moses as the author of the Pentateuch, of David as the writer of the Psalms, and there are no grounds for questioning his acceptance of the opening chapters of Genesis as the historic story of how this physical world came into being.

Nothing is to gained by blinking these facts, and similarly nothing is to be lost by frankly admitting them. Not long ago a book came into my hands which claimed for Jesus the distinction of being the world's greatest scientist. Such a claim can scarcely be established. Jesus did not reveal to men a knowledge of medicine and astronomy and biology and the like. It is as the world's spiritual leader and guide that he has challenged the world's conscience in every century and won the devoted allegiance of men of every social class and virtually every race.

These matters of science and history merely furnished the thought forms by which his own spiritual vision expressed itself. They are not to be identified with that moral and spiritual vision. To use an illustration: Jesus' plea that men should be generous and forgiving would be quite as effective if illustrated and enforced by the thought of God's impartial distribution of the recently discovered rays from inter-stellar space, as by the ancient thought of the daily rising and setting of the sun.

In the second place, when it is claimed that Jesus' teachings are applicable to our own day, one must be careful to make it clear that the assertion does not mean that they are valid as specific rules of conduct. It cannot be claimed that Jesus gave to the world a set of rules defining for all time the particular acts or deeds which good people should perform in various circumstances.

This is obvious when one examines the content of the teaching. For one thing, its range is very limited. If one is thinking in terms of the various moral problems of the twentieth century, one must admit that Jesus' sayings cover only a very few of the actual situations which men have to face. There is nothing in his teaching, for example, about the duties of a citizen—except to pay taxes; nothing which deals with the terrific modern economic problems, nothing specific on the questions of war, race relations, prohibition, etc. Then again many of his sayings, if these are rules, deal with situations which have ceased to exist. "Wash ye one another's feet"— what value can that have to-day? "Whosoever shall compel thee to go one mile, go with him two"—as a rule of behavior that is useless for us to-day.

But this, of course, is to read Jesus' teachings in the wrong way. He not only did not give a moral law code for our day, he did not give one for his own day. That was the error of Pharisaism, to insist upon a series of definite acts which one should perform in stated circumstances. Over against such a conception of righteousness Jesus insisted on a goodness of inner purpose and motive. It is unfair to Jesus' whole outlook on life to claim for his teaching that it is a code of rules of permanent validity. Turning the other cheek may not always be the best course of action in the twentieth century any more than it was not always the best course in the first century. I myself doubt whether the saying about divorce can be erected into an arbitrary rule of permanent and unvarying authority.

These two negative considerations point to the true way in which Jesus' teachings are to be regarded. His knowledge on matters secular and scientific was not infallible, but his instinctive sense for the noblest values in living was unerring. He did not lay down rules or laws, but he stated principles or attitudes which should dominate the life. Slowly at first, but with increasing unanimity, men have proclaimed him the supreme religious genius of all time. In his statement of the ends in life to be sought, the kind of life of eternal value, the attributes and ideals which should guide and direct men's actions, his teaching is of permanent value.

It was because Jesus dealt with these basic problems of life that time has not rendered his message antiquated or outgrown. It was remarked above that his teaching really consists of a very few principles which he states quite simply. But these principles are those which are deepest in life and have to do with its basic problems. Thus the fact that Jesus taught men and women who knew nothing about modern scientific discoveries and inventions is beside the point. For he did not deal with the surface problems, but with the underlying, permanent ones. His theme was the kind of life that is pleasing to God and brings one into the kingdom of God's fellowship and blessedness. It is obvious that such a theme would not be rendered out of date by the invention of the automobile or the radio.

And the answers that he gave to these deepest problems of life are still the final ones, nor can one conceive of their being surpassed. One thinks of his teaching that brotherhood is the secret of living, that one should love one's neighbor as one's self, that it is better to give than to receive, that the ethical ideal is to do unto others as one would have them do unto oneself—all this in order that one might become a son of the heavenly Father, whose desire is to give good gifts unto his children. Can this teaching become antiquated or be surpassed by some better and nobler conception?

But this does not yet quite answer the problem of the *authority* of this teaching. Are the commands of Jesus authoritative, binding on men? And if so, why? How do we know that his teaching is true?

Many of us used to think that Jesus' teaching was necessarily true because Jesus worked miracles. We have also been taught that the teaching should be accepted because Jesus was divine and hence one must believe what he said. Neither of these arguments is completely satisfactory. With regard to the first, it has already been noted that Jesus himself preferred for his hearers not to be distracted from his thoughts by his wonderful works and instructed those whom he healed to tell no one. As concerns the second, one recalls that Jesus did not proclaim his Messiahship to the world, but presented his teaching of God and duty and the coming kingdom without resting them upon any claim as to himself. Wherein, then, is the proof of the truth of this teaching of Jesus?

There is only one answer—the response which each individual makes in his own heart to these matchless sayings. The only proof that Jesus himself ever offered was the inherent worth of the ideas which he presented. Of external proof or authority he made no use. What proof could there be that love is the supreme way of life? Could a miracle prove it? Could the pomp of David's throne have made its proclamation any more convincing? Or could its truth be made apparent only by one who had no place to lay his head, but who gave his gentle but strenuous life in devotion to the cause of his fellow men?

Men have built great churches to Jesus, cathedrals in

which stained glass, great columns, vaulted roofs, and lofty pinnacles have embodied man's aspiration for the divine. Sometimes when one enters these great buildings, or when one reads the statistics of denominational greatness, one recalls the simple story of the widow's gift. The true Church of Christ is the Church of the heart. And the final proof of the truth of what he taught has been the fact that when the Man of Narazeth has stood outside, lowly and unadorned, the Church of the heart has opened and has taken him in.

TOPICS FOR DISCUSSION

1. The data of ethics.

2. The originality of Shakespeare as illustrative as that of Jesus.

3. The doctrine of the Church as the ultimate moral authority. The difficulties of the doctrine.

4. Conscience as the ultimate moral authority. Its limitations as a moral guide.

5. The relation of the moral authority of conscience to that of Jesus.

6. Sayings of Jesus which have had great influence in the struggle of underprivileged groups for equal opportunities.

7. The unique place of Jesus in history.

SUPPLEMENTARY READINGS

On the originality of Jesus:
> Dickey, in *The Outline of Christianity,* Vol. I, pp. 140-153.
> Montefiore: "The Originality of Jesus," in *The Hibbert Journal,* Vol. XXVIII, No. 1 (Oct., 1929), pp. 98 ff.
> Scott: "The Originality of Jesus' Ethical Teachings," in *The Journal of Biblical Literature,* Vol. XLVIII (1929), pp. 109 ff.
> Klausner: *Jesus of Nazareth,* pp. 363-376.

On the authority of conscience as related to that of Jesus' teaching:
> Rashdall: *Conscience and Christ,* Ch. 1 (particularly from p. 13).

On the finality of the Christian religion:
> Morgan: *The Nature and Right of Religion,* Ch. X.
> Scott: *The Ethical Teaching of Jesus,* Ch. XVII.

GENERAL INDEX

A

ABRAHAMS, 244
Adler, 245
Angus, 24
Antioch in Syria, 60 f.
Apocalypticism, origin of, 121 f.
Apostolic church orders, 20
Authority of Jesus' teaching, 369 ff.

B

BARNABAS, 60 ff.
Barton, 356
Baruch, apocalypse of, 21
Bevan, 128
Bosworth, 97, 145, 301, 319
Bousset, 97, 111, 145, 161, 356
Branscomb, 301, 302
Brown, 282
Bundy, 145, 162, 211, 268, 270, 281, 282
Burkitt, 41, 71

C

CADBURY, 39, 72
Cadoux, 194, 227, 245
Case, 24, 210, 356
Clement of Alexandria, 20
Clement of Rome, 42 f., 48, 50, 73, 77
Cohon, 344 f.
Courage, Jesus' demand for, 204

D

DALMAN, 254
Dickey, 114, 213, 219, 220, 227, 302, 319
Dionysus of Alexandria, 87
Discipleship, requirements of, 346 ff.
Divorce, 239 ff., 298 f.
Dougall and Emmett, 265
Drummond, 88

E

EDERSHEIM, 319
Ellwood, 194, 245
Emmett, 162
Eternal life, 254 ff.
Eusebius, 31, 49, 67, 73, 87
Evangelism, 191

F

FAIRWEATHER, 128
Faith, Jesus', 209 f.
Family, Jesus' teaching on the, 229
Fasting, Jesus' attitude toward, 307
Forgiveness, Jesus' teaching on, 183 ff.
Fosdick, 145, 272, 282

G

GENTILES, 320 ff.
Glover, 162, 234, 245, 282
God, Fellowship with, 262
God, Jesus' conception of, 146, 176 f.
Goguel, 24
Goodspeed, 172
Grant, 110, 228
Grenfell and Hunt, 21
Groves, 245

H

HASTINGS, 72, 111, 128, 319
Headlam, 97
Hebrews, Gospel to the, 48
Herford, 16, 301
Hillel, 91, 232, 287
Holtzman, 97, 336
Humanitarian Service, 189 ff.
Humility, 195 f.

I

INDIVIDUALISM of Jesus, 364 ff.
Irenæus, 21, 50, 67, 68

375

INDEX TO SCRIPTURE PASSAGES

READING ASSIGNMENTS IN THE NEW TESTAMENT

(NOTE.—The danger of using any textbook on the teachings of Jesus is that the student will read the textbook instead of the gospels. Even though the passages for the most part are quoted in the text, there is a value in looking them up in their setting and familiar wording. To facilitate class work the following assignments are suggested. Passages occurring in more than one gospel are, for the sake of simplicity, listed only once. Instructors therefore who wish to stress the allocation of passages to the different sources will have to supplement the lists in this respect.)

Chapter I

(a) Rom. 1: 3, Gal. 1: 19, 4: 4, 1 Cor. 9: 5.
(b) 1 Cor. 7: 10, 9: 14, 11: 23-25, 1 Thess. 4: 15, Acts 20: 35.
(c) 1 Cor. 15: 3-8, Gal. 3: 1, 5: 11, 6: 12, 14, Phil. 2: 8, Heb. 12: 2, 13: 12, 1 Pet. 5: 1.
(d) 1 Pet. 2: 21-24, Heb. 5: 7 f., 1 John 3: 16.

Chapter II

(a) Acts 13: 1, 1 Cor. 12: 28, Eph. 4: 11, Jas. 3: 1, 1 Tim. 6: 3.
(b) Mark 1: 40, 2: 14, 15, 18, 23, 3: 1, etc.; Luke 14: 1, 25, 15: 1 f., 16: 1, 14, 18, etc.

Chapter III

(a) Compare Matt. 3: 7-10 with Luke 3: 7-9.
Compare Matt. 23: 37-39 with Luke 13: 34, 35.
Compare Matt. 6: 9-15 with Luke 11: 2-4, note differences.
(b) Mark 1: 14-3: 6. Note the episodic character of the narrative.

Chapter IV

(a) Compare Mark 1: 40-44 with Matt. 8: 1-4 and with Luke 5: 12-14.
Compare Mark 2: 1-12 with Matt. 9: 1-8 and with Luke 5: 17-26.

(b) Matt. 1: 1, 4: 14 f., 21: 4, 7: 28 f., 11: 1, 26: 1, 28: 18-20.
(c) Luke 3: 1, 3: 23, 3: 38, 4: 24-27, 7: 36-50, 15: 11-24.

Chapter V

(a) John 20: 30 f., 1: 1-4, 14, 4: 25, 6: 33-35, 8: 12, 10: 30.
(b) John 3: 10-16, 9: 5-7, 16: 12 f.

Chapter VI

Matt. 10: 34-36, Mark 6: 14-16, Luke 9: 57-62, 10: 17, 13: 31-33, 14: 25-35.

Chapter VII

Matt. 5: 31-48, 6: 1-13, Mark 9: 33-37, Luke 15: 1-10.

Chapter VIII

Joel 3: 1-3, 9-17, Mal. 4: 1-6, Isa. 65: 17-25, Dan. 12: 1-4, Ezek. 37: 21-23.

Chapter IX

(a) Matt. 13: 17, 24 f., 36-43, 47-50, Matt. 25: 34, Matt. 8: 11.
(b) Luke 17: 21, Mark 4: 26-32, 12: 34.
(c) Luke 17: 20, Mark 13: 32.

Chapter X

(a) Matt. 5: 45, 48, 11: 25, Mark 10: 6, 27, 12: 29, 14: 36.
(b) Matt. 6: 26-32, 7: 11, 10: 29, 18: 14, Luke 12: 6 f., 15: 4-10.

383

(c) Matt. 7: 13, 21, 13: 30, 23: 33, Mark 11: 25, Luke 12: 5, 13: 1 f.

(d) Matt. 5: 4, 8, 9, 6: 1, 3 f., Luke 16: 14 f., 18: 9-14.

Chapter XI

(a) Matt. 5: 1-16, 21-48, 6: 1-6, 19-21, 25 f., Mark 10: 17-30.

(b) Matt. 7: 12, 23: 11, Mark 10: 42-45, 12: 31.

(c) Matt. 5: 44, Mark 12: 30.

Chapter XII

(a) Gal. 5: 13 f., Jas. 2: 8, 1: 27, 1 Pet. 4: 8, 1 John 3: 11, 4: 7 f.

(b) Matt. 5: 38-47, 6: 12-14, 18: 21-35, Mark 11: 25, Luke 17: 4.

(c) Matt. 6: 1-4, 25: 31-46, Luke 10: 30-37, 12: 15, 33 f., 19: 2, 8-10.

(d) Matt. 5: 9 f., 16: 26, Mark 8: 34-37, 10: 17-30, Luke 10: 41.

Chapter XIII

(a) Matt. 5: 3, 5, 6, 23: 12, 27, Luke 14: 7-11, 17: 7-10.

(b) Matt. 5: 33-37, 6: 1-6, 16-18, 12: 33 f.

(c) Matt. 5: 10-12, 10: 24 f., Mark 8: 34, Luke 9: 57-62.

Chapter XIV

(a) Mark 10: 17-31, Luke 12: 16-21, 14: 33, 16: 19-26.

(b) Matt. 6: 19-21, 24-34, Luke 12: 13-15, 16: 1-9.

(c) Mark 12: 41-44.

Chapter XV

(a) Matt. 23: 8, Mark 3: 35, 7: 9-13, 10: 13-16.

(b) Matt. 5: 31 f., 19: 3-9, Mark 10: 2-12, Luke 16: 18.

(c) Matt. 5: 46 f., 10: 34-37, Luke 9: 59-62, 14: 26.

Chapter XVI

Matt. 5: 3-12, 6: 11, 8: 11 f., 10: 42, 11: 29, 13: 44-46, 16: 26, Mark 9: 42-47, 10: 29-31, 12: 25 f.

Chapter XVII

(a) Matt. 7: 7-11, 17: 20, Mark 11: 24, Luke 11: 5-13, 17: 6, 18: 3-8.

(b) Matt. 6: 5-15, Mark 11: 25 f., Luke 11: 2-4.

(c) Matt. 9: 36-38, Mark 14: 36, Luke 3: 21, 5: 16, 22: 31 f., 23: 34.

Chapter XVIII

(a) Deut. 5: 6-21, 6: 4 f., Lev. 19: 17 f., Ps. 23, Isa. 55: 6-13, Jer. 31: 31-34, Hab. 3: 17-19, Mal. 2: 10 f.

(b) Matt. 5: 17-44, 12: 9-14, Mark 2: 13-17, 7: 1-15, 10: 2-19

Chapter XIX

Matt. 5: 23 f., 6: 16-18, 23: 16-23, 25, Mark 7: 1-15, 11: 15-18.

Chapter XX

(a) Matt. 6: 7, 10: 5 f., 15: 21-28, Mark 7: 24, 10: 42.

(b) Matt. 8: 11 f., Mark 12: 13-17, Luke 9: 52-55, 10: 33-36, 17: 12-16.

Chapter XXI

(a) Mark 1: 25, 34, 3: 12, 8: 30, 9: 9, Mark 6: 4, Luke 13: 33.

(b) Mark 6: 14, 8: 28, Matt. 21: 11, Luke 7: 16.

(c) Mark 8: 29-38, 10: 37, 14: 61 f., 15: 2, 9, 26, Matt. 11: 3-6.

(d) Mark 10: 21, Matt. 5: 11 f., 10: 39.

(e) Mark 12: 32, 9: 38 f., Luke 9: 51-56.